# lotus

# *Illustrated*
# DICTIONARY
# *of*

# ECONOMICS

Compiled and Edited by:
*Julie Parson*

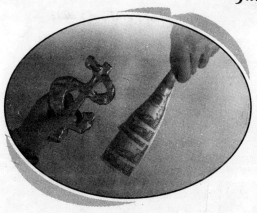

## lotus
## PRESS

4263 / 3,  Ansari  Road,
Daryaganj, New Delhi-02

# Lotus Illustrated DICTIONARY of ECONOMICS

Compiled and Edited by:
**Michelle Cooper**

First Published : 2004

© Reserved

ISBN 81 89093 28 2

Published by :
**LOTUS PRESS**
4263 / 3, Ansari Road,
Daryaganj, New Delhi-110002
Ph: 30903912, 23290047

Printed at :
**Saras Graphics**
Delhi

# PREFACE

Economics, the science that deals with the production, distribution and consumption of wealth, is one of the most important and widely discussed topics in the field of growth and development. It not only provides pointers to the present and future growth at a macro level, like national income or balance of payments, but also throws light on the micro aspects such as individual incomes and expenditures. It works towards finding the problems prevailing in the economy and suggesting alternative solutions to such issues and thereby fostering a holistic and healthy development of the economy.

There are basically two schools of thought that have emerged in the field of economics, the Classical and the Modern. The theories propounded by the economists of these two schools have, to a great extent, been able to solve all kinds of problems and queries that have come up in this area. Renowned economists including the likes of Ricardo, Malthus and Keynes have done exemplary work in this field and have laid down, what can be termed as, the golden rules of economics. Still, as human wants and needs are endless and insatiable, the research and development process has never been ceased and several great economists are working on such problems, day in and day out, towards formulating new theories that are more customised to the present and anticipated economic problems. In their endeavour, they are churning out yet new solutions, taking the theories already in place as the ground rules.

This dictionary is an attempt to give an access to the whole paraphernalia of economic terms in a concise package. The terms have been explained in simple and comprehensible manner, with relevant pictures and illustrations to bring clarity. The dictionary can be taken as a comprehensive and cognisable set of economic terms to be used as a referral. Since economics is a vast subject and consists of several sub components, a complete repertoire of the terms can hardly be claimed in one dictionary, but nonetheless, an attempt has been made towards providing a gamut of terms, which form a part and parcel of the subject.

■ **a fair trader/fair traders**
contrasted with free trader, a fair
trader is a holder of the point of
view that one's country's government must prevent foreign companies from having artificial advantages over domestic ones.

■ **abandoned option**
the event when a buyer does not
exercise his share option because
the price is not in his favour.

■ **abatement cost**
the cost incurred for lessening a
problem like pollution or conges-
tion.

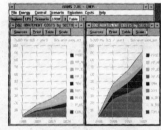
*Abatement Cost*

■ **abilene principle**
a description of a group's inability
to manage its agreement. Nobody
wants to reach a particular destination (Abilene), but for fear of
offending or contradicting each
other, they all end up there.

*Abilene Principle*

■ **ability to pay**
an individual's capacity to bear the
cost of something. The governments all over the world are trying
to make the taxation system equi-
table and just, which is only possible if the people are taxed according to their ability to pay.

*Ability to Pay*

■ **abrasion**
a reduction in the weight of coins,
brought about by wear and tear.

*Abrasion*

■ **absentee landlord**
a person who owns a land, but
does not reside in it and administers the property through an agent.

■ **absenteeism**
to absent oneself from work without giving any reasonable cause,

like sickness and without any prior intimation or consent of the employer.

■ **absolute advantage**
a term used in the international trade theory, according to which a country specialises in producing such goods and services that it is able to produce more efficiently (more output per unit of input) than any other country. In other words, absolute advantage is the ability to produce a good at lower cost, in terms of real resources, than another country. In a Ricardian model, cost is in terms of only labour.

■ **absolute cost advantage**
means that a nation is in an advantageous position to produce an article, as compared to another nation.

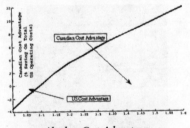

*Absolute Cost Advantage*

■ **absolute monopoly**
also known as perfect monopoly, is a market situation wherein the sales of a particular item is controlled by a single seller and he therefore, takes advantage of his state by charging extremely high prices.

■ **absorption**
the total demand for goods and services by all residents (consumers, producers and government) of a country, in contrast to the total demand for that country's output.

■ **absorption approach**
a way of understanding the determinants of the balance of trade, noting that it is equal to the earnings less absorption.

■ **absorption costing**
in accounting terms, to allocate all the costs of a business to the goods or services produced, without making any distinction between the fixed and variable costs.

*Absorption Costing*

■ **abstinence**
the giving up of the current consumption in order to increase the future consumption, often by directing the available resources towards the production of capital goods. Due to this, the future production of the consumer goods will increase.

■ **abstinence or agio theory of interest**
a theory that identifies interest as

a payment for abstaining from current consumption.

# abundant
available in a plentiful supply. Usually meaningful only in relative terms, compared to demand and/or to supply at another place or time.

# abundant factor
the factor that is available in abundant supply in a country relative to other countries. Can be defined both with respect to quantity and price.

# Academic Consortium on International Trade (ACIT)
a group of academic economists and lawyers who are specialised in international trade policy and international economic law. Its purpose is to prepare and circulate policy statements and papers that deal with important, current issues of international trade policy.

# ACAS
Advisory Conciliation and Arbitration Service.

# accelerated depreciation
a new asset's depreciation over a period that is much shorter than the normal. The firms operating in the developing areas are authorised to follow this method of depreciation.

# accelerating inflation
a sudden increase in the inflation rate. Accelerating inflation is the result of the government's efforts to hold the employment level below its natural rate.

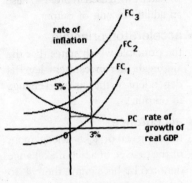

*Accelerating Inflation*

# acceleration principle
suggests a relationship between income and output and the investment effects associated with the changing output. The size of the accelerator depends on the marginal capital/output (C/O) ratio (i.e. how much new investment is needed in response to the changing demand for output) and on a variety of other factors influencing investment decisions.

# accelerator
the process in which changes in the demand for consumer goods leads to an even larger change in the demand for the capital equipment used to produce them.

# accelerator co-efficient
states that any incrase in the output is always accompanied by an increase in the capital, like machinery etc., that is used to produce it. The incremented capital output ratio depicts the amount of capital that

should be increased in order to raise an additional unit of output.

■ **accelerator principle**
the principle which states that the aggregate net investment level is dependent on the expected change in output.

■ **acceptance**
the approval or acknowledgement of the drawee of a bill of exchange denoted by his signing the bill, to fulfil the drawer's order.

■ **acceptance credit**
a manner in which payment is done in international trade. In case the accepting house finds the credit of a foreign import merchant satisfactory, it may open an acceptance credit for him in London.

■ **accepting house**
the establishments whose business is to accept or guarantee bills of exchange. Besides this, such establishments are also involved in several other services and functions.

■ **access / accessibility**
a crucial locational quality expressing the ease with which a location can be reached and interacted with from other locations.

■ **accession**
the process of adding a country to an international agreement, such as the ATT, WTO, EU or NAFTA.

■ **accession country**
a country that is waiting to become a member of the European Union.

■ **accession rate**
also referred to as the hiring rate. The total number of employees whose names are added to the payroll in a given period of time. It acts as an important indicator of the future business conditions.

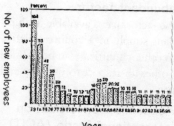

■ **accessions tax**
the tax that the government levies on the receiver of gifts and inherited property.

■ **accident insurance**
the insurance against the injury to life, property, vehicle or third party, as a result of an accident.

■ **accommodating movements**
the meeting of balance of payment deficits of a country by transferring gold and convertible currency abroad.

■ **accommodation bill**
that bill, which is drawn, accepted or endorsed with the sole aim of discounting it and thereby, making some cash available for a short term, without receiving any goods in return.

■ **accommodation endorsement**
the endorsing of a note or any

other bill of credit by one individual to another, thereby granting him the right to obtain a loan.

■ **account day**
the day on which the workers receive their wages. With reference to a stock exchange, it is the settlement day on which all transactions that are due for a given period in the past are settled.

*Account Day*

■ **account period**
in the context of a stock exchange, that period during which transactions are entered into.

■ **accountant**
one whose work is to keep accounts.

*Accountant*

■ **accounting**
the practice of recording the transactions of a business in a systematic manner, so as to reveal a company's financial position, enable the computation of tax and provide the management with the essential information for controlling the business of a company effectively.

■ **accounting period**
the period for which an operating statement is prepared.

■ **accounting standards committee**
an autonomous board that was set up in 1969 by the institute of chartered accountants in England and Wales due to the demands for developing the accounting profession and improving a set of consistent standards in financial reporting.

■ **accounts**
a financial statement in which the transactions of a firm are recorded.

| | Student Accounts | Sponsored Programs | Other Receivables | Total |
|---|---|---|---|---|
| Gross Accounts Receivable | $191,000 | $6,966,000 | $1,721,000 | $8,878,000 |
| Less: Allowance for Doubtful Accounts | 64,000 | 0 | 88,000 | 152,000 |
| Net Accounts Receivable | $127,000 | $6,966,000 | $1,633,000 | $8,726,000 |
| Accounts Receivable Greater than 120 Days Past Due | $117,000 | $164,000 | $287,000 | $568,000 |

■ **accounts payable**
the amount that a business owes to its suppliers and other parties, who give the customers a period of 10 to 90 days to pay for the goods already transported.

*Accounts Payable*

■ **accounts receivable**
the amount that a business is entitled to receive from its customers, who are generally given a period of 10 to 90 days to pay for the goods already transported.

■ **accounts receivable financing**
the application of money that a firm is entitled to receive from its debtors towards obtaining funds to finance the current operating expenses or some other expense.

■ **accrual basis**
in the context of accounting, a method in which the income and expenses are not charged to the period in which they are actually received, but instead are charged to the period in which they earned or incurred.

*Accrual Basis*

■ **accrued**
relating to the earnings, sales, expenses or other items of income or expenditure, which are already made or incurred, but not yet received or paid.

■ **accrued expenses**
an accounting entry wherein the cost of the services used but not paid for are recorded as a liability.

■ **accumulation**
the acquisition of an increasing quantity of something.

■ **ACP countries**
a group of African, Caribbean and Pacific less developed countries that were included in the Lomé Convention and now the Cotonou Agreement.

■ **acquittance**
a written receipt that acknowledges the discharge of full payment of a debt or other financial obligation.

■ **across-the-board tariff changes**
a state when all the tariffs in a country are raised or lowered by an equal percentage.

*Across the Border Tariff Changes*

■ **ACT**
Advance Corporation Tax

■ **action lag**
the delay between the formulation of a policy decision (particularly in macro economics) and its execution.

■ **actionable subsidy**
A subsidy that is not prohibited by the World Trade Organisation (WTO), but the member countries are permitted to levy compensating duties against.

■ **active balance**
a balance of payments that is favourable for a country, which occurs when the revenue earned from exports is higher than the expenditure incurred on the import of goods and services. The given graph shows favourable balance of trade of Russia, as compared to ukraine and Romania

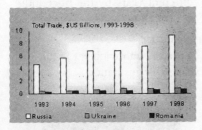

■ **active circulation**
that part of the RBI's issue which is in circulation at any given time.

■ **active market**
a market which is designated for a specific set of stock or shares whose dealings are quite frequent and regular in nature.

■ **activity rate**
the percentage of people in a given population age group that are not employed in the defence forces of a country.

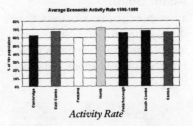
*Activity Rate*

■ **actual protection rate**
implicit tariff.

■ **actuals**
in a stock exchange, the items which are bought with the intent of an immediate delivery.

■ **actuary**
a person whose job is to statistically calculate the risks, premiums, etc. for insurance.

■ **ad valorem**
proportionate to the value. A term used to refer to the taxes and duties levied on goods, etc. as a percentage of their value.

■ **ad valorem equivalent**
The ad valorem tariff that would be equivalent, in terms of its effects on trade, price or some other measure, to a non tariff barrier.

■ **ad valorem tariff**
tariff defined as a percentage of the value of an imported good.

■ **ad valorem tax**
a tax or duty that is calculated on

the basis of the value of a transaction. It is generally taken as a percentage of price at the selling or production stage.

## ■ Adam Smith

an economist who was the first to discuss the problems of economics in a scientific manner in his book 'wealth of nations' published in 1979.

*Adam Smith*

## ■ adaption & adoption dichotomy

a part of A.A. Alchian's and Charles M. Tiebout's rationalisation of classical economic theory. The argument is that active, deliberately optimal (adaptive) behaviours are not needed for the viability of optimising theories, since economic actors would be either 'adopted' by the competitive environment or would fail.

## ■ ADB

Asian Development Bank

## ■ addition rule

a rule used to determine the derivative of a function with respect to a variable, where the function constitutes the linear sum of two or more different functions of the variable.

## ■ adjustable peg

an exchange rate that is pegged, but for which it is understood that the par value will be changed occasionally. Such system can be subject to extreme speculative attack and financial crisis, as speculators may easily anticipate these changes.

## ■ adjusted for inflation

corrected for price changes, to yield an equivalent in terms of goods and services. The adjustment divides nominal amounts for different years by the price indices for those years.

## ■ adjuster

a person whose job is to settle the claims of insurance.

*Adjuster*

■ **adjustment assistance**
a government program to assist those workers and/or firms whose industry has declined, either due to competition from imports (trade adjustment assistance) or from other causes. Such programs usually have two (conflicting) goals, which include, to lessen hardship for those affected and to help them change their behaviour.

■ **adjustment lags**
the time that a variable, like capital stock, takes to adjust to the changes in its determinants.

■ **adjustment mechanism**
the theoretical process by which a market changes in disequilibrium, moving toward equilibrium if the process is stable.

■ **administered price**
also called managed price. A price that is although set by a seller, but is not totally under his control.

■ **administered price**
a price for a good or service that is set and maintained by government, usually requiring accompanying restrictions on trade, if the administered price differs from the world price.

■ **administered protection**
protection resulting from the application of any one of several statutes that respond to specified market circumstances or events, usually as determined by an administrative agency.

■ **administrative agency**
a unit of government, charged with the administration of particular laws.

■ **administrative lag**
a delay between the time of implementation and the resulting effect of a monetary policy. It refers to the time that is lapsed between the recognition by the authorities that action is necessary and the actual implementation of the action. The duration of this time depends upon how efficient the authorities are in implementing the policies formulated.

■ **advance**
an amount that is paid before its due time, which is synonymous to a loan. For example, advance payments received by authors against future royalties to help them meet the expenses while finishing a manuscript.

■ **advance deposit requirement**
a requirement that a percentage of the value of imports or of import duties should be deposited prior to the payment, without competitive interest being paid.

■ **advance refunding**
a prospect for the bond holders whose bonds' expiry date is approaching, to exchange such bonds for new bonds on quite advantageous terms.

■ **advanced countries**
the dividing line between advanced

countries and developing countries is usually based on per capita income.

■ **adverse balance of payment**

an unfavourable balance of payment, characterised by an excess of aggregate imports of goods and services over the aggregate exports of goods and services of a country.

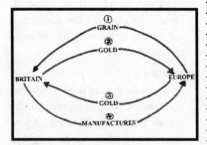

■ **adverse selection**

the tendency for insurance to be purchased only by those who are most likely to need it, thus raising its cost and reducing its benefits.

■ **adverse terms of trade**

a term of trade that is considered unfavourable relative to some benchmark or to past experience.

■ **advertising**

promoting goods and services publicly to enhance the sales.

■ **advertising-sales ratio**

the ratio of the advertising outlay of a firm to its total sales revenue.

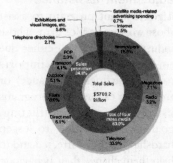

■ **advice**

a report that one merchant sends to another requesting him to send or deliver the goods ordered.

■ **affidavit**

a written statement made on oath before a court officer or other authority.

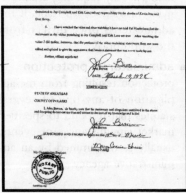

*Affidavit*

■ **African development bank**
established in 1964, a bank for promoting the economic development and social progress of the member states. It has 31 members.

■ **African Economic Community (AEC)**
an organisation of African countries that aims to promote economic, cultural and social development among the African economies.

■ **Africanisation**
a term used to refer to the employment in Africa, for describing the change of any type of employment from non-Africans (usually Asians or Europeans) to African.

■ **AFTA**
ASEAN Free Trade Area

■ **Agency for International Development (US)**
an agency that works under the supervision of the US department of state, whose job is to look after the administration of the economic assistance programmes of the US Government.

■ **agency shop**
the prerequisite for the employees joining a firm to pay the union dues without being a part of the trade union. This kind of an arrangement is generally found in the US between the ones who are of the view that the employees should be free to decide about joining a union or not and those who state that the employees should not be allowed to enjoy the benefits of a union without paying for them.

■ **agenda 21**
A plan of action adopted at the Rio Summit to promote sustainable development.

■ **age-specific fertility rates**
number of births to women of a certain age (or age group e.g. 20-24) per 1000 women of that age (group).

■ **agglomeration**
1. a geographical concentration of people and/or activities.
2. the phenomenon of economic activity congregating in or close to a single location, rather than being spread out uniformly over space.

■ **agglomeration economies (of scale or scope)**
benefits, savings or (average) cost reductions resulting from the clustering of activities. Generally, the concept of agglomeration economies refers to savings or benefits derived from the clustering of activities external to the 'firm' and are therefore a part of 'external economies'.

■ **agglomeration economy**
any benefit that accrues to economic agents as a result of having large numbers of other agents geographically close to them, thus tending to lead to agglomeration.

- **aggregate concentration**
  the extent to which the goods produced in one sector of the economy or the whole is centralised around a few large corporations.

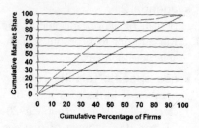

*Aggregate Concentration*

- **aggregate demand**
  the total level of demand in the economy. It is the total of all desired expenditure at any time by all groups in the economy. The main groups who spend are consumers (consumption), firms (who spend on investment), government (government expenditure) and overseas (exports).

- **aggregate demand**
  the total demand for a country's output, including demands for consumption, investment, government purchases and net exports.

- **aggregate demand curve**
  in macroeconomic theory, the aggregate demand curve relates the level of real national income (GDP) demanded (the total quantity of goods and services demanded) to the price level (as measured by the GDP deflator).

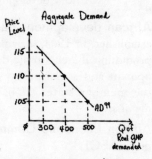

- **aggregate expenditure**
  in macroeconomic theory, aggregate expenditure is the total amount of desired spending by households, governments, Firms and foreign buyers (net of spending on imports) at each level of real national income (GDP).

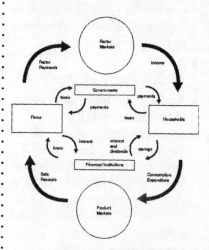

*Aggregate Expenditure*

- **aggregate measure of support**
  the measure of subsidy to agriculture used by the WTO as the basis for commitments to reduce the subsidisation of agricultural prod-

ucts. It includes the value of price supports and direct subsidies to specific products, as well as payments that are not product specific.

- **aggregate supply**
the total quantity supplied at every price level. It is the total of all goods and services produced in an economy in a given time period. In the given diagram, as is Aggregate Supply, P is the price and RGNP is the Production.

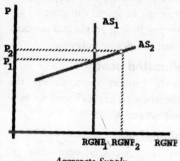

*Aggregate Supply*

- **aggregate supply curve**
in macroeconomic theory, the short run aggregate supply curve relates the total quantity of goods and services supplied and the price level (as measured by the GDP deflator) *ceteris paribus.*

- **aggregation**
1. the accumulation or summing up of primary data. For example, the aggregate demand is an aggregate, in contrast with the demand of an individual.
2. the combining of two or more kinds of an economic entity into a single category. Data on interna-

tional trade necessarily aggregate goods and services into manageable groups. For macroeconomic purposes, all goods and services are usually aggregated into just one.

- **aggregative model**
a model used in econometrics wherein the variables are created by using groups of individual variables.

- **agio**
a payment. It generally refers to the premium that is paid for exchanging one currency for another or for a foreign bill of exchange.

- **agistment**
to feed or look after cattle with the aim of getting a reward.

- **AGOA**
African Growth and Opportunity Act

- **agreement on textiles and clothing**
the 10-year transitional program of the WTO to phase out the quotas on textiles and apparel of the MFA.

- **agricultural banks**
the banks that are specifically established to grant funds to the agricultural sector.

- **agricultural good**
a good that is produced in the agricultural sector, as compared to manufactured good.

- **agricultural subsidies**
the amount paid by the govern-

ment to the farmers to supplement their income and increase food production.

*Agricultural Subsidies*

*Aid*

■ **agricultural wages board**
a statutory body that fixes and negotiates the basic rates of wages for the agricultural workers of Scotland, England and Wales, quite similar to the wages councils.

■ **agriculture**
production that relies essentially on the growth and nurturing of plants and animals, especially for food, usually with land as an important input.

■ **agriculture agreement**
the agreement within the WTO that commits member governments to improve market access and reduce the trade-distorting subsidies in agriculture.

■ **aid**
assistance provided by countries and by international institutions, such as the World Bank, to developing countries in the form of monetary grants, loans at low interest rates, in kind or a combination of these.

■ **aid-tying**
a condition imposed by a donor government on the recipient government to spend the granted aid for purchasing goods and services from the donor country.

■ **allocated cost**
in the context of accounting, the allocation of expenditures to various accounts.

■ **allocation**
an assignment of economic resources to uses. Thus, in general equilibrium, an assignment of factors to industries producing goods and services, together with the assignment of the resulting final goods and services to consumers, within a country or throughout the world economy.

■ **allocative efficiency**
the allocation of resources in such a manner that there is no better reallocation possible.

■ **allonge**
a sheet of paper that is attached to a bill of exchange as a means to provide an additional space for endorsements, if required.

**all-or-none order (US)**
a market or limited price order for buying or selling of shares and stocks, with the condition of being executed entirely, if used.

**allotment**
the allotting of shares or debentures issued by a company to those applicants who have responded positively to a subscription offer.

**allotment letter**
a letter that certifies the number of shares allotted to an applicant and also includes the information about the dates of payment and the manner in which further amounts that are due need to be paid.

**allowances and expenses for corporation tax**
some permissible costs that are deducted from revenue to obtain the taxable income.

**allowances and expenses for income tax**
the costs and expenses that are deducted from the gross income to obtain the taxable income.

**allowed-or standard-times**
the preset time, calculated on the basis of time-study data, within which a specific task needs to be completed.

**altruism**
concern for others' welfare.

**amalgamation**
the union or merging of two independent firms or companies to form a single business entity.

**amber box**
the category of subsidies in the WTO Agriculture Agreement, the total value of which is to be reduced. It includes most domestic support measures that distort production and trade.

**American Depository Receipt (ADR)**
a document that is issued by the US Bank, when a shareholder deposits his shares in it.

**amortisation**
used in relation to the payment of a loan in advance, over a specified time period. Such fund can also be created when equated instalments are deposited at regular intervals of time, so as to accumulate an amount equivalent to the amount of debt including interest.

**amplitude**
the extent of the up and down movements of a fluctuating economic variable, that is, the difference between the highest and lowest values of the variable.

**AMS**
Aggregate Measure of Support.

**Andean community**
An organisation of five Andean countries, including Bolivia, Colombia, Ecuador, Peru and Venezuela, formed in 1997 out of the Andean Pact. It provides for economic and social integration, in-

cluding regional trade liberalisation and a common external tariff, as well as harmonisation of other policies.

■ **Andean Pact**

The Cartagena Agreement of 1969, which provided for economic cooperation among a group of five Andean countries.

■ **angel investor**

a venture capitalist with a social conscience. Similar to venture capitalists, 'angels' are looking for high growth potential with a five-to-ten-year cash-out. Angel investors often look for 'psychic income beyond just balance sheet and income statement- the chance to help other entrepreneurs, assist with inner city problems, for example.

Starting a Company ?

Need Funding ?

Want Investor Advice ?

Need Business Services ?

You've come to the right place.

■ **anglo-saxon bias**

the way in which Walter Isard characterised the 19th century in a spatial economic theory in Britain, in contrast to the 'Germanic Bias' in the development of the classical location theory.

■ **Annual General Meeting (AGM)**

is an important yearly meeting of all the share holders of a public limited company.

*Annual General Meeting*

■ **annual report**

The statement of a company's finances and, often, prospects for the future.

■ **annuity**

A type of life insurance contract that guarantees periodic payments to the insured at some future time, usually retirement.

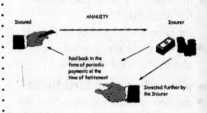

■ **antedate**

to date a document with a date that is earlier than the current one, such as a life insurance policy, so that it matures or takes effect sooner.

■ **anticipation**

in the context of acFTHE counting, to record the earnings or profit before they are actually realised. For example, the total proceeds of an instalment have actually been made.

**anti-dumping duty**
tariff levied on dumped imports. The threat of an anti-dumping duty can deter imports, even when it has not been used and anti-dumping is therefore a form of non-tariff barrier.

**anti-dumping suit**
a complaint by a domestic producer that imports are being dumped and the resulting investigation.

**antitrust legislation**
a law formulated to restrict monopolistic practices followed by a private business, so as to ensure a healthy competition.

**anti-trust policy**
the US term for competition policy.

**ANZCERTA**
Australia-New Zealand Closer Economic Relations Trade Agreement

**APEC**
Asia Pacific Economic Cooperation Members: Members of ASEAN, NAFTA, ANZCERTA, Chile, China, Hong Kong, Taiwan, Japan, South Korea, Russia, Vietnam and Peru.

**APM**
Average Propensity to Import

**apparel**
clothing.

**apparent consumption**
production plus imports minus exports, sometimes also adjusted for changes in inventories. The intention here is not to distinguish different uses for a good within the country, but only to infer the total that is used there for any purpose.

**appellate body**
the standing committee of the WTO that reviews decisions of dispute settlement panels.

**application money**
the sum that needs to be paid along with an application for a new issue of stocks or shares.

**applied economics**
a branch of economics that deals with the study of practical problems, using the principles and tools of economic analysis.

**applied tariff rate**
the actual tariff rate in effect at a country's border.

**appraisal**
an assessment of the worth, especially that of a property or business, for the determination of insurance, taxes, tariffs, sale price, etc.

**appraiser**
one who is trained and experienced in the valuation of the property.

**appreciation**
1. an increase in the value of

something, particularly said in terms of currency, whose appreciation leads to the increase in the purchasing power.
2. a rise in the value of a country's currency on the exchange market, relative either to a particular other currency or to a weighted average of other currencies. The currency is said to appreciate.

■ **appreciative theory (Nelson)**
attempts to structure qualitative notions about the nature of a firm and its activities, in a manner that is less rigorous but richer than at the formal level.

■ **apprenticeship**
a practice that requires young trainers, who are receiving training in a particular occupation, to serve a specified period of time before being recognised as skilled.

*Apprenticeship*

■ **appropriability problem**
problems related to the ability of the firm to capture acceptable levels of benefits, associated with the exploitation of its own technological innovation through confidentiality, patent etc.

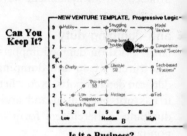

Can You Keep It?

Is it a Business?

*Appropriability Problem*

■ **appropriate technology**
the applying of an appropriate technology according to the factor endowments that exist in country. Developing countries generally have relatively larger labour force as compared to investment capital and therefore labour-intensive industry is more appropriate for such countries.

■ **appropriation**
money or materials set aside or spent for a specific purpose or allocating the resources between the numerous uses.

■ **arbitrage**
1. the simultaneous buying of currency, securities or goods from one market and selling them in another market at a higher price.
2. a combination of transactions designed to profit from an existing discrepancy among prices, exchange rates and/or interest rates on different markets without risk of these changing.

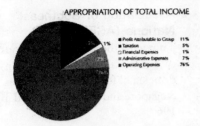

APPROPRIATION OF TOTAL INCOME

| | |
|---|---|
| ■ Profit Attributable to Group | 11% |
| ■ Taxation | 5% |
| □ Financial Expenses | 1% |
| ▨ Administrative Expenses | 7% |
| ▨ Operating Expenses | 76% |

*Appropriation*

■ **arbitration**
a means of settling the dispute between two parties, by a third person who has no interest in the matter.

■ **argument for protection**
a reason given for restricting imports by tariffs.

■ **Armington assumption**
the assumption that internationally traded products are differentiated by the country of origin.

■ **articles of association**
an official document that the promoters of a public limited company are legally required to file with the Registrar.

■ **arubaito**
part-time work

■ **as is**
the used or damaged goods that are sold without any warranty by the seller.

■ **ASEAN**
Association of Southeast Asian Nations

■ **Asian Development Bank**
A multilateral institution based in Manila, Philippines, that provides financing for development needs in countries of the Asia-Pacific region.

■ **Asia-Pacific Economic Cooperation**
an organisation of countries in the Asia-Pacific region, launched in 1989 and devoted to promoting open trade and practical economic cooperation.

■ **assessment**
the calculation of the tax liability of an individual, firm or a company. An assessment makes an individual aware of his tax liability along with the manner in which it is calculated.

■ **asset**
an item of property, such as land, capital, money, a share in ownership or a claim on others for future payment, such as a bond or a bank deposit.

■ **asset stripping**
the selling of such assets of a company that it does not require in its day to day functioning.

■ **assignment**
the right to transfer the benefit of the loan that a person is entitled to receive from another person, for instance Mr. X has given a loan to Mr. Y, then he can authorise another person to recover loan from Mr. Y.

■ **assignment problem**
how to use macroeconomic policies to achieve both internal bal-

ance and external balance, specifically, with only monetary and fiscal policies available under fixed exchange rates.

■ **assimilative capacity**
the extent to which the environment can accommodate or tolerate pollutants.

■ **assisted areas**
those areas which are recognised by the concerned administration or the government as being eligible to receive special assistance due to their relative backwardness and poverty.

*Assisted Areas*

■ **associated company**
an independent company that is connected or related to another independent company in a particular manner.

■ **Association of International Bond Dealers**
an organisation established in 1969, whose job is to compile and publish the current market quotations and yields for Eurobond issues.

■ **Association of Southeast Nations (ASEF)**
a union of the developing nations of South East Asia, including Indonesia, Malaysia, Philippines, Singapore and Thailand formed in 1967.

■ **asymmetric information**
the failure of two parties to a transaction to have the same relevant information.

■ **asymptote**
a value towards which a function's dependent variable inclines or moves when the independent variable becomes very large or very small, but it never reaches it.

■ **asymptotic distribution**
the probability distribution towards which a statistic moves or inclines when the sample size reaches infinity. Generally used in econometrics in assessing the large sample properties of its estimators.

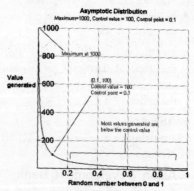

*Asymptotic Distribution*

■ **at best**
in relation to the stock market, an abbreviation for the lowest possible price in respect of a buying order and 'at the highest possible price' in respect of a selling order.

■ **at discretion**
a term that qualifies an instruction that a client gives to his stockbroker for buying or selling stocks or shares, granting the broker to exercise his own judgement for the price at which to buy.

■ **at limit**
a term that qualifies an instruction that a client gives to his stockbroker for buying or selling stocks or shares, placing a limit on the highest price that may be paid or the lowest price for making a sale.

■ **at par**
at equality. Two currencies are said to be 'at par' if they are trading one-for-one.

■ **at sight**
the payment of a bill of exchange or promissory note on demand.

■ **at the market**
a term that qualifies an instruction that a client gives to his stockbroker for buying or selling stocks or shares, permitting the broker to buy or sell at a price that is around the market price prevailing at the time.

■ **ATC**
Agreement on Textiles and Clothing

■ **atomistic competition**
a structure of market characterised by a large number of firms, who compete independently.

■ **attribute**
an individual's qualitative characteristic, like sex is an attribute, age is a variable.

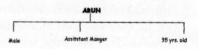

ATTRIBUTES

ARUN

Male          Assistant Manger          35 yrs. old

■ **auction**
a public sale of items in which the item is sold to the highest bidder.

■ **auctioneer**
1. a representative of a seller, who is authorised to sell his goods at an auction.
2. an agent whose job is to bring about the fixing of a mutually acceptable price between buyer(s) and seller(s).

■ **audit**
the periodic checking of the accounts of an organisation, so as to ascertain their accuracy.

■ **auditor's report**
the report that a person who audits a company's accounts submits after examining the accounts and relevant records of the company.

■ **autarky**
1. national economic self-suffi-

ciency and independence.
2. the situation of not engaging in international trade.

■ **autarky price**
price in autarky, that is, the price of something within a country when it is not traded by that country.

■ **authorised capital**
the maximum amount of capital that can be raised by a public limited company by public issue of shares. This amount is also stated in the memorandum of association, which is filed along with the articles of association with the registrar.

■ **authorised clerk**
the clerk employed by a stockbroker, who is authorised to deal on the floor of the stock exchange.

■ **authority constraints**
it states where and when individual or joint activities occur and who can participate in such activities is constrained. Participation in such activities is dicated by authority constraints, which are related to who controls the particular piece of time-space: working hours, land owners' property rights, zoning, curfew, public transportation schedules and routes, office hours of governments and organisations, etc.

■ **autocovariance**
The jth autocovariance of a **stochastic process** $y_t$ is the **covariance** between its time t value and

the value at time t-j. It is denoted as gamma below and E[ means **expectation** or mean:]
and E[ ] means expectation or mean: gammajt $= E[(y_t - E_y)(Yt_j - E_y)]$.

## The Autocovariance function

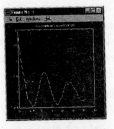

■ **automatic licensing**
the licensing of imports or exports for which licenses are assured, for gathering information or a holdover from when licenses were not automatic. Depending on how the licensing is administered, automatic licensing can add to the bureaucratic and/or time cost of trade.

■ **automatic stabilisers**
the means through which the fluctuations in the different economic variables are streamlined or can be avoided without any specific effort of the government.

■ **automatic stabiliser**
government spending programs, which respond to changes in the level of national income in such a way as to offset those changes.

■ **automation**
the mechanisation of the various

operations of an economy.

■ **autonomous expenditures**
those expenditures that are not affected by the level of income, in the income expenditure model. For example, government expenditure, investment expenditure, etc.

■ **autoregression**
a set of data wherein the value of each observation partially depends on the value of the observation that immediately precedes it.

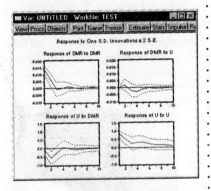

*Autoregression*

■ **average cost**
the amount spent on producing each unit of output. The average cost is calculated by dividing the total cost by the number of units of output produced.

■ **average cost pricing**
setting the price equal to the average cost.

■ **Average Fixed Cost (AFC)**
1. total fixed cost divided by the output. The average fixed cost will decline as the output increases.

This is because as output increases the fixed costs are spread further and further.
2. in the theory of the firm, fixed costs are the costs of production, which are constant, whatever the level of output. Average fixed costs are total fixed costs divided by the number of units of output, that is, fixed cost per unit of output.

■ **average product**
the average product of a factor in a firm or industry is its output divided by the amount of the factor employed.

■ **average propensity to import**
is determined as a ratio of the aggregate value of goods and services that a country imports in a year to the national income.

■ **Average Revenue Product (ARP)**
in the theory of factor pricing, average revenue product is the total revenue (TR) divided by the number of units (N) of the factor employed.
$$ARP = {}^{TR}/_{N}$$

■ **average tariff**
an average of a country's tariff rates. This can be calculated in several ways, none of which are ideal for representing how protective the country's tariffs are.

■ **Average Total Cost (ATC)**
the amount spent on producing each unit of output. The average

cost is obtained by dividing the total cost by the number of units produced. The average total cost is made up of two elements, the average fixed cost and the average variable cost.

■ **Average Variable Cost (AVC)**

1. the variable cost per unit of output. It is calculated by dividing the average variable cost by the number of units of output produced.
2. in the theory of the firm, average variable cost is the total variable cost divided by the number of units of output.

■ **averaging**

to purchase more of a security in the event of a decrease in its price so as to lower the average cost of a holding.

■ **axes**

the fixed lines on a graph, which carry the scales against which the coordinates are plotted.

■ **axiom**

propositions which form a set of relationships (and are specific in terms of the direction of the relationships) and are assumed to be true as a basis for argument or inference (but may not be true in actuality).

■ **backbone firms**

an originally Japanese concept to describe medium-sised firms which exhibit the effects of strong entrepreneurial leadership and vitality. In such firms, strategies are shaped by technological innovation, marketing and attention given to skilled and participatory workforces.

■ **backhaul transportation**

utilisation of otherwise empty cargo space on the return trip, after a primary transport activity has taken place. Since the primary transport function may have paid for the partial or full cost of return transportation, the price of backhaul utilisation may be relatively low.

■ **back-office functions**

record-keeping and analytical functions that do not require frequent personal contact with clients or business associates.

*Back-office Functions*

■ **backward bending**

a curve that reverses direction, usually if, after moving out away from an origin or axis, it then turns back towards it. The term is used most frequently to describe supply curves for which the quantity supplied declines as price rises above some point, as may happen in a labour supply curve, the supply curve for foreign exchange or an offer curve.

■ **backward linkages**
linkages to suppliers of inputs. A useful concept to differentiate direction of flows in complex economies.

■ **balance of merchandise trade**
the value of a country's merchandise exports minus the value of its merchandise imports.

■ **balance of payments**
1. A list or accounting of all the international transactions of a company, for a given time period, usually one year. Payments into the country (receipts) are entered as positive numbers called credits and payments out of the country (payments) are entered as negative numbers called debits.
2. a single number summarising all the international transactions of a country.

■ **balance of payments argument for protection**
a common reason for restricting imports, especially under fixed exchange rates, when a country is losing international reserves due to a trade deficit.

■ **balance of payments equilibrium**
under a pegged exchange rate, it is the equality of credits and debits in the balance of payments, using the traditional definition of the capital account. A surplus or deficit implied changing official reserves, so that something would ultimately have to change.

■ **balance of payments surplus**
a number summarising the state of a country's international transactions, usually equal to the balance on current account plus the balance on capital account.

■ **balance of trade**
the value of a country's exports minus the value of its imports. Unless specified as the balance of merchandise trade, it normally incorporates trade in services, including earnings (interest, dividends, etc.) on capital.

**Balance of earnings (in billion CHF)**

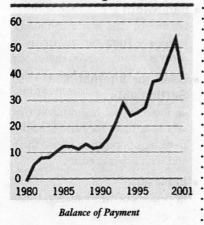

*Balance of Payment*

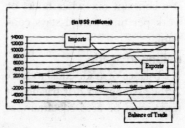

■ **balance on capital account**
a country's receipts minus payments for capital account transactions.

■ **balance on current account**
a country's receipts minus payments for current account transactions. Equals the balance of trade plus net inflows of transfer payments.

■ **balanced budget**
such budget rises when the government receives the same amount of money from taxation as it is spending. Classical economists argued that this should always be the aim of government policy. Keynesians on the other hand said that in times of low economic activity, the government should run a deficit (spending more than its revenue) to boost the economy and when the economy is booming they could run a surplus (spending less than revenue). In this way, they could balance the budget in the long-run.

■ **balanced growth**
a macroeconomics model exhibits balanced growth if consumption, investment and capital grow at a constant rate while hours of work per time period stays constant.

■ **balanced trade**
1. a balance of trade equal to zero.
2. the assumption that balance of trade must be zero equilirium, as wouldbe the case with a floating exchange rate and no cash flows.

■ **baldwin envelope**
the consumption possibility frontier for a large country, constructed as the envelope formed by moving the foreign offer curve along the country's transformation curve.

■ **banana war**
a trade dispute between the European Union (EU) and the US over EU preferences for bananas from former colonies. On behalf of US-owned companies exporting bananas from South America and the Caribbean, the U.S. complained to the WTO, which ruled in favour of the US.

■ **bancor**
the international currency proposed by Keynes to be used as the basis for the international monetary system that was being constructed at the end of World War II.

■ **bandwidth**
volume of data that a communications system can transmit or process.

■ **Bank for International Settlements**
an international organisation that acts as a bank for central banks, fostering cooperation among them and with other agencies.

■ **bank note**
in periods of free banking, banks

could issue their own money called bank notes. A bank note was a risky, perpetual debt claim on a bank, which paid no interest and could be redeemed on demand at the original bank, usually in gold.

■ **Bank of Canada**
federal agency, which controls interest rates and the money supply in Canada. It influences interest rates by setting rates on short-term loans that it makes to chartered banks.

■ **barriers to entry**
factors that prevent firms from entering a market, such as government rules or patents

■ **barter**
the exchange of goods for goods, without using money.

■ **barter economy**
an economic model of international trade in which goods are exchanged for goods without the existence of money.

■ **base money**
monetary base.

■ **base year**
The year in which calculations, usually indexes, commence and with which other years are compared. For example, Consumer Price Index.

■ **basic balance**
one of the more frequently used measures of the balance of payments surplus or deficit under pegged exchange rates, the basic balance was equal to the current account balance plus the balance of long-term capital flows.

■ **basic competitive model**
the model of the economy that pulls together the assumptions of self-interested consumers, profit maximis-ing firms and perfectly competitive markets.

■ **basic import price**
see **minimum price system.**

■ **basing-point pricing**
a pricing method under which prices are quoted to include transportation from one (or more) given point(s), regardless of the location from which the actual shipment is made.

■ **bayesian analysis**
developed to provide a subjectively- rational framework for decision-making under uncertainty.

■ **bear market**
a market characterised by falling stock prices.

■ **beggar thy neighbour**
for a country to use a policy for its own benefit that harms other countries. Examples are optimal tariffs and, in a recession, tariffs and/or devaluation to create employment.

■ **behavioural environment**
related to a firm or organisation. Consists of that part of the 'objective' environment defined by the firm's operating location(s) with associated communities and by the

various functional linkages to suppliers, customers, governments, consumers and other interactive stakeholders.

■ **behavioural matrix**
1. addresses the role of information use in behavioural approaches to location.
2. differentiates the amount of information available

■ **benchmarking**
1. setting reference points or standards by which behaviours or developments can be measured at a point in time or over time
2. a particular tool for impriving performance by learning from best practices by which they they are achieved.

*Benchmarking*

■ **benign neglect**
doing nothing about a problem, in the hope that it will not be serious or will be solved by others.

■ **bequest savings motive**
people save so that they can leave an inheritance to their children.

■ **Bertrand competition**
an oligopoly in which each firm believes that its rivals are committed to keeping their prices fixed and that customers can be lured away by offering lower prices. It is an assumption that is be made by firms in an oligopoly, that other firms hold their prices constant as they themselves change behaviour. Contrasts with Cournot competition. Both are used in models of international oligopoly, but Cournot competition is used more often.

■ **beta index (in network analysis)**
the ratio between the number of links (edges) and the number of nodes in a network.

■ **bias**
bias of technology, either change or difference, refers to a shift towards or away from use of a factor. The exact meaning depends on the definition of neutral used to define absence of bias. Factor bias matters for the effects of technological progress on trade and welfare.

■ **bicycle theory**
with regard to the process of multilateral trade liberalisation, the theory that if it ceases to move forward (i.e., achieve further liberalisation), then it will collapse (i.e., past liberalisation will be reversed).

■ **bid price (or rent) function**
a set of combinations of land prices and distances among which

the individual (or firm) is indifferent. It describes prices that the household (firm) would be willing to pay at varying locations and for varying amounts of land, in order to achieve a given level of satisfaction (utility/ profits).

■ **bid/ask spread**
the difference between the price that a buyer must pay on a market and the price that a seller will receive for the same thing. The difference covers the cost of and provides profit for the broker or other intermediary, such as a bank on the foreign exchange market.

■ **bilateral**
between two countries.

■ **bilateral agreement**
an agreement between two countries.

■ **bilateral exchange rate**
the exchange rate between two countries' currencies, defined as the number of units of either currency needed to purchase one unit of the other.

■ **bilateral quota**
an import (or export) quota applied to trade with a single trading partner, specifying the amount of a good that can be imported from (exported to) that single country only.

■ **bilateral trade**
the trade between two countries, that is, the value or quantity of one country's exports to the other or the sum of exports and imports between them.

■ **bill of exchange**
1. a contract entitling an exporter to receive immediate payment in the local currency for goods that would be shipped elsewhere.
2. any document demanding payment.

■ **bill of lading**
the receipt given by a transportation company to an exporter, when the former accepts goods for transport. It includes the contract specifying what transport service will be provided and the limits of liability.

■ **binding**
see **tariff binding**.

■ **birth rate**
the number of live births per 1000 of the population. The birth rate is also often called the 'crude birth rate'.

■ **BIS**
Bank for International Settlements.

■ **black market**

an illegal market, in which something is bought and sold outside of official government-sanctioned channels. Black markets tend to arise when a government tries to fix a price without itself providing all of the necessary supply or demand.

■ **bloc**

see **trading bloc**

■ **blue box**

a special category of subsidies permitted under the WTO Agriculture Agreement, it includes payments that are linked to production but with provisions to limit production through production quotas or requirements to set aside land from production.

■ **bond**

a debt instrument, issued by a borrower and promising a specified stream of payments to the purchaser, usually regular interest payments plus a final repayment of principal.

■ **bonded warehouse**

see **foreign trade zone.**

■ **boolean operator**

a reference to the three search rules: 'AND', 'OR' & 'NOT'. It is derived from Boolean Logic referring to the logical relationship among search terms (named after the British mathematician George Boole).

■ **boom**

a period of time when resources are being fully used and the GDP is growing steadily.

■ **BOP**

Balance of Payments

■ **border tax adjustment**

rebate of indirect taxes (taxes on other than direct income, such as a sales tax or VAT) on exported goods and levying of them on imported goods.

■ **bound rate**

see **tariff binding.**

■ **box**

used with a colour, a category of subsidies based on the status in WTO: red=forbidden, amber=go slow, green=permitted, blue = subsidiestied to production limits. Terminology seems only to be used in agriculture, where in fact there is no red box.

■ **boycott**

to protest by refusing to purchase from someone or otherwise do business with them. In international trade, a boycott most often takes the form of refusal to import a country's goods.

■ **BP-Curve**

in the Mundell-Fleming model, the curve representing balance of payments equilibrium. It is normally upward sloping because an increase in income increases imports while an increase in the interest rate increases capital inflows.

# BRAC
the Base Closure and Realignment Commission. It recommended military bases for closure in 1988, 1991, 1993 and 1995.

# brain drain
the migration of skilled workers out of a country.

# branding
the development of the identity of a product through name selection and related marketing strategies, involving consideration of Nomenclature Strategy, Name Creation or Brand Extension, Trademark Screening, Target Audience Market, Graphical Elements, etc.

## break-of-bulk point
the location (usually a port) where a shipment is divided into parts. This usually happens where a transfer of the shipment between transport modes occurs, such as between water and land at a port.

## broker's fee
the fee for a transaction charged by an intermediary in a market, such as a bank in a foreign-exchange transaction.

## Brussels Tariff Nomenclature (BTN)
an international system of classification for goods that was once widely used for specifying tariffs. It was changed, in name only, to the CCCN in 1976 and later superseded by the Harmonised System of Tariff Nomenclature.

# bubble
a rise in the price of an asset, based not on the current or prospective income that it provides but solely on expectations by market participants, that the price will rise in the future. When those expectations cease, the bubble bursts and the price falls rapidly.

# bubble economy
term for an economy in which the presence of one or more bubbles in its asset markets is a dominant feature of its performance. Japan was said to be a bubble economy in the late 1980s.

# budget
the annual announcement of the government's fiscal policy changes by the Chancellor of the Exchequer. It usually takes place in the month of March each year. In the budget, the Chancellor will announce the tax changes he proposes for the following tax year and also how the government plans to spend that revenue. He will also give the medium-term forecast for the economy.

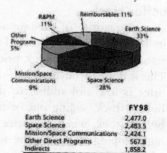

| | FY98 |
|---|---|
| Earth Science | 2,477.0 |
| Space Science | 2,483.5 |
| Mission/Space Communications | 2,424.1 |
| Other Direct Programs | 567.8 |
| Indirects | 1,858.2 |
| Total | 9,810.6 |

*Budget*

■ **budget constraint**
for an individual or household, the condition that income equals expenditure (in a static model) or that income minus expenditure equals the value of increased asset holdings (in a dynamic model).

■ **budget deficit**
the negative of the budget surplus, thus the excess of expenditure over income.

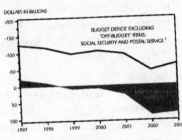

DOLLARS IN BILLIONS

BUDGET DEFICIT EXCLUDING
"OFF-BUDGET ITEMS:
SOCIAL SECURITY AND POSTAL SERVICE '

*Budget Deficit*

■ **budget surplus**
in general, an excess of income over expenditure, but usually refers specifically to the government budget, where it is the excess of tax revenue over expenditure (including transfer payments).

■ **buffer stock**
a large quantity of a commodity held in storage to be used to stabilise the commodity's price. This is done by buying when the price is low and adding to the buffer stock, selling out of the buffer stock, when the price is high, hoping to reduce the size of price fluctuations.

■ **building block**
see **stumbling block**

■ **bundles and bundling**
concepts used by Hägerstrand to refer to the needs of people and goods to 'travel' together in daily time-space prisms (in bundles), such as in meetings or on public buses.

■ **bundling**
term used by software companies to refer to the trend in Microsoft and other PC software firms 'to bundle together multiple products into a smaller number of unified or integrated product offerings.'

■ **business climate**
an often used, nevertheless rather ambiguous concept referring to collection of location factors, directly or indirectly expressing the general or governmental attitude towards business and/or various local qualities or attributes which affect business operations, such as taxes, labour costs, union activities, utilities and business representation in local decision-making.

*Business Climate*

### business cycle

the pattern followed by macroeconomic variables, such as GDP and unemployment that rise and fall irregularly over time, relative to trend.

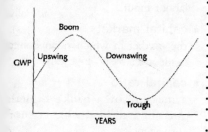

### Business Cycle Dating Committee

see **National Bureau of Economic Research.**

### business services

services which are forwardly linked to other business activities. Such services tend to perform functions, which are more efficiently 'externalised' by the client firms, i.e. cannot be efficiently performed in-house. For examples banking, insurance, etc.

### buyer's market

a market for a good (stocks, housing, etc.) where prices are falling and there are more parties interested in selling than in buying.

### CACM

Central American Common Market. Founded in 1960, preceded by Organisation of Central American States.

### cain rule

a rule used to determine the derivative of a function in relation to a variable, where the function consists of another function.

### calculus

in the field of mathematics, a system of calculation that is done using special symbolic notations, generally concerned with the calculation of derivatives and integration.

### call

in the stock exchange terminology, an option to purchase a specific amount of some stock at a quoted price, known as the striking price, within a specified period of time.

### call loan

a loan that can be concluded or 'called' at any point of time by the creditor or the debtor.

### capability constraints

constraints on human activities in time and space, imposed by nature or available tools. Part of Hägerstrand's time-geographic conceptualisation.

### capital

1. monetary capital: the money used for investment purposes.
2. real or invested capital: the capital goods (machines and production- & distribution infrastructure) needed for the production of goods and services.

*Capital*

■ **capital account**
a part of the balance of payments where flows of savings, investment and currency are recorded.

■ **capital consumption**
in national accounts, capital consumption is the amount by which gross investment exceeds the net investment. It is the same as replacement investment.

■ **capital deepening**
an increase in capital intensity, normally in a macro context, where it is measured by something analogous to the capital stock available per labour hour spent. In a micro context, it could mean the amount of capital available for a worker to use, but this use is rare. Capital deepening is a macroeconomic concept of a faster-growing magnitude of capital in production than in labour.

■ **capital gain**
increase in the value of an asset between the time it is purchased and the time it is sold.

■ **capital intensity**
the amount of capital per unit of labour input.

■ **capital market**
the market in which savings are made available to investors.

■ **capital ratio**
a measure of a bank's capital strength used by the U.S. regulatory agencies.

■ **capital structure**
of a firm is broadly made up of its amounts of equity and debt.

■ **capital-augmenting**
one of the ways in which an effectiveness variable could be included in a production function in a Solow model. If effectiveness A is multiplied by capital K but not by labour L, then we say the effectiveness variable is capital-augmenting.

■ **capitation**
the system of payment for each customer served, rather than by the service performed.

■ **Carnegie School of Economic Behaviour**
set of ideas about the internal workings of firms, developed by Herbert Simon, his colleagues and those who were at one time or another at Carnegie-Mellon University and who were influenced by his ideas.

■ **cartel**

a group of producers with an agreement to collude in setting prices and output.

■ **cash-in-advance constraint**

a modelling idea. In a basic Arrow-Debreu general equilibrium there is no need for money because exchanges are automatic, through a Walrasian auctioneer. To study monetary phenomena, a class of models was made in which money was required to make purchases of other goods. In such a model the budget constraint is written so that the agent must have enough cash on hand to make any consumption purchase. Using this mechanism, money can have a positive price in equilibrium and monetary effects can be seen in such models.

■ **categorical assistance**

public assistance aimed at a particular category of people, like the elderly or the disabled.

■ **causation**

relationship that results when a change in one variable is not only correlated with, but actually causes the change in another one.

■ **CBI**

Confederation of British Industry

■ **CD**

Certificate of Deposit

■ **censored dependent variables**

a dependent variable in a model is censored, if observations of it cannot be seen when it takes on values in some range. That is, the independent variables are observed for such observations, but the dependent variable is not.

■ **Center for Research in Security Prices (CRSP)**

a standard database of finance information at the University of Chicago. Has daily returns on NYSE, AMEX and NASDAQ stocks.

■ **central bank**

the bank that oversees and monitors the rest of the banking system and serves as the bankers' bank.

■ **central place**

the focus of central place theory. A central place is a market centre supplying the inland with goods and services. The size of the inland and the order of the goods and services provided, determine the economic base of the central place and thereby its size and economic structure.

*Central Place*

■ **central place theory**

a body of theory associated with the names Walter Christaller, August Lösch and others, suggesting specific hierarchical explanations (anchored in micro-economic demand and production theory) for the organisation of economic landscapes of cities, towns and market areas.

■ **central planning**
the system in which central government bureaucrats determine what will be produced and how it will be produced.

■ **centralisation**
an organisational structure in which decision making is concentrated at the top.

■ **centrally planned economy**
an economy in which most decisions about resource allocation are made by the central government.

■ **Certificate of Deposit (CD)**
an account in which money is deposited for a preset length of time, that must yield a slightly higher return to compensate for the reduced liquidity.

■ **CES Production Function**
CES stands for Constant Elasticity of Substitution. This is a function describing production, usually at a macroeconomic level, with two inputs, which are usually capital and labour.

■ **CES Utility**
a kind of utility function. A synonym for CRRA or isoelastic utility function. Often written this way, presuming a constant g not equal to one:

■ **cessation closure**
a form of plant closure, which is based on the decision by a firm to abandon an activity/activity mix or the production of a specific product or product mix. In more complex situations, several plants may be closed in the context of such an abandonment.

■ **ceteris paribus**
all other things remaining the same, the assumption that all other variables within an economic model remain constant whilst one change is being considered.

■ **chaebol**
one of a small number of very large, highly diversified and centralised Korean firms, owned and controlled by the founding patriarch's family through a central holding company.

■ **chained**
an index number that is frequently reweighted. An example is an inflation index made up of prices weighted by the frequency with which they are paid and the frequent recomputation of weights makes it a chained index.

■ **chaotic**
a description of a dynamic system that is very sensitive to initial conditions and may evolve in wildly different ways, from slightly different initial conditions.

■ **characteristic equations**
a polynomial whose roots are eigenvalues.

## characteristic functions

denoted here as PSI(t) or $PSI_X(t)$. A characteristic function is defined for any random variable X with a pdf f(x). PSI(t) is defined to be $E[e^{itX}]$, which is the integral from minus infinity to infinity of $e^{itX}f(x)$.

## characteristic roots

is a synonym for eigenvalues.

## chartalism

also known as 'state theory of money' — 19th century monetary theory, based more on the idea that legal restrictions or customs can or should maintain the value of money, not intrinsic content of valuable metal.

## chicago school

Refers to a perspective on economics of the University of Chicago circa 1970. Variously interpreted to imply:

## chi-square distribution

a continuous distribution, with natural number parameter r. Is the distribution of sums of squares of r standard normal variables. Mean is r, variance is 2r, **pdf** and **cdf** is difficult to express in html and moment-generating function (mgf) is $(1-2t)^{-r/2}$.

## choice

economic choices involve the alternative uses of scarce resources.

## choke price

the lowest price at which the quantity demanded is zero.

## cholesky decomposition

given a symmetric positive definite square matrix X, the Cholesky decomposition of X is the factorisation X=U'U, where U is the square root matrix of X and satisfies:

1 U'U = X

2 U is upper triangular (that is, it has all zeros below the diagonal)

Once U has been computed, one can calculate the inverse of X more easily because $X^{-1} = U^{-1}(U')^{-1}$ and the inverses of U and U' are easier to compute.

## cholesky factorisation

see **cholesky decomposition**.

## choropleth maps

maps, in which each spatial unit is filled with a uniform colour or pattern. They are appropriate for the data that have been scaled or normalised. For example, economic geographers may apply a spatial perspective to economic data using such maps. A choropleth map may show the per-capita GDP differences between areas.

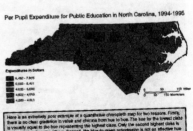

Per Pupil Expenditure for Public Education in North Carolina, 1994-1995

*Choropleth Maps*

■ **chow test**

a particular test for structural change. An econometric test to determine whether the coefficients in a regression model are the same in separate subsamples. In reference to a paper of G.C. Chow (1960), "the standard F test for the equality of two sets of coefficients in linear regression models" is called a Chow test.

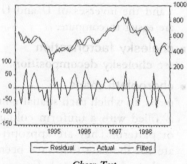

*Chow Test*

■ **circuit**

description of a network with one or more loops, creating alternative paths between nodes and thereby network redundancy.

*Circuit*

■ **circular flow**

the manner in which funds move through the capital, labour and product markets between households, firms, the government and the foreign sector.

■ **circulating capital**

the flows of value within a production organisation. Includes stocks of raw material, work in process, finished goods inventories and cash in hand, needed to pay workers and suppliers before the products are sold.

■ **classical**

according to Lucas (1998), a classical theory would have no explicit reference to preferences. Contrast to **neoclassical.**

■ **classical economists**

economists prevalent before the Great Depression, who believed that the basic competitive model provided a good description of the economy and that if short periods of unemployment did occur, market forces would quickly restore the economy to full employment.

■ **classical unemployment**

unemployment that results from too-high real wages. It occurs in the supply-constrained equilibrium, so that rightward shifts in the aggregate supply reduce the level of unemployment.

■ **Clayton Act**

a 1914 U.S. law on the subject of antitrust and price discrimination.

■ **clears**

in this context it is a verb. A market clears if the vector of prices for goods is such that the excess demand at those prices is zero. That is, the quantity demanded of every good at those prices is met.

■ **cliometrics**

the study of economic history.

■ **closed economy**

an economy that neither exports nor imports.

■ **closed I/O model**

an input-output model is either open or closed with respect to certain sectors or activities, i.e. such activities either remain 'exogenous' to the model or are made 'endogenous'.

■ **cluster**

a concept associated with Michael Porter's work, who defines a 'cluster' as a geographically proximate group or geographic concentration of 'interconnected companies, specialised suppliers and service providers, firms in related industries and associated institutions linked by commonalities and complementarities. The geographic scope of a cluster can range from a single city or state to a country or even a group of neighbouring countries.

■ **Coase theorem**

informally, the theorem states that in the presence of complete competitive markets and the absence of transactions costs, an efficient set of inputs to production and outputs from production will be chosen by agents, regardless of how property rights over the inputs were assigned to the agents.

■ **Cobb-Douglas Production Function**

relates the productivity of labour to the capital intensity (capital-labour ratio) under the condition of a constant profit wage ratio.

■ **cobweb model**

a theoretical model of an adjustment process that, on a price/quantity or supply/demand graph, spirals towards equilibrium.

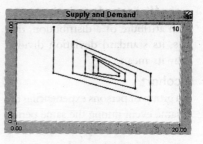

*Cobweb Model*

■ **Cochrane-Orcutt Estimation**

an algorithm for estimating a time series linear regression in the presence of auto correlated errors. The implicit citation is to Cochrane-Orcutt (1949).

■ **coefficient cf localisation**

a simple method of determining the extent to which an industry is localised compared with the spatial (multi-regional) distribution of all (or at least a larger set of) economic activities. The coefficient is calculated by subtracting for each region, the percentage employment share of the industry in question from the total regional employment share (the region's share of national employment in all activities). The sum of the positive (or the negative, not both) deviations, divided by 100 represents the coefficient (potentially varying between 0 and 1).

■ **coefficient of specialisation**
this coefficient is calculated just like the coefficient of localisation, except that regions become industries and industries become regions.

■ **coefficient of variation**
an attribute of a distribution, that is, its standard deviation divided by its mean.

■ **cohort**
a group of persons experiencing the same event during the same period of time. Cohort analysis traces those persons born during the same time period, as they age and live through common time-specific experiences and life stages. Among the most important experiences of an aging cohort are the cohort birth rates and cohort death rates.

*Cohort*

■ **collusion**
an agreement between parties to refrain from participating in an activity that they normally would, in order to reduce competition and gain higher profits.

■ **commerical paper**
another term for commoditised short-term corporate debt.

■ **commodity**
a good that is generally a primary good used in manufacturing such as timber, cotton, wool and copper.

■ **common markets**
group of countries between which there is free trade in products and factors of production and which imposes a common external tariff on imported goods from outside the market.

■ **compact sets**
a closed and bounded set.

■ **comparative advantage**
a country's ability to produce a good relatively more efficiently than another country.

■ **compensating variation**
the price a consumer would need to be paid or the price the consumer would need to pay, to be just as well off after (a) a change in prices of products that the consumer might buy and (b) time to adapt to that change.

■ **compensating wage differentials**
the additional amount paid for a

job that has certain unattractive features, such as risk of injury, as compared with a job that requires similar skills but lacks these negative features.

■ **competition**
that which develops when two or more producers are providing a similar product or service.

■ **competitive equilibrium price**
the price at which the quantity supplied and the quantity demanded are equal to each other.

■ **complement**
a good for which demand decreases when the price of a closely related good increases.

■ **complementarity**
refers to both, the similarities and the differences (between regions or countries) needed to bring about interaction. Regions have to be sufficiently similar with respect to cultural and other facets, to be able to engage in the kind of communication needed for interaction.

■ **complete markets**
a market in which the complete set of possible gambles on future states-of-the-world can be constructed with the existing assets.

■ **complete/completeness**
1. according to economic theory: a model's markets are complete if the agents can buy insurance contracts to protect them against any future time and state of the world.

2. according to statistics: in a context where a distribution is known except for parameter?, a minimal sufficient statistic is complete if there is only one unbiased estimator of? using that statistic.

■ **Completed Fertility Rate (CFR)**
number of children actually born per woman in a cohort of women by the end of their childbearing years (normally, women of 45 or over are considered to have completed their childbearing years. In some countries, this end-year is often set at 49).

■ **composite quasi-rent**
a quasi rent is the excess above the return necessary to maintain a resource's current service flow, which can be the means to recover sunk costs. Composite quasi- rent is that portion of the quasi- rent of resources that depends on continued association with some other specific, currently associated resources.

■ **compound**
to increase in value. Compound interest is calculated on the principal amount (the amount you originally invested) and also on the interest earned on that interest in previous years. For example, a deposit (or loan) compounded at 10 per cent annually will double in about seven years if no money is taken out (or paid in).

- **concavity of distribution functions**

a property of a distribution function-utility function pair. It is assumed to hold in some principal-agent models so as to make certain conclusions possible.

- **concentration ratio**

a way of measuring the concentration of market share held by particular suppliers in a market. It is the percentage of total market sales accounted for by a given number of leading firms.

- **concept**

a word or group of words that summarises or classifies certain facts, events or ideas into one category. Concepts are labels or categories or selected properties of objects. They are the bricks from which theories are constructed. Theories are constructed by linking concepts representing different attributes or belonging to different classes and by developing sets of interrelated statements concerning the relationship(s) between such concepts.

- **conceptual framework for economic geography**

the structure which serves to hold the conceptual parts (concepts) together and within which the ideas, facts, principles, insights and circumstances of Economic Geography exist and are related to each other.

- **condition number**

a measure of how close a matrix is to being singular. Relevant in estimation if the matrix of regressors is nearly singular, the data are nearly collinear and (a) it will be hard to make an accurate or precise inverse, (b) a linear regression will have large standard errors.

- **conditional**

it has a special use in finance, when used without other modifiers. Often means 'conditional on time and previous asset returns'. In that context, one might read 'returns are conditionally normally distributed.'

- **conditional factor demands**

a collection of functions that give the optimal demands for each of the several inputs as a function of the output expected and the prices of inputs. Often the prices are taken as given and incorporated into the functions and so they are only the functions of the output.

- **conformable**

generally used in conjunction with matrices. A matrix may not have the right dimension or shape to fit into some particular operation with another matrix. Take matrix addition — the matrices are supposed to have the same dimensions to be summed. If they don't, we can say that they are not conformable for addition. The most common application of the term comes in the context of multiplication.

- **conglomerates**
  a firm operating in several industries.

- **connectivity**
  an aggregate measure of the extent to which the nodes of a network are linked (directly or indirectly) to other nodes. Connectivity always refers to characteristics of a whole network, not to those of a single node.

- **consistent estimators**
  an estimator for a parameter is consistent if the estimator converges in probability to the true value of the parameter.

- **Consolidated Metropolitan Statistical Area (CMSA)**
  an area that meets the requirements for recognition as a 'Metropolitan Statistical Area' (MSA) and also has a population of one million or more can be recognised as a CMSA if separate component areas can be identified within the entire area by meeting statistical criteria specified in the standards and local opinion indicates that there is support for the component areas.

- **Constant Absolute Risk Aversion (CARA)**
  also called exponential utility, it is a class of utility functions. Has the form for some positive constant 'a':
  $$u(c)=-(1/a)e^{-ac}$$
  Under this specification the elasticity of marginal utility is equal to '-ac' and the instantaneous elasticity of substitution is equal to '1/

ac'. The coefficient of absolute risk aversion is 'a', thus the abbreviation CARA for Constant Absolute Risk Aversion.

- **Constant Relative Risk Aversion (CRRA)**
  a property of some utility functions, also said to have isoelastic form. CRRA is a synonym for **CES**.

- **constant returns to scale**
  when all inputs are increased by a certain proportion, output increases by the same proportion.

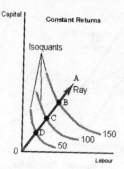

- **consultant**
  someone who assembles information, creates a knowledge base and provides professional advise relating to a problem of an individual, group or organisation on a volunteer basis or for remuneration.

*Consultant*

■ **consumer confidence**

a measure of the level of optimism that the consumers have about the performance of the economy. Generally, consumer confidence is high when the unemployment rate is low and GDP growth is high.

■ **consumer price index**

a price index in which the basket of goods is defined by what a typical consumer purchases.

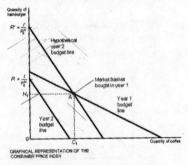

*Consumer Price Index*

■ **consumer protection legislation**

laws aimed at protecting consumers, for instance by assuring that consumers have more complete information about items they are considering to buy.

■ **consumer sovereignty**

1. the principle that holds that each individual is the best judge of what makes him better off.
2. when resources are allocated according to the wishes of consumers, i.e. in a perfectly free market.

■ **consumer surplus**

the difference between what a person would be willing to pay and what he actually has to pay in order to buy a certain amount of a good.

■ **consumer, consumption**

the individuals and corporations that buy products and services. In economics, consumption refers only to consuming that involves a monetary transaction.

■ **consumption function**

the relationship between disposable income and consumption.

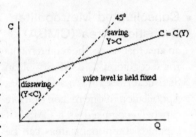

*Consumption Function*

■ **consumption set**

the set of affordable consumption bundles. One way to define a consumption set is by a set of prices, one for each possible good and a budget. Or, a consumption set could be defined in a model by some other set of restrictions on the set of possible consumption bundles.

■ **contingency clauses**

statements within a contract that make the level of payment or the work to be performed conditional upon various factors.

■ **contingency theory**
regards the design of an effective organisation, as necessarily having to be adapted to cope with the 'contingencies' which derive from the circumstances of environment, technology, scale, resources, work task and other factors.

■ **contingent valuations**
the use of questionnaires about valuation, to estimate the willingness of respondents to pay for public projects or programs.

■ **contract curve**
the same as the Pareto set, with the implication that it is drawn in an Edgeworth box.

■ **contractionary fiscal policy**
a government policy of reducing the spending and raising taxes. In the language of some first courses in macroneconomics, it shifts the IS curve (investment/saving curve) to the left.

■ **contractionary monetary policy**
a government policy of raising interest rates charged by the central bank. In the language of some first courses in macroeconomics, it shifts the LM curve (liquidity/money curve) to the left.

■ **control variables**
a variable in a model controlled by an agent in order to optimise something.

■ **convergence in quadratic mean**
a kind of convergence of random variables. If $x_t$ converges in quadratic mean, it converges in probability but it does not necessarily converge.

■ **convolution**
the convolution of two functions $U(x)$ and $V(x)$ is the function: $U*V(x)$ = (integral from 0 to x of) $U(t)V(x-t)$ dt.

■ **Cook's Distance**
a metric for deciding whether a particular point alone affects regression estimates much. After a regression is run, one can consider, for each data point, how far it is from the means of the independent variables and the dependent variable. If it is far from the means of the independent variables, it may be very influential and one can consider whether the regression results are similar without it.

■ **cooperative game**
a structure in which the players have the option of planning as a group, in advance of choosing their actions.

■ **core**
in terms of original allocations of goods among agents with specified utility functions, it is the set of possible reallocations such that no subset of agents could break off from the others and all do better just by trading among themselves.

- **corner solutions**
  a choice made by an agent that is at a constraint and not at the tangency of two classical curves on a graph, one characterising what the agent could obtain and the other characterising the imaginable choices that would attain the highest reachable value of the agents' objective.

- **corporate income tax**
  a tax based on the income or profit received by a corporation.

- **corporate welfare**
  when a government gives money or a monetary break (like tax cuts or subsidies) to a business. Governments give money to businesses that are very profitable to keep them from moving to other provinces or countries.

- **correlation**
  relationship that results when a change in one variable is consistently associated with a change in another.

- **cost**
  1. the price one pays in exchange for something. In economics, cost is usually defined simply as how much money you pay for something. However, there are costs beyond monetary price and many prices do not reflect the true cost of items. For example, the price of petrol does not reflect the environmental costs associated with driving a car.
  2. the value that must be given up to acquire a good or service.

- **Cost and Freight (CAF)**
  a price quotation inclusive of both the merchandise cost and the freight charges for its shipment to a given destination.

- **cost curve**
  a graph of total costs of production as a function of total quantity produced.

- **cost function**
  a function of input prices and output quantity. Its value is the cost of making that output, given those input prices.

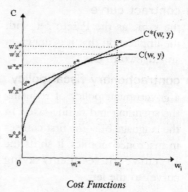

*Cost Functions*

- **costate variables**
  a Lagrangian multiplier or Hamiltonian multiplier.

- **cost-of-living index**
  measures the changing cost of a constant standard of living. The index is a scalar measure for each time period. Usually, it is a positive number, which rises over time to indicate that there was inflation. Two incomes can be compared across time by seeing whether the incomes changed as much as the index did.

## cost-push inflation
inflation whose initial cause is a rise in the production costs.

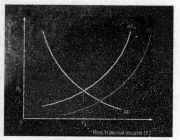

*Cost Push Inflation*

## countable additivity property
the third of the properties of a measure.

## countertrading
the bilateral international trading relationships between companies.

## countervailing power
J.K.Galbraith' thesis of the tendency of market (monopoly) power to be reduced by the emergence of countervailing groups and forces.

## coupling constraints
the need to join with other people organisations or capital investments (as 'bundles') to accomplish an objective.

## coupon bonds
a bond that pays the holder of the bond a specified amount of money at given dates until maturity. Then, the face value of the bond is paid at maturity. The total value of the coupons in a year, over the face value of the bond, is called the coupon rate.

## coupon strips
a bond can be resold into two parts that can be thought of as components: (a) a principal component that is the right to receive the principal at the end date and (b) the right to receive the coupon payments. The components are called strips. The right to receive coupon payments is the coupon strip.

## Cournot's competition
an oligopoly in which each firm believes that its rivals are committed to a certain level of production and that rivals will reduce their prices in order to sell that amount.

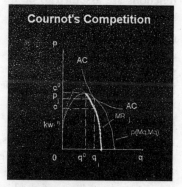

## Cournot Duopoly
a pair of firms that split a market, modelled as in the Cournot Game.

## Cournot Game
a game between two firms. Both produce a certain good, say widgets. No other firms do. The price they receive is a decreasing function of the total quantity of widgets that the firms produce. That function is known to both the

firms. Each chooses a quantity to produce, without knowing how much the other will produce.

# ■ Cournot Models

a generalisation of the Cournot Game, to describe industry structure. Each of the N firms will choose a quantity of output. Price is a commonly-known decreasing functions of total output. All firms know N and take the output of the others as given. Each firm has a cost function $c_i(q_i)$. Usually, the cost functions are treated as common knowledge. Often the cost functions are assumed to be the same for all firms.

# ■ covariance stationary

a stochastic process is covariance stationary, if neither its mean nor its autocovariances depend on the index.

# ■ Cowles Commission

a 1950s panel on econometrics, which focused attention on the problem of simultaneous equations. In some tellings of the history, this had an impact on the field — other problems such as errors-in-variables (measurement errors in the independent variables), were set aside or given lower priority elsewhere too because of the prestige and influence of the Cowles Commission.

# ■ credentials competition

the trend in which prospective workers acquire higher educa-

tional credentials, not so much because of anything they actually learn in the process, but to convince potential employers to hire them by signalling that they will be more productive employees than those with weaker credentials.

# ■ credit constraint effect

when prices fall, firms' revenues also fall, but the money they owe to creditors remains unchanged, as a result, firms have fewer funds of their own to invest. Due to credit rationing, firms cannot make up the difference and accordingly, investment decreases.

# ■ credit rationing

credit is rationed when no lender is willing to give loan to a borrower or the amount lenders are willing to lend to borrowers is limited even if the borrower is willing to pay more than other borrowers of comparable risk who are being granted loans.

# ■ credit unions

an organisation that takes deposits and makes loans. Credit unions are non-profit and run as a co operative by the depositors of the union.

# ■ criterion function

see **loss function**.

# ■ critical isodapane

that isodapane (out of the family of isodapanes) which signifies th outer limit for alternative location (alternative to the location wit minimum aggregate transport costs) in a Weberian locational triangle or other polygon. Its specification is dependent on the savings (labour cost, scale- or agglomeration economies) associated with such an alternative.

■ **critical region**
see **rejection region**.

■ **Cronbach's Alpha**
a test for a model or survey's internal consistency. Called a 'scale reliability coefficient' sometimes. Cronbach's alpha assesses the reliability of a rating, summarising a group of test or survey answers, which measure some underlying factor (e.g., some attribute of the test-taker). A score is computed from each test item and the overall rating called a 'scale' is defined by the sum of these scores over all the test items. Then reliability a is defined to be the square of the correlation between the measured scale and the underlying factor that the scale was supposed to measure.

■ **cross subsidisation**
the practice of charging higher prices from one group of consumers, in order to subsidise lower prices for another group.

■ **cross-levelling of knowledge**
any new concept which has been created, justified and modelled, moves on to a new cycle of knowledge creation at a different ontological level. This interaction and spiral process takes place both intra-organisationally and inter-organisationally.

■ **cross-section data**
is the parallel data on many units such as individuals, households, firms or governments.

■ **cross-validation**
a way of choosing the window width for a kernel estimation. The method is to select, from a set of possible window widths, one that minimises the sum of errors made in predicting each data point, by using a kernel regression on the others.

■ **crude birth rate**
the number of life births per 1000 population (male + female) in a given year.

■ **cryptography**
used to encode information to conceal secret messages from unauthorised parties. It has traditionally been used for military and national security purposes. Cryptography makes use of algorithms to transform data, which then cannot be retrieved, unless one has access to the cryptographic key.

■ **CSO**
Central Statistical Office

■ **CTT**
Capital Transfer Tax

■ **cubic splines**
a particular nonparametric estimator of a function. Given a data set $\{X_i, Y_i\}$, it estimates the values of Y for X's other than those in the

sample. The process is to construct a function that balances the twin needs of (a) proximity to the actual sample points, (b) smoothness.

- **cumulative causation**
  a self-reinforcing process during which impulses activate a positive feedback, leading to further growth, decline or other kinds of change with the same direction as the original impulse.

- **Cumulative Distribution Function (CDF)**
  this function describes a statistical distribution. It has the value, at each possible outcome, of the probability of receiving that outcome or a lower one. A CDF is usually denoted in capital letters.

- **current account**
  a part of balance of payments, where payments for the purchase and sale of goods and services are recorded.

- **current account balance**
  the difference between a country's savings and its investment. If the current account balance is positive, it measures the portion of a country's saving invested abroad and if it is negative, it measures the portion of the domestic investment financed by foreigners' savings.

- **current balance**
  difference between total exports and total imports.

- **CWO**
  Cash With Order

- **de minimis**
  a legal term for an amount that is small enough to be ignored, too small to be taken seriously. Used to restrict legal provisions, including laws regarding international trade, to amounts of activity or trade that are not trivially small.

- **deadweight loss**
  the net loss in economic welfare that is caused by a tariff or other source of distortion, defined as the total losses to those who lose, minus the total gains to those who gain. Usually identified in a supply-and-demand diagram in terms of change in consumer and producer surplus, together with government revenue. The net of these appears as one or two welfare triangles.

- **debenture**
  1. a debt that is not backed by collateral, but only by the credit and good faith of the borrower.
  2. a certificate issued by customs authorities, entitling an exporter of imported goods to be paid back duties that have been paid when they were imported. Such a refund is called a drawback.

- **debit**
  recorded as negative (-) in the balance of payments. Any transaction that gives rise to a payment out of the country, such as an import, the purchase of an asset (including official reserves) or lending to foreigners.

■ **debt crisis**

a situation in which a country, usually a Least Developed Country (LDC), finds itself unable to service its debts.

■ **debt overhang**

a situation in which the external debt of a country is larger than the sum that such country will be able to repay, often due to having borrowed in foreign currency and then having its own currency depreciate.

■ **debt service**

the payments made by a borrower on their debt, usually including both interest payments and partial repayment of principal.

■ **debt/equity swap**

an exchange of debt for equity, in which a lender is given a share of ownership to replace a loan. Used as a method of resolving debt crises.

■ **debtor nation**

a country whose assets owned abroad are worth, less than the assets within the country that are owned by foreigners.

■ **decentralised decision-making**

the locus of decision-making is decentralised to the extent to which there are multiple decision-makers involved, with their own goals and objectives and to the extent to which they follow their own expectations about the developments in the environment, including the activities of other actors and competitors.

■ **decile**

one of the ten segments of a distribution that has been divided into tenths. For example, the second-from-the-bottom decile of an income distribution consists of those whose income exceeds the incomes of 10% to 20% of the population.

■ **decision rules**

1. a function that maps from the current state to the agent's decision or choice.
2. a mapping from the expressed preferences of each of a group of agents to a group decision.
The first is more relevant to decision theory and dynamic optimisation, while the second is relevant to game theory.

■ **Decision Support Systems (DSS)**

A computer based system that helps the decision maker utilise data and models to solve unstructured problems.

■ **decision tree**

the use of the network-theoretical concept of 'tree' to the uncertainty-related structuring of decision options. A tree is a fully connected network without circuits, i.e. every node is connected to every other node, but

*Economics*

only once. A decision tree distinguishes between nodes, from which decision options branch off and nodes, which have branches representing 'environmental' options, i.e. environmental states, which are associated with alternative decisions.

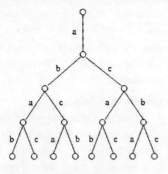

*Decision Tree*

■ **decouple**
the provision of support to an enterprise, usually a farm, in a manner that does not provide an incentive to increase production. Farm subsidies that are decoupled are included in the green box and are therefore permitted by the WTO.

■ **decreasing cost**
average cost that declines as the output increases, due to increasing returns to scale.

■ **decreasing returns to scale**
a property of a production function such that changing all the inputs by the same proportion changes the output less than in proportion. Example: a function homogeneous of degree less than

one. Also called simply decreasing returns.

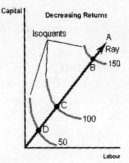

■ **deduction**
also known as deductive reasoning. A process of inference, which leads from general principles or universal premises via logical reasoning to expectations or conclusions about particular cases.

■ **deductive**
characterises a reasoning process of logical reasoning from the stated propositions.

■ **deep integration**
economic integration that goes well beyond the removal of formal barriers to trade and includes various ways of reducing the international burden of differing national regulations, such as mutual recognition and harmonisation.

■ **deep markets**
a capital market may be said to be deep if it has great depth. May less formally be used to describe a market with a large total market capitalisation.

■ **default**
failure to repay a loan. International loans by governments and private agents lack mechanisms to deal with default, comparable to the legal mechanisms that exist within countries.

■ **deficiency payment**
payment to a producer of an amount equal to the difference between a guaranteed price and the market price, with the latter often determined on the world market. A form of subsidy to production.

■ **deficit**
in the balance of payments or in any category of international transactions within it, the deficit is the sum of debits minus the sum of credits or the negative of the surplus.

■ **deflation**
1. a fall in the general level of prices. Unlikely unless the rate of inflation is already low, it may then be due either to a surge in productivity or, less favourably, to a recession.
2. occurs when the prices are declining over time. This is the opposite of inflation. When the inflation rate is negative, the economy is in a deflationary period.

■ **degressive**
declining with income or over time. A degressive income tax takes a smaller fraction of higher incomes. Degressivity in trade policy might be a tariff the ad valorem size of which is scheduled to decline over time or a quota that is scheduled to expand faster than demand for imports.

■ **de-industrialisation**
a decline, over time, in the share of the manufacturing in an economy, usually accompanied by growth in the share of services. Typically, accompanied by an increase in manufactured imports.

■ **delivered price**
the price which includes freight charges to the location of the buyer.

■ **delta**
used with respect to options. The rate of change of a financial derivative's price with respect to changes in the price of the underlying asset. Formally, this is a partial derivative. A derivative is perfectly delta-hedged if it is in a portfolio with a delta of zero. Financial firms make some effort to construct delta-hedged portfolios.

■ **delta method**
gives the distribution of a function of random variables for which one has a distribution. In particular, for the function $g(b,l)$, where b and l are estimators for true values $b_0$ and $l_0$:
$$g(b,l) \sim N(g(b_0,l_0), g'(b,l) \, var \, (b,l) \, g'(b,l)')$$

■ **demand**
1. want or desire to possess a good

or service with the necessary goods, services or financial instruments, necessary to make a legal transaction for those goods or services.

2. the act of offering to buy a product.

■ **demand curve**
the graph of quantity demanded, as a function of price, normally downward sloping, straight or curved and drawn with the quantity on the horizontal axis and price on the vertical axis.

■ **demand deposit**
1. a bank deposit that can be withdrawn 'on demand'. The term usually refers only to checking accounts, even though depositors in many other kinds of accounts may be able to write checks and regard their deposits as readily available.
2. the money stored in the form of checking accounts at banks.

■ **demand elasticity**
normally, the price elasticity of demand.

■ **demand price**
the price at which a given quantity is demanded. The demand curve viewed from the perspective of price as a function of quantity.

■ **demand schedule**
a list of prices and corresponding quantities demanded or the graph of that information. Thus, a demand curve.

■ **demand set**
in a model, the set of the most-preferred bundles of goods that an agent can afford. This set is a function of the preference relation for this agent, the prices of goods and the agent's endowment.

■ **demographic transition**
a model of population change based on European experiences. The model describes the effects of changes in fertility and mortality, associated with industrialisation, urbanisation and health care improvements.

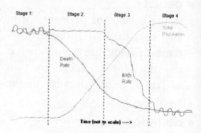

*Demographic Transition*

■ **demography**
the study of the size, growth and age and geographical distribution of human populations and births, deaths, marriages and migrations.

■ **dependency theory**
the theory which states that the less developed countries are poor because they allow themselves to be exploited by the developed countries through international trade and investment.

■ **dependent variable**
the variable to be 'explained' with

the help of 'independent variables'. These independent variables serve as the 'explanatory' variables, however, the extent to which this relationship or 'explanation' actually implies 'causality' varies. It may merely refer to a statistical relationship. Thus, the relationship is often expressed as: a dependent variable is a function of one or more 'independent' variable(s).

■ **depreciate**
see **depreciation**.

■ **depreciation**
1. a fall in the value of a country's currency in the exchange market, relative either to a particular other currency or to a weighted average of other currencies. The currency is said to depreciate.
2. the decline in value or usefulness of a piece of capital over time and/or with use.

■ **depressions**
a severe downturn in economic activity. These are considerably worse than recessions.

■ **depth**
an attribute of a market. In securities markets, depth is measured by the size of an order flow innovation, required to change the prices by a given amount.

■ **deregulation**
reducing or eliminating government intervention to control particular market activities, especially of private firms. For example, removing price controls or monopoly privileges.

■ **deregulation**
the lessening or complete removal of government regulations on an industry, especially concerning the price that firms are allowed to charge and leaving the price to be determined by the market forces.

■ **derivatives**
securities whose value is derived from some other time-varying quantity. Usually, that other quantity is the price of some other asset such as bonds, stocks, currencies or commodities. It could also be an index or the temperature.

■ **derived demand**
the demand that arises or is defined indirectly from some other demand or underlying behaviour.

■ **derogation**
as used in the trade literature, this seems to mean a departure from the established rules, as when a country's policies are said to constitute a derogation from the GATT.

■ **de-skilling**
a decrease in the level and scope of skills within a local/regional labour market, resulting from mainly two corporate strategies: (a) mechanisation and computeri-sation of production and office activities (b) truncation of corporate activities within the region.

- **destabilising speculation**
speculation that increases the movements of the price in the market where the speculation occurs. Movement may be defined by amplitude, frequency or some other measure.

- **deterioration**
the process or occurrence of an asset's declining productivity as it ages. This is a component of depreciation.

- **deterministic functions and variables**
a deterministic function or variable often means one that is not random, in the context of other variables available.

- **devaluation**
1. depreciation.
2. a fall in the value of a currency that has been pegged, either because of an announced reduction in the par value of the currency with the peg continuing or because the pegged rate is abandoned and the floating rate declines.
3. a fall in the value of a currency, in terms of gold or silver, meaningful only under some form of gold standard or silver standard.

- **developed country**
a country whose per capita income is high by the world standards.

- **developing country**
a country whose per capita income is low by the world standards. Same as LDC. As usually used, it does not necessarily connote that the country's income is rising.

- **development**
economic development.

- **development economics**
a sub-discipline within economics specialising in the processes of long term growth and change, especially in the case of the less developed economies.

- **DFI**
Direct Foreign Investment

- **DFS Model**
one of the continuum-of-goods models of Dornbusch, Fischer and Samuelson (1977, 1980).

- **Dickey-Fuller test**
an econometric test for whether a certain kind of time series data has an autoregressive unit root.

- **differential effect**
in shift & share analysis, that part of the total regional shift which is due to the fact that local/regional industries may develop differently from their counterparts, in the larger (usually the national) benchmark region. Thus, these shift effects arise from the fact that some industries in some regions are (relatively) expanding or contracting more rapidly than the same industries in other regions.

- **differential treatment**
see **special and differential treatment**.

- **differentiated product**
1. a firm's product that is not identical to the products of other firms

in the same industry.

2. sometimes applied to products produced by a country, even though there are many firms within the country whose products are the same, if buyers distinguish products based on the country of origin. This is called the Armington assumption.

■ **diffuse priors**

in Bayesian statistics, the investigator has to specify a prior distribution for a parameter, before the experiment or regression that is to update that distribution. A diffuse prior is a distribution of the parameter with equal probability for each possible value, coming as close as possible to representing the notion that the analyst hasn't a clue about the value of the parameter being estimated.

■ **digital nervous system**

the digital processes that enable a company to perceive and react to its environment, to sense competitive challenges and customer needs and to organise timely responses.

■ **Dillon Round**

the fifth round of multilateral trade negotiations that was held under GATT auspices, that commenced in 1960 and completed in 1961. It was the first to be given a name, after C. Douglas Dillon, U.S. Undersecretary of State under Eisenhower and Treasury Secretary under Kennedy.

■ **diminishing returns**

the fall in the marginal product of a factor or factors that eventually occurs as the input of that factor rises, holding the input of at least one other factor fixed, according to the Law of Diminishing Returns.

■ **direct factor content**

a measure of factor content that includes only the factors used in the last stage of production, ignoring factors used in producing intermediate inputs.

■ **direct foreign investment**

see **foreign direct investment**

■ **direction of trade**

the particular countries and kinds of countries towards which a country's exports are sent and from which its imports are brought. Thus, the pattern of a country's bilateral trade.

■ **directly unproductive profit-seeking activities**

activities that have no direct productive purpose (neither increasing consumer utility nor contributing to the production of a good or service that would increase the utility) and are motivated by the desire to make profit, typically from market distortions created by government policies. Examples include rent seeking and revenue seeking.

■ **direct-plus-indirect factor content**

a measure of factor content that

includes factors used in producing the intermediate inputs and so forth. That is, it includes all the primary factors that contributed, however indirectly, to the production of a good.

■ **DISC**

Domestic International Sales Corporation

■ **discount bonds**

a bond bought at a discount or at a price less than its face value. The face value is the amount of money that the holder of the bond receives at the expiry date of the bond. Unlike coupon bonds, discount bonds only pay the bearer once, when the bond expires.

■ **discount factor**

in a multi-period model, agents may have different utility functions for consumption (or other experiences) in different time periods. Usually, in such models they value future experiences, but to a lesser degree than present ones. For simplicity, the factor by which they discount next period's utility may be a constant between zero and one and if so, it is called a discount factor.

■ **discount rate**

1. the interest rate at which an agent discounts future events in preferences, in a multi-period model. Often denoted as 'r'. A present-oriented agent discounts the future heavily and so has a 'High' discount rate.

2. the rate, per year, at which future values are diminished to make them comparable to the values in the present. Can be either subjective (reflecting personal time preference) or objective (a market interest rate).

■ **discrete choice linear models**

an econometric model: $\Pr(y_i=1) = F(X_i'b) = X_i'b$. See **discrete choice model**.

■ **discrete choice model**

an econometric model in which the actors are presumed to have made a choice from a discrete set. Their decision is modelled as endogenous. Often the choice is denoted $y_i$.

■ **discrete regression models**

econometrics models in which the dependent variables assumes discrete values.

■ **discrete time**

the division of time into indivisible units. In economic models, these units represent periods, such as days, quarters or years.

■ **discretionary licensing**

see **licensing**.

■ **discriminatory tariff**

a higher tariff against one source of imports than against another. Except in special circumstances, such as anti-dumping duties, this is a violation of MFN and is prohibited by the WTO against the other members.

## diseconomies of scale
similar to economies of scale, but with the implication that they are negative, so larger scale would increase the cost per unit.

## diseconomies of scale, scope or agglomeration
cost increases or other disadvantages associated with the scale or scope of operation or with the agglomeration of population or economic activities.

## disembodied technological change
alters the production function without requiring gross investment to carry it into place.

## disequilibrium
1. inequality of supply and demand.
2. an untenable state of an economic system, from which it may be expected to change.

## disinflation
occurs when the inflation rate is declining over time. Deflation occurs when the inflation rate becomes negative.

## disintegration
another term for fragmentation. Used by Feenstra (1998).

## disintermediation
1. the prevention of banks from flowing money from savers to borrowers as an effect of regulations.
2. circumventing intermediaries or middlemen from transactions between businesses or between businesses and consumers, now often involving direct digital transactions via 'ecommerce' on the Internet.

## disjointed incrementalism
decision strategy of 'muddling through' by responding to immediate short-term problems in an incremental fashion.

## dismal science
refers to economics, which because it is so often used in reference to tradeoffs, is widely thought to be depressing to study.

## disparity
inequality, usually income disparity.

## disposable income
the income a person or household has left to dispose off, after income tax has been deducted from personal income. Disposable income may either be spent on consumption or can be saved.

## dispute settlement
in the GATT, the adjudication of disputes among parties. In the WTO this is done by the dispute settlement mechanism.

## dispute settlement body
the entity within the WTO that formally deals with disputes between members. It consists of all WTO members meeting together to consider reports of panels and the Appellate Body.

- **dispute settlement mechanism**

  the procedure by which the WTO settles disputes among members, primarily by means of a three-person panel that hears the case and issues a report, subject to review by the Appellate Body.

- **dissaving**

  if individuals or households spend more than their current income, they are said to be dissaving.

- **distance decay**

  the diminishing level of interaction or value of a variable, with increasing distance, largely resulting from the effect of various forms of distance-sensitive transaction costs on demand or cost patterns or functions.

- **distance elasticity of demand**

  the relative response of effective demand to a change in the distance (or transport costs) that a consumer (or consumers) has (have) to overcome, in order to purchase a good or service at a given price.

- **distance learning**

  a learning environment in which the teacher (facilitator) and the student are separated in space and connected via one or more forms of telecommunication.

- **distortion**

  any departure from the ideal of perfect competition that interferes with economic agents, maximising social welfare when they maximise their own. Includes taxes and subsidies, tariffs and NTBs, externalities, incomplete information and imperfect competition.

- **diversification**

  1. a policy designed to reduce the dependence of a regional economy on specialised types of activities or markets, by shifting to a broader range of activities or markets.

  2. an important concept in the discussion of the advantages and shortcomings of different regional economic structures, including specialised and diversified structures.

- **diversification cone**

  for the given prices in the Heckscher-Ohlin Model, a set of factor endowment combinations that are consistent with producing the same set of goods and having the same factor prices. Such a set has the form of a cone.

- **diversified portfolio**

  a portfolio that includes a variety of assets whose prices are not likely to change together. In international economics, this usually means holding assets denominated in different currencies.

- **diversion**

  see **trade diversion**.

- **dividend taxes**

  a tax that the government levies on shareholders of a corporation when that corporation distributes a dividend. Normally a dividend tax is a percentage of the total dividend issued.

## dividends

the amount of money, normally a portion of the profits, a board of directors distributes to the ordinary shareholders of the corporation.

## Dixit-Stiglitz function

really just a symmetric CES function, the innovation of Dixit and Stiglitz (1977) was to allow the number of arguments to be variable. Used originally as a utility function, with elasticity of substitution greater than one the function displays a preference for variety. Used as a component of a production function, the same property implies that costs fall with variety.

## Dixit-Stiglitz utility

the Dixit-Stiglitz function used as a utility function.

## Doha Declaration

the document agreed upon by the trade ministers of the member countries of the WTO at the Doha Ministerial meeting. It initiates negotiations on a range of some 21 subjects. A distinctive feature is the emphasis placed on the interests of developing countries.

## Doha Ministerial

the WTO ministerial meeting held in Doha, Qatar, in November 2001, at which it was agreed to begin a new round of multilateral trade negotiations, the Doha Round.

## Doha Round

the round of multilateral trade negotiations begun in January 2002 as a result of agreement at the Doha Ministerial. Also called the Doha Development Round.

## dollar standard

an international financial system in which the US dollar is used by most countries as the primary reserve asset, in contrast to the gold standard in which gold played this role.

## dollarisation

the official adoption by a country other than the United States of the US dollar as its local currency.

## Domar Aggregation

the principle that the growth rate of an aggregate is the weighted average of the growth rates of its components, where each component is weighted by the share of the aggregate it makes up. The idea comes up in the context of national accounts and national statistics.

## domestic

from or in one's own country. A domestic producer is one that produces inside the home country. A domestic price is the price inside the home country. Opposite of 'foreign' or 'world'.

## domestic content requirement

a requirement that goods sold in a country contain a certain minimum of domestic value added.

■ **domestic credit**
credit extended by a country's central bank to domestic borrowers, including the government and commercial banks. In the United States, the largest component by far is the Fed's holdings of US government bonds, but it also makes some short-term loans to banks to use as their reserves.

■ **domestic distortions argument for protection**
see **second best argument**.

■ **domestic law**
a measure, in terms of real resources, of the opportunity cost of producing or saving foreign exchange. It is an ex ante measure of comparative advantage, used to evaluate projects and policies.

■ **domestic support**
a policy that assists domestic industry, including a subsidy to production, payment not to produce, price support and other means of increasing the income of producers.

■ **domestic resource cost**
measure, in terms of real resources, of the opportunity cost of producing or saving foreign exchange. It is an ex ante measure of comparative advantage, used to evaluate projects and policies.

■ **dominant designs**
after a technological innovation and a subsequent era of ferment in an industry, a basic architecture of a product or process that becomes the accepted market standard. Dominant designs may not be better than the alternatives nor can it be promised that they will be innovative. They have the benchmark features to which subsequent designs are compared.

■ **double coincidence of wants**
a problem that is generally related to the Barter System. Refers to a situation where the supplier of good X wants good Y and the supplier of good Y wants good X.

■ **downstream dumping**
the export of a good whose cost is reduced by access to a domestically produced intermediate input that is sold below cost. This is not (yet) eligible under any anti-dumping statute for an anti-dumping duty.

■ **drawback**
rebate of import duties when the imported good is re-exported or used as input to the production of an exported good.

■ **DRAM**
Dynamic Randon-Access Memory

■ **DRC**
Domestic Resource Cost

■ **DSM**
Dispute Settlement Mechanism

■ **dual economy**
an economy which is supposed to consist of two relatively distinct parts, in terms of specific distinguishing attributes. In the devel-

opment literature, numerous theories use this proposed dualism to isolate relationships between the two parts, which are suggested to reinforce the dualism.

# dual labour market

a segmented labour market in which one part is, usually and in broad terms, characterised by high skills and wages, job security and desirable working and career development conditions, while the other part has low wages, no or inferior benefits, a temporary or unstable nature, no or little chance of advancement and otherwise poorer working conditions.

# dummy variables

in an econometric model, a variable that marks or encodes a particular attribute. A dummy variable has the value zero or one for each observation, e.g. 1 for pass and 0 for fail .

# dumping

export price that is 'unfairly low', defined as either below the home market price (normal value) hence, price discrimination or below cost. With the rare exception of successful predatory dumping, dumping is economically beneficial to the importing country as a whole (though harmful to competing producers) and often represents normal business practice.

# dumping margin

in a case of dumping, the difference between the 'fair price' and the price charged for export. Used as the basis for setting anti-dumping duties.

# duopoly

an oligopoly with two firms.

# DUP Activities

see **directly unproductive profit-seeking activities.**

# Durbin's h test

an algorithm for detecting autocorrelation in the errors of a time series regression. The implicit citation is to Durbin (1970). The h statistic is asymptotically distributed normally, if the hypothesis is that there is no autocorrelation.

# Durbin-Watson statistic

a test for first-order serial correlation, in the residuals of a time series regression. A value of 2.0 for the Durbin-Watson statistic indicates that there is no serial correlation. This result is biased towards the finding that there is no serial correlation if lagged values of the regressors are in regression.

# Dutch disease

the adverse effect on a country's other industries that occurs when one industry substantially expands its exports, causing a real appreciation of the country's currency.

# dutiable imports

imports on which a positive duty or tariff is levied.

# duty

tax, that is, an import duty is a tariff.

- **duty drawback**
  see **drawback**.

- **duty-free**
  without tariff, usually applied to imports on which normally a tariff would be charged, but that for some reason are exempt. Travellers, for example, may be permitted to import a certain amount duty-free.

- **dynamic comparative advantage**
  a changing pattern of comparative advantage over time due to changes in factor endowments or technology.

- **dynamic economies of scale**
  a form of increasing returns to scale in which average cost declines over time as producers accumulate experience, so that average product rises with total output of the firm or industry accumulated over time.

- **dynamic effects**
  certain poorly understood effects of trade and trade liberalisation, including both multilateral and preferential trade agreements, that extend beyond the static gains from trade. Such dynamic effects are thought to make the gains from trade substantially larger than in the static model.

- **dynamic gains from trade**
  the hoped-for benefits from trade that accrue over time, in addition to the conventional static gains from trade of trade theory. Sources of these gains are not well understood or documented, although there exist a variety of possible theoretical reasons for them and some empirical evidence that countries have benefited more than the static gains alone would suggest.

- **dynamic inconsistency**
  a possible attribute of a player's strategy in a dynamic decision-making environment. When the best plan that a player can make for some future period will not be optimal when that future period arrives, the plan is dynamically inconsistent. Monetary policy is sometimes said to suffer from a dynamic inconsistency problem.

- **dynamic model**
  any model with an explicit time dimension. To be meaningfully dynamic, however, it should include variables and behaviour that, at one time, depend on variables or behaviour at another time. Models may be formulated in discrete time or in continuous time.

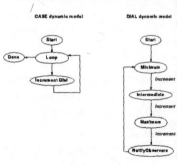

*Dynamic Models*

**dynamic multipliers**
the impulse responses in a distributed lag model.

**dynamic optimisations**
the maximisation problems to which the solution is a function.

**dynamic programming**
the study of dynamic optimisation problems through the analysis of functional equations like value equations. This phrase is normally used, analogously to linear programming, to describe the study of discrete problems.

**early harvest**
a term, in trade negotiations, for agreeing to accept the results of a portion of the negotiations, before the rest of the negotiations are completed.

**earth summit**
see **Rio Summit**

**EC**
European Communities

**ECB**
European Central Bank

**Eco-dumping**
Environmental dumping

**econometrics**
the application of statistical methods to the empirical estimation of economic relationships. Econometric analysis is used extensively in international economics, to estimate the causes and effects of international trade, exchange rates and international capital movements.

**Economic and Monetary Union (EMU)**
a currency area formed in 1999, as a result of the Maastricht Treaty. Members of the EMU share the common currency, the Euro.

**economic contraction**
the downward phase of the business cycle, in which GDP is falling and unemployment is rising over time.

**economic development**
increase in the economic standard of living of a country's population, normally accomplished by increasing its stocks of physical and human capital and improving its technology.

**economic expansion**
the upward phase of a business cycle, in which GDP is rising and unemployment is falling over time.

**economic freedom**
freedom to engage in economic transactions, without government interference, but with the support of the government institutions necessary for that freedom, including rule of law, sound money and open markets.

**economic geography**
see **new economic geography**.

**economic growth**
the increase over time in the capacity of an economy to produce goods and services and to improve the well-being of its citizens.

■ **economic integration**
see **integration.**

■ **Economic Overhead Capital (EOC)**
economic infrastructure, such as roads, railways, port facilities, power facilities.

■ **economic rent**
any return that a factor of production receives, in excess of its opportunity cost.

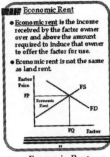

*Economic Rent*

■ **economic sanction**
the use of an economic policy as a sanction.

■ **economic union**
a common market with the added feature that additional policies: monetary, fiscal, welfare, are also harmonised across the member countries.

■ **economies of agglomeration**
see **agglomeration economies.**

■ **economies of flexibility**
the advantages accruing to a producer with many plants of different sizes, in allocating increases or decreases in operations to that plant whose size is such as to handle the total output change of the producer most efficiently.

■ **economies of massed resources**
those scale economies which flow from the fact that a firm is large, employing numbers of workers, with a large management, buying materials on a large scale, raising capital on a large scale and often able to use and keep busy large units of moderately versatile equipment on a variety of comparatively similar jobs.

■ **economies of scale**
if all the inputs in a production process are increased and the output increases proportionately, by more amount than the increase in the inputs, economies of scale are being realised. There may also be diseconomies of scale, which occur when an increase in all the inputs brings about a less than proportionate increase in output.

■ **economies of scale**
see **increasing returns to scale**

■ **economy, economies**
two meanings of 'economies' need to be distinguished:
1. the economies of regions (as aggregates of interrelated economic activities).
2. in the sense of economising savings, cost reductions, etc. a used in agglomeration economies scale economies, localisation economies.

## edge cities

cities at the outskirts of large urban centres. They encompass residential, commercial and industrial districts. They provide jobs and entertainment, both for those who live there and those who come in from outside.

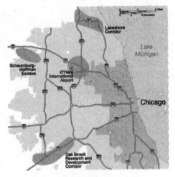

*Edge Cities*

## Edgeworth box

a geometric device showing allocations of two goods to two consumers in a rectangle, with dimensions equal to the quantities of the goods. Preferences are entered as indifference curves, relative to opposite corners of the box, tangencies defining efficient allocations and the contract curve.

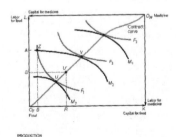

*Edgeworth*

## Edgeworth production box

a variation of the consumption Edgeworth box that instead represents the allocations of two factors to two industries, for use in production functions. Efficient allocations now appear as tangencies between isoquants, while the contract curve becomes the efficiency locus.

## effect of trade

the effect of a change in some policy or other exogenous variable that will increase the quantity of trade. Since in trade models, trade itself is endogenous, the effects associated with a change in trade depend on what caused it.

## effective protection

the concept that the protection provided to an industry depends on the tariffs and other trade barriers on both its inputs and its outputs, since a tariff on inputs raises cost. Measured by the effective rate of protection.

## effective protective rate

Same as **effective rate of protection**.

## Effective Rate of Protection (ERP)

a measure of the protection provided to an industry by the entire structure of tariffs, taking into account the effects of tariffs on inputs, as well as on outputs.

## effective tariff

effective rate of protection.

■ **efficiency locus**

the set of efficient allocations in an Edgeworth production box. It is usually a curve, similar to a contract curve and in fact, is sometimes known by that name.

■ **efficient allocation**

an allocation that it is impossible unambiguously to improve upon, in the sense of producing more of one good without producing less of another.

■ **efficient market**

a market in which, at a minimum, current price changes are independent of past price changes or, more strongly, price reflects all (publicly) available information. Some believe the foreign exchange markets to be efficient, which in turn implies that future exchange rates cannot profitably be predicted.

■ **elastic**

having an elasticity greater than one. For price elasticity of demand, this means that expenditure rises as price falls. For income elasticity, it means that expenditure share rises with income, a superior good.

■ **elastic offer curve**

an offer curve along which import demand is always elastic. It is therefore not backward bending.

■ **elasticity**

when used without a modifier (such as 'cross' or 'income'), elasticity usually refers to price elasticity, which is the percentage change in the quantity demanded of a good or service, divided by the percentage change in its (own) price.

■ **elasticity**

a measure of responsiveness of one economic variable to another. Usually, the responsiveness of quantity to price along a supply or demand curve — comparing percentage changes (%D) or changes in logarithms (d ln).

■ **elasticity of demand for exports**

the price elasticity of demand for exports of a country, either for a single industry or for the aggregate of all imports. Equals the rest of world's elasticity of demand for imports.

■ **elasticity of demand for imports**

this is normally the price elasticity of demand for imports of a country, either for a single industry or for the aggregate of all imports. The latter plays a critical role in determining how the country's balance of trade responds to the exchange rate.

■ **elasticity of substitution**

the elasticity of the ratio of two inputs to a production (or utility) function, with respect to the ratio of their marginal products (or utilities). With competitive demands, this is also the elasticity with respect to their price ratio.

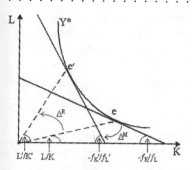

*Elasticity of Substitution*

## elasticity of supply

the (price) elasticity of supply is the percentage change in the quantity supplied of a good or service divided by the percentage change in its (own) price.

## embargo

the prohibition of some category of trade. May apply to exports and/or imports, of particular products or of all trade, vis a vis the world or a particular country or countries.

## embeddedness

the idea that economic behaviour is influenced by the dominant norms, institutions and social practices which, in turn are culturally embedded.

## emigration

the migration of people out of a country.

## empirical finding

something that is observed from real-world observation or data, in contrast to something that is deduced from theory.

## employment argument for protection

the use of a tariff or other trade restriction to promote employment, either in the economy at large or in a particular industry. This is a second best argument, since other policies, such as a fiscal stimulus or a production subsidy, could achieve the same effect at lower economic cost.

## enabling clause

the decision of the GATT in 1979 to give developing countries special and differential treatment.

## endogenous growth

economic growth whose long-run rate depends on behaviour and/or policy.

## endogenous protection

protection that is explained as the outcome of economic and/or political forces. See political economy of protection.

## endogenous variable

an economic variable that is determined within a model. It is therefore not subject to direct manipulation by the modeller, since that would override the model. In trade models, the quantity of trade itself is almost always endogenous.

## endowment

the amount of something that a person or country simply has, rather than their having somehow to acquire it. In the H-O Model of trade theory, endowments refer to primary factors of production, ignoring the fact that some of them, especially capital and skill, are deliberately accumulated.

# Engel's Curve

a general reference to the line which shows the relationship between various quantities of a good that a consumer is willing to purchase at varying income levels (ceteris paribus).

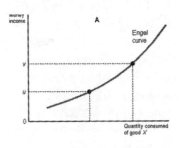

AENGEL CURVES: VARIOUS SHAPES

*Engle's Curve*

# engine of growth

sometimes used to describe the role that exports may have played in economic development, both of some of the regions of recent settlement in the nineteenth century and of today's NICs.

# enterprise or empowerment zones

specifically targeted, relatively small areas which benefit from tax abatement, other monetary aid or exemptions from selected regulations designed to attract new investments and jobs and thereby stimulate economic development.

# entrepôt trade

the import and then export of a good without further processing, usually passing through an entrepôt, which is a storage facility from which goods are distributed.

# entrepreneurship

the ability and willingness to undertake the task of organising and managing production, along with making the usual business decisions. Entrepreneurship is often associated with the functions of innovating and bearing risks.

# envelope

the outermost points traced out by a moving curve.

# envelope curve

a curve enclosing, by just touching, a number of other curves.

# environmental dumping

export of a good from a country with weak or poorly enforced environmental regulations, reflecting the idea that the exporter's cost of production is below the true cost to society, providing an unfair advantage in international trade. Also called eco-dumping.

# Environmental Kuznets Curve

an inverse U-shaped relationship hypothesised between per capita income and environmental degradation. Named after the Kuznets Curve dealing with inequality.

■ **environmental subsidy**
a subsidy intended for environmental purposes. A subsidy for adapting existing facilities to new environmental laws or regulations is non-actionable under WTO rules.

■ **equilibrium**
1. a state of balance between offsetting forces for change, so that no change occurs.
2. in competitive markets, the equality of supply and demand.

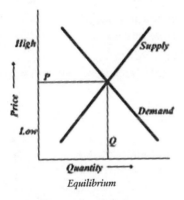
*Equilibrium*

■ **equilibrium condition**
a condition which must be satisfied for the equilibrium to exist, equilibrium being defined as a situation in which there is no tendency for change. For example, in the Keynesian expenditure model, the equilibrium condition is that the planned spending just equals the current level of national income. Once that condition is satisfied, there is no tendency for the level of national income to change.

■ **equilibrium price**
a price at which the quantity supplied equals the quantity demanded. At this price, there is no excess of quantity demanded or supplied, nor is there any deficiency of either and consequently, the price will remain at this level.

■ **equity**
1. in the context of income distribution theory, an objective, goal or principle implying 'fairness'.
2. in a financial context, a share in the ownership of a corporation, more commonly called a stock, as in the stock market.

■ **equivalent tariff**
see **tariff equivalent**.

■ **equivalent variation**
the amount of money that, paid to a person, group or whole economy, would make them as well off as a specified change in the economy. Provides a monetary measure of the welfare effect of that change, which is similar to, but not in general, the same as the compensating variation.

■ **escalation**
1. regarding the structure of tariffs, see tariff escalation.
2. in the context of a trade war, the increase in tariffs that occurs as countries retaliate again and again.

■ **escape clause**
1. the portion of a legal text that permits departure from its provisions in the event of specified ad-

verse circumstances.

2. the US statute (section 201, 1974 trade act) that permits imports to be restricted, for a limited time and on a nondiscriminatory basis, if they have caused injury to US firms or workers.

■ **EU enlargement**

the process of taking more member countries into the EU.

■ **Euratom**

the European Atomic Energy Community, created in 1956, along with the EEC.

■ **euro**

the common currency of a subset of the countries of the EU, adopted on January 1, 1999.

*Euro*

■ **Euro Interbank Offered Rate (EURIBOR)**

a euro-denominated interest rate charged by large banks, among themselves, on euro-denominated loans.

■ **euro zone**

the countries of the EMU, that is, the group of European countries, members of the EU, that adopted the common currency, the euro.

*Euro Zone*

■ **eurobond**

a bond that is issued outside of the jurisdiction of any single country, denominated in a eurocurrency.

■ **eurocurrency**

see **eurodollar**.

■ **eurodollar**

originally referred to US dollar-denominated deposits in commercial banks, located in Europe. Over time, the term came to include deposits in a commercial bank in any country, denominated in any currency other than that of the country. Now, sometimes called eurocurrencies.

■ **Europe Agreement**

an agreement between the EU and each of the ten Eastern European countries (starting with Hungary and Poland in 1994), creating free trade areas and establishing additional forms of political and economic cooperation in the preparation for these countries' eventual membership in the EU.

■ **European Central Bank**

the central bank of the Euro Zone, which includes the group of countries using the euro as their currency.

*European Central Bank*

■ **European Coal and Steel Community (ECSC)**

an economic agreement in 1951 among six countries of Western Europe — Belgium, France, Germany, Italy, Luxembourg and Netherlands — that preceded the formation of the EEC and ultimately the EU.

■ **European Currency Unit (ECU)**

a composite currency that is a basket of most of the currencies of the countries in the European Union. Conceived in 1979, it has been used as a unit of account of the European Monetary System.

■ **European Economic Area(EEA)**

the group of countries comprised of the EU, together with EFTA. The two groups have agreed to deepen their economic integration.

■ **European Economic Community (EEC)**

a customs union formed in 1958 by the Treaty of Rome, among six countries of Europe: Belgium, France, Germany, Italy, Luxembourg and Netherlands.

■ **European Free Trade Association (EFTA)**

a free trade area, made up of countries in Europe that did not join the European Economic Community. EFTA was established in 1960 among Austria, Denmark, Norway, Portugal, Sweden, Switzerland and the United Kingdom. As of 2000, it includes Iceland, Liechtenstein, Norway and Switzerland.

■ **European Monetary Agreement (EMA)**

an intergovernmental organisation, administered by the OECD that facilitated settlement of balance of payments accounts among its member states from 1958 to 1972. It replaced the EPU and its functions were taken over by the IMF in 1972.

■ **European Monetary System (EMS)**

a currency union, formed by some of the members of the EEC in 1979 that continued with changing membership, until replaced by the EMU and the euro in 1999.

■ **European Payments Union (EPU)**

an international arrangement for settling payments among member countries in Europe, during a period in which many of the countries' currencies were not convertible. The EPU functioned from 1950 to 1958, after which it was replaced by the EMA.

■ **European Recovery Program**
see **Marshall Plan**.

■ **European Union (EU)**
a group of European countries that have chosen to integrate many of their economic activities, including forming a customs union and harmonising many of their rules and regulations.

■ **even case**
in international trade models with multiple goods and factors, this is the special case of an equal number of goods and factors. It is convenient for analysis because the matrix of factor input requirements is square and therefore, potentially invertible.

■ **Everything But Arms**
the name given by the EU to its decision in 2001, to eliminate quotas and tariffs on all products except arms from the world's 48 poorest countries.

■ **ex ante analysis**
analysis of the effects of a policy, such as trade liberalisation or formation of a PTA, based only on the information available, before the policy is undertaken.

■ **ex post analysis**
analysis of the effects of a policy, such as trade liberalisation or formation of a PTA, based on the information available, after the policy has been implemented and its performance observed.

■ **ex post tariff**
see **implicit tariff**.

■ **excess demand**
demand minus supply. Thus, a country's demand for imports of a homogeneous good is its excess demand for that good.

■ **excess profit**
the profit of a firm over and above what provides its owners with a normal return to capital.

■ **excess reserves**
the difference between the amount of cash that a bank wishes or is required to hold, in relation to its deposit liabilities and the amount it actually holds.

■ **excess supply**
supply minus demand. Thus, a country's supply of exports of a homogeneous good is its excess supply of that good.

■ **exchange**
transaction(s) between economic units.

■ **exchange control**
rationing of foreign exchange, typically used when the exchange rate is fixed and the central bank is unable or unwilling to enforce the rate by the exchange-market intervention.

■ **exchange market**
1. the market on which national

currencies are exchanged for one another.

2. the actual exchange market, which exists primarily among large international banks. Others, who wish to exchange currencies do it through these banks.

3. the theoretical representation of the exchange market as, either the interaction of supply and demand arising from exchange-market transactions or as an asset market equilibrium between currencies.

■ **exchange rate**
the price of one country's currency, in terms of another's.

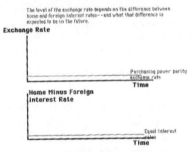

*Exchange rate*

■ **Exchange Rate Mechanism (ERM)**
a system that was operated by some central banks within the European Union, which intervened in exchange markets to limit the fluctuations of their currencies relative to one another, while letting all of them collectively float.

■ **exchange rate overshooting**
the response of an exchange rate to a shock, by first moving beyond where it will ultimately settle. Thought to help explain exchange rate volatility, this was first modelled by Dornbusch (1976).

■ **exchange rate regime**
the rules under which a country's exchange rate is determined, especially the way the monetary or other government authorities do or do not intervene in the exchange market. Regimes include floating exchange rates, pegged exchange rate, managed float, crawling peg, currency board and exchange controls.

■ **exchange rate risk**
see **exchange risk**.

■ **exchange rationing**
see **exchange control** or **ration foreign exchange**.

■ **exchange risk**
uncertainty about the value of an asset, liability or commitment, due to uncertainty about the future value of an exchange rate. Unless they cover themselves in the forward market, traders, with commitments to pay or receive foreign currency in the future, bear exchange risk. So do holders of assets and liabilities denominated in the foreign currency.

■ **exchange stabilisation fund**
a government institution sometimes used to handle exchange market intervention, charged with the explicit function of smoothing exchange rate fluctuations.

■ **exchange-market intervention**

usually done by a country's central bank, this is the purchase and sale of the country's currency on the exchange market, in order to influence or fully determine its price. These transactions, unless they are sterilised, change the monetary base of the country and thus, its money supply.

■ **exhaustion**

in intellectual property regimes, the transaction at which rights terminate.

■ **exogenous growth**

economic growth that occurs without being the result of deliberate policy or behaviour. The term arises because neoclassical growth models converge to a steady state, in which the per capita income is constant over time. Growth, then, requires exogenous technical progress.

■ **exogenous variable**

a variable that is taken as given by an economic model. It therefore is subject to direct manipulation by the modeller. In most models, policy variables such as tariffs and par values of pegged exchange rates are exogenous.

■ **expansion**

see **economic expansion**

■ **expectation**

the expectation of a variable is the same as its expected value and is also used with both meanings.

■ **expected value**

1. the mathematical expected value of a random variable. Equals the sum (or integral) of the values that are possible for it, each multiplied by its probability.
2. what people think a variable is going to be. In general, the expectation in this second sense may be more important than the first, for determining behaviour on a market, such as the exchange market.

■ **expected value maximisation principle**

the most widely advocated rule in decision theory. It suggests that the option with the largest expected value should be chosen. Calculation of the expected value of a decision option requires the availability of the probabilities attached to each possible environmental state (e.g. probability of any specific action taken by the competitor out of all possible actions). Thus, the EV is the sum of the products of all environmental states multiplied by their respective probabilities.

■ **experience good**

a product whose value can be better known after having consumed it. Producers of experience goods may temporarily charge a price lower than the marginal cost, to induce buyers to try the product. Done with an export, this would be legally considered dumping.

■ **explicit cost**
the amount spent to obtain or produce something.
1. a good that crosses out of a country's border for commercial purposes.
2. a product, which might be a service, that is provided to foreigners by a domestic producer.
3. to cause a good or service to be an export under the definitions 1 and/or 2.

■ **export bias**
any bias in favour of exporting. Most often applied to growth that is based disproportionately on accumulation of the factor used intensively in the export industry and/or technological progress favouring that industry.

■ **export credit**
a loan to the buyer of an export, extended by the exporting firm when shipping the good prior to payment or by a facility of the exporting country's government. In the latter case, by setting a low interest rate on such loans, a country can indirectly subsidise exports.

■ **export credit insurance**
a program to guarantee payment to exporting firms who extend export credits.

■ **export led growth**
growth of an economy over time that is thought to be caused by expansion of the country's exports. See **export promotion, engine of growth**.

■ **export licensing**
see **licensing**.

■ **export limitation**
any policy that restricts exports.

■ **export multiplier**
the multiplier for a change in exports, that is, the increase in GDP caused by one-unit increase in exports.

■ **export pessimism**
the view that efforts to expand exports by the LDCs will lead to a decline in their terms of trade because of an inability (due to weak demand) or unwillingness (expressed via protection) of developed countries to absorb these exports.

■ **export platform**
describes the role of a host country, as a production location designed to serve international markets, possibly including the home market of the parent firm.

■ **export price index**
price index of the goods that a country exports.

■ **Export Processing Zone (EPZ)**
a designated area or a country in which firms can import duty-free, so long as the imports are used as inputs to production of exports.

■ **export promotion**
a strategy for economic development that stresses on expanding exports, often through policies to assist them, such as export subsi-

dies. The rationale is to exploit a country's comparative advantage, especially in the common circumstance, where an over-valued currency would otherwise create bias against exports.

■ **export quota**
a quantitative restriction on exports, often the means of implementing a VER.

■ **export requirement**
a requirement by the government of the host country for FDI, that the investor should export a certain amount or percentage of its output.

■ **export subsidy**
1. a subsidy to exports, that is, a payment to exporters of a good, per unit of the good exported.
2. sometimes applied to any payments to producers that lead to an increase in exports.

■ **export substitution**
a shift to the export of increasingly processed products. The export of more or less processed raw materials is substituted for the export of raw or relatively unprocessed materials contributing to local (or national) employment and the creation of value added.

■ **export tax**
a tax on exports.

■ **external balance**
1. balance of payments equilibrium.
2. any target value for the balance on current account, balance on capital account or balance of payments.

■ **external debt**
the amount that a country owes to foreigners, including the debts of both the country's government and its private sector.

■ **external diseconomy**
see **negative externality**.

■ **external economies of scale**
a form of increasing returns to scale, in which productivity and thus costs of individual firms depend on the output of their entire industry, rather than just their own. Unlike more conventional (internal) scale economies, these are consistent with perfect competition.

■ **external economy**
see **positive externality**.

■ **externalities**
a benefit or cost associated with an economic transaction, which is not taken into account by those directly involved in making it. A beneficial or adverse side effect of production or consumption.

■ **externality**
an effect of one economic agent's actions on another, such that one agent's decisions make another better or worse off, by changing their utility or cost. Beneficial effects are positive externalities, while the harmful ones are negative externalities.

# F Distribution/F-Distribution

defined in terms of two independent chi-squared variables. Let u and v be independently distributed chi-squared variables with $u_1$ and $v_1$ degrees of freedom, respectively.

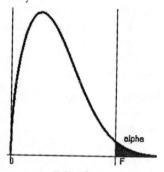

*F Distribution*

# F Test/ F-Tests

a test for the joint hypothesis that a number of coefficients are zero. Large values generally reject the hypothesis, depending on the level of significance required.

# factor

1. primary factor.
2. sometimes refers to any input to production.

# factor abundance

the abundance or scarcity of a primary factor of production. Because, in the short run at least, the supplies of primary factors are more or less fixed, this can be taken as given for determining much about a country's trade and other economic variables. Fundamental to the H-O Model.

# factor augmenting

said of a technological change or technological difference, if production functions differ by scaling of a factor input only.

# factor bias

see **bias**.

# factor content

the amounts of primary factors used in the production of a good or service or a vector of quantities of goods and services, such as the factor content of trade or the factor content of consumption. Can be either direct or direct-plus-indirect.

# factor cost

the cost of the factors used in production. The term is used especially when the value of economic activity in a sector or an economy can be measured or valued either at 'factor cost', adding up payments to factors or at 'market value', adding up revenues from goods sold.

# factor endowment

the quantity of a primary factor present in a country. See **endowment**.

# factor intensity

the relative importance of one factor versus others in production, in an industry, usually compared across industries. Most commonly defined by ratios of factor quantities employed at common factor prices, but sometimes by factor shares or by marginal rates of substitution between factors.

■ **factor intensity reversal**
a property of the technologies for two industries such that their ordering of relative factor intensities is different at different factor prices. For example, one industry may be relatively capital intensive compared to the other at high relative wages and labour intensive at low relative wages.

■ **factor intensity uniformity**
the absence of factor intensity reversals.

■ **factor movement**
see **international factor movement**.

■ **factor of production**
the input or resource which is combined with other factors of production in a production process, to produce a good or service.

■ **factor price**
the price paid for the services of a unit of a primary factor of production per unit time. Includes the wage or salary of labour and the rental prices of land and capital. Does not normally refer to the price of acquiring ownership of the factor itself, which might be called the 'purchase price'.

■ **Factor Price Equalisation (FPE)**
the tendency for trade to cause factor prices in different countries to become identical.

■ **factor price equalisation theorem**
one of the major theoretical results of the Heckscher-Ohlin Model, with at least as many goods as factors, showing that free and frictionless trade will cause factor price equalisation between two countries, if they have identical linearly homogeneous, technologies and their factor endowments are sufficiently similar to be in the same diversification cone.

■ **factor price equalisation**
an effect observed in models of international trade — that the prices of inputs to production in different countries, like wages, are driven towards equality in the absence of barriers to trade. This happens among other reasons because price incentives cause countries to choose to specialise in the production of goods whose factors of production are abundant there, which raises the prices of the factors towards equality, with the prices in countries where those factors are not abundant.

■ **factor price frontier**
a curve in factor space showing the minimum combinations of factor prices consistent with the absence of profit in producing one or more goods, given their prices. Since, with perfect competition, profit implies disequilibrium, this shows a lower bound on equilibrium factor prices.

**factor proportions model**
the Heckscher-Ohlin model of trade.

**factor scarcity**
see **factor abundance**.

**factor share**
the fraction of payments to value added, in an industry, that goes to a particular primary factor.

**factor space**
a graph in which the axes measure the quantities of factors.

**factor-price space**
a graph with factor prices on the axes.

**factor-saving**
biased in favour of using less of a particular factor.

**factor-using**
biased in favour of using more of a particular factor.

**factory systems**
the idea that factories may have been more efficient by reducing transaction costs.

**fads**
the conjecture that market prices for securities take long swings away from their fundamental values and tend to return to them.

**fair price**
in anti-dumping cases, the price to which the export price is compared, which is either the price charged in the exporter's own domestic market or some measure of their cost, both adjusted to include any transportation cost and tariff needed to enter the importing country's market. See **dumping**.

**fairness argument for protection**
the view that it is unfair to force domestic firms to compete with foreign firms that have an advantage, either in terms of low wages or due to foreign government policies. This misinterprets economic activity as a game, the purpose of which is to win, rather than as a means of using limited resources to satisfy human needs. See **level playing field**.

**Fama-MacBeth Regression**
a panel study of stocks to estimate CAPM or APT parameters.

**family / families**
in an economic study, a family is defined as two or more persons related by blood, marriage or adoption and residing together.

**FAS**
Free Alongside Ship. Same as FOB, but without the cost of loading onto a ship.

**fast track**
a procedure adopted by the US Congress, at the request of the President, committing it to consider trade agreements without amendment. In return, the President must adhere to a specified timetable and other procedures.

■ **fat-tailed distributions**
describes a distribution with excess kurtosis.

■ **favourable exchange rate**
an exchange rate different from the market or official rate, provided by the government on a transaction, as an indirect way of providing a subsidy.

■ **Feasible Generalised Least Squares (FGLS)**
the generalised least squares estimation procedure, but with an estimated covariance matrix, not an assumed one.

■ **Fed**
the Federal Reserve System of the United States.

■ **Fed Funds Rate**
the interest rate at which US banks lend to one another, their excess reserves held on deposit at the US.

■ **Federal Information Processing Standards (FIPS)**
these are encodings defined by the US government and used to encode some data (like states and counties) in US data sets.

■ **Federal Reserve System**
the central bank of the United States.

■ **fertility rates**
births per 1000 (with increasing compositional specificity of underlying population).

■ **fiat money**
1. money that is intrinsically useless and is used only as a medium of exchange.
2. a money whose usefulness results, not from any intrinsic value or guarantee that it can be converted into gold or another currency, but only from a government's order (fiat) that it must be accepted as a means of payment.

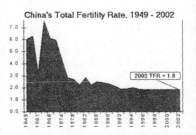

*Fertility Rates*

■ **filters**
a way of treating or adjusting data before it is analysed. More exactly, a filter is an algorithm or mathematical operation that is applied to a time series sample to get another sample, often called the 'filtered' data. For example a filter might remove some high-frequency effects from the data.

■ **final good**
a good that requires no further processing or transformation, to be ready for use by consumers, investors or government.

■ **financial account**
a term used in the balance of payments statistics, since sometime in the 1990s, for what used to be called the 'capital account'. See **capital account**.

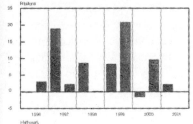

## ■ Financial Accounting Standards Board (FASB)

a board which sets accounting rules for the US.

## ■ financial capital

financial assets, such as stocks, bonds, bank deposits, etc., as opposed to real assets such as buildings and capital equipment.

## ■ financial crisis

a loss of confidence in a country's currency or other financial assets, causing international investors to withdraw their funds from the country.

## ■ financial instrument

a document, real or virtual, having legal force and embodying or conveying monetary value.

## ■ financial intermediary

an institution that provides indirect means for funds from those who wish to save or lend, to be channelled to those who wish to invest or borrow. Examples include banks and other depository institutions, mutual funds and some government programs.

## ■ financial market

a market for a financial instrument, in which the buyers and sellers find each other and create or exchange financial assets. Sometimes these are organised in a particular place and/or institution, but often they exist more broadly through communication among dispersed buyers and sellers, including banks, over long distances.

## ■ FIR

Factor Intensity Reversal.

## ■ first best

see **second best**.

## ■ first degree homogeneous

homogeneous of degree 1.

## ■ first mover advantage

the advantage that a firm may derive from being the first to enter a market or from being the first to use a new technology, advertising technique, etc.

## ■ First Order Condition (FOC)

one of the mathematically necessary conditions for maximisation, used routinely in solving economic models. Typically, it consists of setting equal to zero the derivative of the function being maximised (or its Lagrangian), with respect to a variable that can be controlled.

## ■ first welfare theorem of economics / first theorem of welfare economics

the statement that a Walrasian equilibrium is weakly Pareto optimal.

Such a theorem is true in a large and important class of general equilibrium models (usually static ones). The standard case is if every agent has a positive quantity of every good and every agent has a utility function that is convex, continuous and strictly increasing, then the First Welfare Theorem holds.

## ■ first-order stochastic dominance

usually means stochastic dominance.

## ■ fiscal policy

any macroeconomic policy involving the levels of government purchases, transfers or taxes, usually implicitly focused on domestic goods, residents or firms. A fiscal stimulus is an increase in purchases or transfers or a cut in taxes.

## ■ fiscalist view

an extreme Keynesian view, that money doesn't matter at all as aggregate demand policy. Assumes that investment demand does not respond to interest rate changes. Relevant only in depression conditions.

## ■ Fisher Consistency / Fisher Consistent Estimation

a necessary condition for maximum likelihood estimation to be consistent. Maximising the likelihood function L gives an estimate for parameter b that is Fisher-consistent if:

$E[d(\ln L)/db]=0$ at $b=b_0$, where

$b_0$ is the true value of b.

Another interpretation or phrasing: 'An estimation procedure is Fisher consistent if the parameters of interest solve the population analog of the estimation problem.'

## ■ Fisher Effect

the theory that a change in the expected rate of inflation will lead to an equal change in the nominal interest rate, thus keeping the real interest rate unchanged.

nominal rate of interest = real rate of interest + inflation

## ■ Fisher Hypothesis

the real rate of interest is constant. So, the nominal rate moves with inflation.

## ■ Fisher Index

is a price index, computed for a given period by taking the square root of the product of the Paasche index value and the Laspeyres index value.

## ■ Fisher Information

an attribute or property of a distribution with known form but uncertain parameter values. It is only well-defined for distributions satisfying certain assumptions.

## ■ Fisherian Criterion

for optimal investment by a firm — that it should invest in real assets until their marginal internal rate of return equals the appropriately risk-adjusted rate of return on securities.

## fixed cost

the cost that a firm bears if it produces at all and that is independent of its output. The presence of a fixed cost tends to imply increasing returns to scale. Contrasts with **variable cost**.

## Fixed Effects Estimator / Fixed Effects Estimation (FE)

a linear regression in which certain kinds of differences are subtracted out, so that one can estimate the effects of another kind of difference.

## fixed exchange rate

usually synonymous with a pegged exchange rate. Although 'fixed' seems to imply less likelihood of change, in practice countries seldom if ever achieve a truly fixed rate.

## flexibility strategy

could be considered a strategic 'response to uncertainty'. A flexible firm, investment, set of skills, residential arrangement, etc. is more responsive to unpredictable futures than a rigid firm, etc. Pursuing a flexibility strategy would mean to build appropriate flexibilities into projects and organisations, even if that means higher project or organisational costs, as long as the benefits of possible future adjustments outweighs these costs.

## flexible exchange rate

Same as **floating exchange rate**.

## flexible specialisation

a company- level strategy of 'permanent innovation', 'accommodation to ceaseless change' (rather than to control it). This strategy is based on flexible multi-use equipment, skilled workers and the creation, through politics, of an industrial community that restricts the forms of competition to those favouring innovation.

## flexible work force

a work force which can be adapted to changing circumstances. In the context of segmented, dual labour markets, it's been suggested that a flexible work force may have two meanings: One part of the labour force is given the chance to be flexible itself, i.e. to be considered functionally sufficiently diversified so that employees can be used for different functions or in different jobs, whereas the other part of the labour force can be hired and fired with ease or employed with variable hours as needed.

## flexible-accelerator model

a macro model in which there is a variable relationship between the growth rate of output and the level of net investment. The relation between the change in output and the level of net investment is the accelerator principle.

## floating exchange rate

a regime in which a country's exchange rate is allowed to fluctuate freely and be determined, without intervention in the exchange market, by the government or the central bank.

■ **floor**
see **price floor**.

■ **fob**
the price of a traded good excluding the transport cost. It stands for 'free on board', but is used only as these initials. It means the price after loading onto a ship, but before shipping, thus not including transportation, insurance and other costs needed to get a good from one country to another.

■ **FOGS Negotiations**
in the Uruguay Round, this portion of the negotiations dealt with the functioning of the GATT System and resulted ultimately in the formation of the WTO and its dispute settlement mechanism.

■ **footloose activity**
an activity which is viable at many different locations. It does not depend on any specific location factor. An industry is footloose if its long run profitability is the same for any location in an economy.

■ **footloose factor**
a factor that can move easily across national borders, in contrast to one that, due to inclination or constraints, cannot. Footloose factors are sometimes thought to have an advantage in a globalised economy.

■ **footloose industry**
an industry that is not tied to any particular location or country and can relocate across national borders, in response to changing economic conditions. Many manufacturing industries seem to have this characteristic.

■ **foreign asset position**
the amount of assets that residents of a country own abroad. Also used to mean the net foreign asset position.

■ **Foreign Corrupt Practices Act**
US law that prohibits US firms from bribing foreign officials.

■ **Foreign Direct Investment (FDI)**
1. acquisition or construction of physical capital by a firm from one (source) country in another (host) country.
2. investments undertaken by multinational firms in pursuit of their own organisational objectives.
3. a component of a country's national financial accounts. Foreign direct investment is the investment of foreign assets into domestic structures, equipment and organisations. It does not include foreign investment into the stock markets. Foreign direct investment is thought to be more useful to a country than investments in the equity of its companies because equity investments are potentially 'hot money' which can leave at the

first sign of trouble, whereas FDI is durable and generally useful whether things go well or badly.

■ **foreign exchange**
foreign currency. Any currency other than a country's own.

■ **foreign exchange market**
the exchange market.

■ **foreign investment argument for protection**
the use of protection, to attract FDI from abroad. It does work, since much FDI has been motivated by firms trying to get behind a tariff wall to sell their products. In an otherwise nondistorted economy, however, the cost in terms of more expensive goods is higher than the benefit from additional capital.

■ **foreign repercussion**
the feedback effect on a domestic economy, when its macroeconomic changes cause large enough changes abroad for those in turn to cause further changes at home.

Most commonly, a rise in income stimulates imports, causing an expansion abroad that in turn raises the demand for the home country's exports.

■ **Foreign Sales Corporation (FSC)**
a provision of the US tax code that grants income-tax rebates to American exporters, if they form what may be a largely artificial foreign subsidiary called an FSC. This has been the subject of a trade dispute with the EU which complained to the WTO that this constitutes an illegal export subsidy.

■ **Foreign trade deficit**
see **trade deficit**

■ **foreign trade zone**
an area within a country where imported goods can be stored or processed without being subject to import duty. Also called a 'free zone', 'free port' or 'bonded warehouse'.

■ **formula approach**
a procedure for organising multilateral trade negotiations, using a formula for tariff reductions as a starting point.

■ **forward**
on the forward market.

■ **forward discount**
opposite of **forward premium**.

■ **forward linkages**
linkages between a producer or supplier and her customers. As different from backward linkages,

forward linkages are output-oriented and, in the matrix-context of input-output analysis, are conventionally traced in rows.

■ **forward market**
a market for exchange of currencies in the future. Participants in a forward market enter into a contract to exchange currencies, not today, but at a specified date in the future, typically 30, 60 or 90 days from now and at a price (forward exchange rate) that is agreed upon today.

■ **forward premium**
the difference between a forward exchange rate and the spot exchange rate, expressed as an annualised percentage return on buying foreign currency spot and selling it forward.

■ **forward rate**
also called the forward exchange rate, this is the exchange rate on a forward market transaction.

■ **four-firm concentration ratio**
the percent of an industry's sales that accrue to the largest four firms, a measure of industrial concentration.

■ **fragmentation**
the splitting of production processes into separate parts that can be done in different locations, including in different countries.

■ **free cash flow**
cash flow to a firm, in excess of that required to fund all projects that have positive net present values when discounted at the relevant cost of capital.

■ **free enterprise**
a system in which economic agents are free to own property and engage in commercial transactions. See **laissez faire**, **economic freedom**.

■ **free entry**
the assumption that new firms are permitted to enter an industry and can do so costlessly. Together with free exit, it implies that profit must be zero in equilibrium.

■ **free entry condition**
an assumption posted in a search and matching model of a market. The assumption is that there is no institutional constraint on firms entering the market (e.g. to hire workers). There is no fixed number of firms. The number of firms is determined in equilibrium, by the costs of starting up.

■ **free exit**
the assumption that firms are permitted to leave an industry and can do so costlessly. See **free entry**.

■ **free good**
goods which are unlimited in supply and which therefore have no opportunity cost.

■ **free list**
a list of goods that a country has designated as able to be imported without being subject to tariff or import licensing.

■ **free market economy/free market economies**

an economy in which the allocation for resources is determined only by their supply and the demand for them. This is mainly a theoretical concept as every country, even capitalist ones, places some restrictions on the ownership and exchange of commodities.

■ **free port**

see **foreign trade zone**.

■ **free reserves**

excess reserves minus borrowed reserves.

■ **free rider**

someone who enjoys the benefits of a public good without bearing the cost. An example, in trade policy, is that trade liberalisation benefits the majority of consumers without their lobbying for it. This may tip policy in the direction of protection, for which there are fewer free riders.

■ **free spatial demand curve**

demand schedule (price/quantity of demand function) of consumers, distributed in space with varying distances from a given, central location, aggregated for a supply location with 'price' (in the mind of consumers) to include transport costs from this location to the consumers.

■ **free trade**

a situation in which there are no artificial barriers to trade, such as tariffs and NTBs. Usually used, often only implicitly, with frictionless trade, so that it implies that there are no barriers to trade of any kind. For a traded homogeneous product, it follows that domestic and world price must be equal.

■ **Free Trade Area (FTA)**

a group of countries that adopt free trade (zero tariffs and no other restrictions on trade) on trade among themselves, while not necessarily changing the barriers that each member country has on trade with the countries outside the group.

■ **Free Trade Area of the Americas (FTAA)**

a preferential trading arrangement being negotiated among most of the countries (all but Cuba) of the western hemisphere.

■ **free trade association**

free trade area.

■ **Free Trade Zone (FTZ)**

an **export processing zone**.

■ **free trader / free traders**

a holder of the political point of view that the best policy is to allow free trade into one's own country.

■ **free zone**

see **foreign trade zone**.

■ **frequency**

the speed of the up and down movements of a fluctuating economic variable, that is, the number of times, per unit of time, that the variable completes a cycle of up and down movement.

■ **frequency function**
the probability of drawing each particular value from a discrete distribution: $p(x) = \Pr(X=x)$.
(Here x is random variable and x is a possible value.)

■ **frictional unemployment**
unemployment that comes from people moving between jobs, careers and locations.

■ **frictionless trade**
the absence of natural barriers to trade, such as transport costs.

■ **Friedman Rule**
in a cash-in-advance model of a monetary system, the Friedman rule for monetary policy is to deflate so that it is not costly to those, who have money, to continue to hold it. Then the cash-in-advance constraint isn't binding on them.

■ **full employment**
occurs when everyone in the economy who is willing to work at the current market rate for someone of his skills have jobs. Full employment does not imply that all adults have jobs.

■ **Full Information Maximum Likelihood (FIML)**
an approach to the estimation of simultaneous equations.

■ **functional / functionals**
a mapping from paths of functions to the reals (e.g. a value function defined by a mapping from possible paths of choices).

■ **functional distribution of income**
how the income of an economy is divided among the owners of different factors of production, into wages, rents, etc.

■ **functional equation**
an equation where the unknown is a function. For example, a value function is the solution to the equation that sets the value function equal to the present discounted value of the current period's utility and the discounted value function of the next period's state.

■ **future-oriented agent**
discounts the future lightly and so has a low discount rate or equivalently a high discount factor.

■ **futures market**
a market for exchange (of currencies, in the case of the exchange market) in the future. That is, participants contract to exchange currencies, not today, but at a specified calendar date in the future and at a price (exchange rate) that is agreed upon today.

■ **G-10**
a group of ten.

■ **G-20**
an international forum of finance ministers and central bank governors from 19 countries and the EU, plus the IMF and World Bank. Created in 1999 by the finance

ministers of the G-7, it meets annually to discuss financial and economic concerns among industrialised economies and emerging markets.

■ **G-24**
a group of developing countries, established in 1971, with the aim of taking positions on monetary and development finance issues.

■ **G-7**
a group of seven major industrialised countries whose heads of state have met annually, since 1976, in summit meetings to discuss economic and political issues. The seven are United States, Canada, Japan, Britain, France, Germany and Italy (plus the EU).

■ **G-77**
a coalition of developing countries within the United Nations, established in 1964, at the end of the first session of UNCTAD, intended to articulate and promote the collective economic interests of its members and enhance their negotiating capacity. Originally with 77 members, it now (in 2001) has 133.

■ **G-8**
the G-7 plus Russia, which have met as a full economic and political summit since 1998.

■ **gains from trade**
the net benefits that countries experience as a result of lowering import tariffs and otherwise liberalising trade.

■ **gains from trade theorem**
the theoretical proposition that (in the absence of distortions) there will be gains from trade for any economy that moves from autarky to free trade, as well as for a small open economy and for the world as a whole if tariffs are reduced appropriately.

■ **game**
a theoretical construct in game theory in which players select actions and the payoffs depend on the actions of all the players.

■ **game theory**
the modelling of strategic interactions among agents, used in economic models where the numbers of interacting agents (firms, governments, etc.) is small enough that each has a perceptible influence on the others.

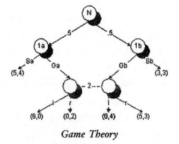

*Game Theory*

■ **gamma index**
a measure of the connectivity of a network comparing (through a ratio) the actual number of links with the maximum number of possible links (edges) in this network.

■ **gastarbeiter**
a guest worker.

- **GATT Articles**

the individual sections of the GATT agreement, conventionally indentified by their Roman numerals. Most were originally drafted in 1947, but are still included in the WTO.

- **GATT-Speak**

variation on GATT-Think.

- **GATT-Think**

a somewhat derogatory term for the language of GATT negotiations, in which exports are good, imports are bad and a reduction in a barrier to imports is a concession. Similar to mercantilism.

- **General Agreement on Tariffs and Trade (GATT)**

a multilateral treaty entered into in 1948 by the intended members of the International Trade Organisation, the purpose of which was to implement many of the rules and negotiated tariff reductions that would be overseen by the ITO. With the failure of the ITO to be approved, the GATT became the principal institution regulating trade policy, until it was subsumed within the WTO in 1995.

- **General Agreement on Trade in Services (GATS)**

the agreement, negotiated in the Uruguay Round, that brings international trade in services into the WTO. It provides for countries to provide national treatment to foreign service providers and for them to select and negotiate the service sectors to be covered under GATS.

- **general equilibrium**

equality of supply and demand in all markets of an economy simultaneously. The number of markets does not have to be large. The simplest Ricardian model has markets only for two goods and one factor, labour, but this is a general equilibrium model. Contrasts with partial equilibrium.

- **generalised system of preferences**

tariff preferences for developing countries, by which developed countries let certain manufactured and semi-manufactured imports from developing countries enter at lower tariffs than the same products from developed countries.

- **gentrification**

the widespread emergence of middle-and upper middle-class enclaves in formerly deteriorated-inner-city neighbourhoods.

- **geobase**

data base or index to the international literature of geography, ecology, earth science and marine science.

- **Giffen good**

a good that is so inferior and so heavily consumed at low incomes that the demand for it rises when its price rises. The reason is that the price increase lowers income sufficiently that the positive income effect (because it is inferior) outweighs the negative substitution effect.

Figure 3.   Percentage change per year in the Gini coefficient and growth in real GDP per capita in selected economies of the ESCAP region

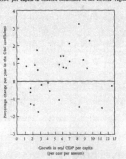

*Gini Coefficient*

■ **Gini Coefficient (or Index of Concentration)**
it is a measure of the income (or some other distributional) inequality in a society. It measures the degree to which two frequency (percentage) distributions correspond. The Gini coefficient is a number between 0 and 100 (or 0 and 1), where 0 means perfect equality (exact correspondence, e.g. everyone has the same income) and 100 (or 1) means perfect inequality (one person has all the income, everyone else earns nothing).

■ **global**
the world-wide presence of a phenomenon or a world-wide spatial pattern of locations of an organisation and/or a pattern of interdependencies.

*Global*

■ **global competitiveness**
Competitiveness, applied internationally.

■ **global optimum**
an allocation that is better, by some criterion, than all others possible.

■ **global quota**
an import quota that specifies the permitted quantity of imports from all sources combined. This may be without regard to the country of origin and thus available on a first-come-first-served basis or it may be allocated to specific suppliers.

■ **globalisation**
1. the increasing world-wide integration of markets for goods, services and capital that attracted special attention in the late 1990s.
2. also used to encompass a variety of other changes that were perceived to occur at about the same time, such as an increased role for large corporations (MNCs) in the world economy and increased intervention into domestic policies and affairs by international institutions such as the IMF, WTO

and World Bank.

3. among countries outside the United States, especially developing countries, the term sometimes refers to the domination of world economic affairs and commerce by the United States.

*Globalisation*

■ **GMO**
Genetically Modified Organism

■ **Gnomes of Zurich**
term used by the British Labour government to refer to Swiss bankers and financiers who engaged in currency speculation that forced the devaluation of the British pound in 1964.

■ **gold standard**
a monetary system in which both the value of a unit of the currency and the quantity of it in circulation are specified in terms of gold. If two currencies are both on the gold standard, then the exchange rate between them is approximately determined by their two prices in terms of gold.

■ **good**
a product that can be produced,

bought and sold and that has physical identity. Sometimes said, inaccurately, to be anything that 'can be dropped on your foot' or also inaccurately, to be 'visible. Contrasts with service. Trade in goods is much easier to measure than trade in services and thus much more thoroughly documented and analysed.

■ **government procurement**
purchase of goods and services by government and by state owned enterprises.

■ **government procurement practice**
the methods by which units of government and state-owned enterprises determine from whom to purchase goods and services. When these methods include a preference for domestic firms, they constitute an NTB.

■ **graduation**
termination of a country's eligibility for GSP tariff preferences, on the grounds that it has progressed sufficiently, in terms of per capita income or another measure, that it is no longer in need of special and differential treatment.

■ **Grandfather clause**
a provision in an agreement, including the GATT but not the WTO, that allows signatories to keep certain of their previously existing laws that otherwise would violate the agreement.

■ **gravity model**
a model of the flows of bilateral trade based on analogy with the law of gravity in physics: $T_{ij} = AY_iY_j/D_{ij}$, where $T_{ij}$ is exports from country $i$ to country $j$, $Y_i, Y_j$ are their national incomes, $D_{ij}$ is the distance between them and $A$ is a constant. Other constants as exponents and other variables are often included.

■ **gray area measure**
a measure whose conformity with existing rules is unclear, such as a VER under the GATT prior to the WTO.

■ **gray market**
goods that are sold for a price lower than or through a distributor different than that intended by the manufacturer. Most commonly, goods that are intended by their manufacturer for one national market that are bought there, exported and sold in another national market.

■ **green box**
category of subsidies permitted under the WTO Agriculture Agreement, includes those not directed at particular products, direct income support for farmers unrelated to production or prices, subsidies for environmental protection and regional development.

■ **green field investment**
FDI that involves the construction of a new plant, rather than the purchase of an existing plant or firm.

■ **Gross Domestic Product (GDP)**
1. the total value of new goods and services produced in a given year, within the borders of a country, regardless of by whom. It is 'gross' in the sense that it does *not* deduct depreciation of previously produced capital, in contrast to NDP.
2. value of all the goods and services produced by workers and capital located within a country (or region), regardless of the nationality of workers or ownership.

■ **Gross National Product (GNP)**
1. total value of all final goods and services produced for consumption in society during a particular time period. The GNP does include allowances for depreciation and indirect business taxes such as those on sales and property.
2. it is the output of labour and property of a country's nationals, regardless of the location of the labour and property. Gross National Product includes income earned by the factors of production (assets and labour) owned by a country's residents but excludes income produced within the country's borders by factors of production owned by nonresidents.

■ **gross output**
the total output of a firm, industry or economy without deducting intermediate inputs. For a firm or industry, this is larger

than its value added, which is net of its own intermediate inputs. For an economy, gross output is greater than net output, which deducts the amount of the good itself, used as an intermediate input.

- **group of ten**
a group of ten countries, members of the IMF, that, together with Switzerland, agreed to make resources available outside their IMF quotas. Since 1963, the governors of the G10 central banks have met on the occasion of the bimonthly BIS meetings.

- **growth**
see **economic growth**.

- **growth accounting**
decomposition of the sources of economic growth, into the contributions from increases in capital, labour and other factors. What remains, called the Solow residual, is usually attributed to technology.

- **Grubel-Lloyd index**
the measure of the intra-industry trade suggested by Grubel and Lloyd (1975). For an industry $i$ with exports $X_i$ and imports $M_i$, the index is $I = [(X_i+M_i) - |X_i-M_i|]100/(X_i+M_i)$. This is the fraction of total trade in the industry, $X_i+M_i$, that is accounted for by IIT (times 100).

- **guest worker**
a foreign worker who is permitted to enter a country temporarily, in order to take a job for which there is shortage of domestic labour.

- **Gulf Cooperation Council (GCC)**
an agreement among six countries of Persian Gulf region — Bahrain, Kuwait, Oman, Qatar, Saudi Arabia and the United Arab Emirates — in 1981, with the aim of coordinating and integrating their economic policies.

- **H Index (The Herfindahl-Hirschman Index)**
stands for Herfindahl-Hirschman index, which is a way of measuring the concentration of market share held by particular suppliers in a market. The H index is the sum of squares of the percentages of the market shares held by the firms in a market. If there is a monopoly, one firm with all sales, the H index is 10000. If there is perfect competition, with an infinite number of firms with near-zero market share each, the H index is approximately zero. Other industry structures will have H indices between zero and 10000.

- **Harberger triangle**
the triangular area or areas in a supply and demand diagram that measures the net welfare loss or deadweight loss due to a market distortion or policy, such as a tariff.

- **Harberger-Laursen-Metzler Effect**
the conjecture or result that a

terms of trade deterioration will cause a decrease in savings due to the decrease in real income and therefore that a real depreciation will cause an increase in real expenditure.

■ **harmful externality**
see **negative externality**.

■ **harmonisation**
the changing of government regulations and practices, as a result of an international agreement, to make those of different countries the same or more compatible.

■ **Harmonised System (HS)**
an international system for classifying goods in international trade and for specifying the tariffs on those goods. It was adopted at the beginning of 1989, replacing the previously used schedules in over 50 countries.

■ **Harold Hotelling**
former Harvard economist (M.A. from UW) who among other contributions, published a famous paper (in 1929) on the stability of spatial competition for the spatial duopoly (competition involving two competitors).

■ **Harrod neutral**
a particular specification of technological change or technological difference that is labour augmenting.

■ **Harrod, Sir Roy F. (1900-78)**
born in Norfolk, England. An influential British economist, educated at Oxford, who was an early proponent of Keynesian economics, a prominent adviser to the British government during the years of World War II and subsequently Keynes official biographer. Harrod wrote extensively on a number of topics such as business cycles, monetary problems, international trade and the theory of economic growth. In the latter field, he pointed out as early as 1939 that in the Keynesian model, investment played the role of an offset to saving-a way of getting spending withdrawn from the income stream by savers back into it. But investment also increases the productive capacity of the economy.

■ **Hat algebra**
the Jones (1965) technique for comparative static analysis in trade models. By totally differentiating a model in the logarithms of its variables, a linear system is obtained relating small proportional changes (denoted by carats (^) or 'hats') in terms of various elasticities and shares. (The published ar-

ticle used *, not ^, because of ty-pographical constraints.)

■ **Havana Charter**

the charter for the never-imple-mented International Trade Organisation. The draft was com-pleted at a conference in Havana, Cuba, in 1948.

■ **Headquarters services**

the activities of a firm that typi-cally occur at its main location and that contribute in a broad sense to its productivity at all of its lo-cations and plants. These may in-clude management, accounting, marketing and R&D.

■ **Heavily Indebted Poor Countries (HIPC)**

the name given to those poor coun-tries with large debts, the target of initiatives to forgive that debt as a means of assisting development.

■ **Heckscher-Ohlin Model (H-O Model)**

a model of international trade in which comparative advantage de-rives from differences in relative factor endowments across coun-tries and differences in relative factor intensities across industries. Sometimes refers only to the text-book or 2x2x2 model, but more generally includes models with any numbers of factors, goods and countries. Model was originally formulated by Heckscher (1919), fleshed out by Ohlin (1933) and refined by Samuelson (1948, 1949, 1953).

■ **Heckscher-Ohlin Theorem**

the proposition of the Heckscher-Ohlin Model that countries will ex-port the goods that use relatively intensively their relatively abun-dant factors.

■ **Heckscher-Ohlin-Samuelson Model (HOS Model)**

usually synonymous with the Heckscher-Ohlin Model, although sometimes the term is used to dis-tinguish the more formalised, math-ematical version that Samuelson used from the more general but less well-defined conceptual treatment of Heckscher and Ohlin.

■ **Heckscher-Ohlin-Vanek Model (HOV)**

the Heckscher-Ohlin Model for the case of identical techniques of production, used to derive the strong prediction about the factor content of trade known as the Heckscher-Ohlin-Vanek Theo-rem.

■ **Heckscher-Ohlin-Vanek Theorem**

the prediction of the H-O-V Model that a country's net factor content of trade equals its own factor endowment minus its world-expenditure share of the world factor endowment. That is, for country i, $F^i = V^i - s^i V^W$, where $F^i$ is the factor content of its trade, $V^i, V^W$ its and the world's factor endowment and $s^i$ its share of world expenditure.

# hedge

to offset risk. In the foreign exchange market, hedgers use the forward market to cover a transaction or open position and thereby reduce exchange risk. The term applies most commonly to trade.

# Hicks, John R. (1904-1989).

one of the leading British economic theorists of the 20th century, Hicks was educated at Oxford to which he returned to teach after holding positions at the London School of Economics, Cambridge and Manchester. Hicks made important contributions on a variety of topics, but is best known for his work on consumer behaviour as published in his major work, *Value and Capital*. In it, Hicks utilised the indifference curve concept first developed by Vilfredo Pareto to construct a theory of demand which was independent of any cardinal measure of utility such as was implicit in the traditional approach perpetuated by Alfred Marshall in his famous *Principles*. Hicks also provided a way of incorporating the interest rate in the Keynesian model which has become a standard feature of intermediate level text-book treatments of the Keynesian model. He was joint winner (with the American economist Kenneth Arrow) of the Nobel prize in economics in 1972.

# ■ Hicksian Demand Function

denoted h(p,u), it refers to the amount of a good that is demanded by a consumer given that it costs p per unit and that the consumer will have utility u from all goods. h(p,u) is the cost-minimising amount.

# ■ Hicks-neutral

said of a technological change or technological difference, if production functions differ by scaling of output only: $F^2(V)=lF^1(V)$, where $F^1(\cdot)$ and $F^2(\cdot)$ are the production functions being compared, V is a vector of factor inputs and l>0 is a constant.

# ■ high dimension

in trade theory, this refers to having more than two goods, factors and/or countries or to having arbitrary numbers of these. Contrasts with the two-ness of the 2x2x2 Model.

# ■ high-powered money

the monetary base or the total of currency in circulation and commercial bank deposits with the central bank.

# ■ high-tech industries or activities

the identification of those industries considered to be high-tech has generally relied on a calculation comparing R&D intensities. R&D intensity, in turn, has typically been determined by comparing industry R&D expenditures and/or numbers of technical people employed (i.e., scientists, engineers, technicians) to industry value added or to the total value of its shipments. See also **technology-based industry**.

■ **Hilbert Space/Hilbert Spaces**

a complete normed metric space with an inner product. So the Hilbert spaces are also Banach spaces. $L^2$ is an example of a Hilbert space. Any $R^n$ with n finite is another.

■ **hinterland**

tributary (factor-supply or product-market) area of a heartland, central region, city or port. A hinterland is delineated by the interdependency relationships with the core region.

■ **Hirsch, Fred (1931-1978)**

born in Vienna, Fred Hirsch graduated from the London School of Economics in 1952. After working as an economic journalist and with the International Monetary Fund, he became a professor of economics at the University of Warwick in 1975. He published a large amount of work on international monetary issues and the subject of inflation, but he became more widely known only at the end of his tragically short life when he published his book, *The Social Limits to Growth*.

■ **hold-up problem / hold-up problems**

one of a certain class of contracting problems. Imagine a situation where there is profit to be made if agents A and B work together, so they consider an agreement to do so after A buys the necessary equipment. The hold-up problem (in this context) is that A might not be willing to take that agreement, even though the outcome would be Pareto efficient, because after A has made that investment, B would have the power and might decide to demand a larger share of the profits than before, since A is now deeply invested in the project but B is not, so B has some bargaining power that wasn't there before the investment. B could demand all of the profits, in fact, since A's alternative is to lose the investment entirely.

■ **home bias**

a preference, by consumers or other demanders, for products produced in their own country compared to otherwise identical imports. This was proposed by Trefler (1995) as a possible explanation for the mystery of the missing trade.

■ **Homogeneous function**

a function with the property that multiplying all arguments by a constant changes the value of the function by a monotonic function of that constant: $F(lV)=g(l)F(V)$, where $F(\cdot)$ is the homogeneous function, V is a vector of arguments, $l>0$ is any constant and $g(\cdot)$ is some strictly increasing positive function. Special cases include homogeneous of degree X and linearly homogeneous.

■ **homogeneous of degree 1**
the same as linearly homogeneous and, for a production function, constant returns to scale. See **homogeneous of degree X**.

■ **homogeneous of degree X**
a homogeneous function where the monotonic function is the constant raised to the exponent X: $F(lV)=l^XF(V)$. For X>1, see **increasing returns to scale** and for X<1, see **decreasing returns to scale**.

■ **homogeneous of degree zero**
the property of a function that, if you scale all arguments by the same proportion, the value of the function does not change. See homogeneous of degree X. In the H-O Model, CRTS production functions imply that marginal products have this property, which is critical for FPE.

■ **homogeneous product**
the product of an industry in which the outputs of different firms are indistinguishable. Contrasts with differentiated product.

■ **homohypallagic**
having a constant elasticity of substitution. One of the inventors of the CES function tried to christen this in Minhas (1962), where he also explored its theoretical and empirical implications for the Heckscher-Ohlin Theorem, but the name did not catch on.

■ **homothetic**
a function of two or more arguments is homothetic if all ratios of its first partial derivatives depend only on the ratios of the arguments, not their levels. For competitive consumers or producers optimising subject to homothetic utility or production functions, this means that ratios of goods demanded depend only on relative prices, not on income or scale.

■ **homothetic demand**
demand functions derived from homothetic preferences. The demand functions are not themselves literally homothetic.

■ **homothetic preferences**
together with identical preferences, this assumption is used for many propositions in trade theory, in order to assure that consumers with different incomes but facing the same prices will demand goods in the same proportions.

■ **homothetic tastes**
see **homothetic preferences**.

■ **horizontal integration**
production of different varieties of the same product or different products at the same level of processing, within a single firm. This may, but need not, take place in subsidiaries in different countries.

■ **horizontal integration**
corporate mergers involving competing firms producing the same or similar production, at the same stage of production. Such merg-

ers tend to reduce competition in the market of such products.

■ **horizontal intraindustry trade**
intraindustry trade in which the exports and imports are at the same stage of processing. Likely due to product differentiation. Contrasts with vertical IIT.

■ **host country**
see **FDI**.

■ **household**
a basic economic unit in which one or more people choose to live together and share resources. Economic thinking is based on this division of society allowing that not all members of a household (for example children) bring in a monetary income.

■ **HRD**
Human Resource Development

■ **Huber Standard Errors**
same as Huber-White Standard Errors

■ **Huber-White Standard Errors**
the standard errors which have been adjusted for specified assumed-and-estimated correlations of error terms across observations.

■ **human agency**
reference to the independent decision-making intentions, opportunities, capabilities and activities of human beings.

■ **human capital**
1. The stock of knowledge and skill, embodied in an individual as a result of education, training and experience that makes them more productive.
2. The stock of knowledge and skill embodied in the population of an economy.

■ **human capital accumulation**
the attributes of a person that are productive in some economic context. Often refers to formal educational attainment, with the implication that education is the investment whose returns are in the form of wage, salary or other compensation. These are normally measured and conceived of as private returns to the individual but can also be social returns.

■ **hyperbolic discounting**
a way of accounting in a model for the difference in the preferences that an agent has over consumption now versus consumption in the future.

■ **hypertextually organised book**
such a book may have the following introduction: This is a book designed "to reward browsing in any direction. Cross-references, for example, point out meaningful links. Zoom in where you feel engaged. Here are some starting points: ....".

## hysteresis
a hypothesised property of unemployment rates: that there is a ratcheting effect, so a short-term rise in unemployment rates tends to persist.

## IC Constraint
stands for 'incentive compatibility constraint'. When solving a principal-agent maximisation problem for a contract that meets various criteria, the IC constraints are those that require agents to prefer to act in accordance with the solution. If the IC constraint were not imposed, the solution to the problem might be economically meaningless, insofar as it produced an outcome that met some criterion of optimality but which an agent would choose not to act in accord with.

## iceberg transport cost
a cost of transporting a good that uses up only some fraction of the good itself, rather than using any other resources. Based on the idea of floating an iceberg, which is costless except for the amount of the iceberg itself that melts. It is a very tractable way of modelling transport costs since it impacts no other market.

## idempotent matrix
a matrix M is idempotent if MM=M. (M times M equals M.)

## identical preferences
the assumption that individuals, either within a country or in different countries, have the same preferences. To be useful, since individuals' and countries' incomes may differ, the assumption is often used together with homothetic preferences.

## identity matrix
a square matrix of any dimension whose elements are ones on its northwest-to-southeast diagonal and zeroes everywhere else. Any square matrix multiplied by the identity matrix with those dimensions, equals itself. One usually says 'the' identity matrix since in most contexts the dimension is unambiguous. It is standard to denote the identity matrix by I.

## idle
sometimes used to name the state of people who are not in school but also not working. Context is usually industrialised countries with established labour markets and the idle are often poor.

## iff
an abbreviation for 'if and only if'.

## imbalance
1. any departure from equality.
2. in the balance of payments, any surplus or deficit.

## IMF Quota
the amount of money that each IMF member country is required to contribute to the institution, partly in their own currency and partly in U.S. dollars, gold or other member-country currencies. A

country's quota is based upon the country's GDP. Countries have voting power in the IMF in proportion to their IMF quotas.

■ **immigration**
the migration of people into a country.

■ **immiserising growth**
economic growth that makes the country worse off. Bhagwati (1958) coined the term for growth that expands exports and worsens the terms of trade sufficiently that its real income falls. Johnson (1955) had shown that a market distorted by a tariff could lose from growth and had also, independently, worked out conditions for Bhagwati's result.

■ **impairment**
see **nonviolation**

■ **imperfect competition**
1. a market situation in which one or more buyers or sellers are important enough to have an influence on price.
2. any departure from perfect competition. However, imperfect competition usually refers to one of the market structures other than perfect competition.

■ **imperfectly competitive**
refers to an economic agent (firm or consumer), group of agents (industry), model or analysis that is characterised by imperfect competition. Contrasts with perfectly competitive.

■ **implicit contract**
a non-contractual agreement that corresponds to a Nash equilibrium to the repeated bilateral trading game other than the sequence of Nash equilibria to the one-shot trading game.

■ **implicit price deflator**
a broad measure of prices derived from separate estimates of real and nominal expenditures for GDP or a subcategory of GDP. Without qualification, the term refers to the GDP deflator and is thus an index of prices for everything that a country produces, unlike the CPI, which is restricted to consumption and includes prices of imports.

■ **implicit tariff**
1. tariff revenue on a good or group of goods, divided by the corresponding value of imports. Often lower than the official or statutory tariff, due both to PTAs and due to failures in customs collection.
2. The difference between the price just inside a border and the price just outside it, especially in the case of a good protected by an import quota.

■ **import**
1. a good that crosses into a country, across its border, for commercial purposes.
2. a product, which might be a service, that is provided to domestic residents by a foreign producer.
3. to cause a good or service to

be an import under definitions 1 and/or 2.

## import authorisation
the requirement that imports be authorised by a special agency before entering a country, similar to import licensing.

## import bias
1. Any bias in favour of importing.
2. Applied to growth, it tends to mean a bias against importing and against trading more generally. Thus growth that is based disproportionately on accumulation of the factor used intensively in the import-competing industry and/or technological progress favouring that industry.

## import demand elasticity
The elasticity of demand for imports with respect to price.

## import elasticity
usually means the import demand elasticity.

## import license
the license to import under an import quota or under exchange controls.

## import licensing
see licensing.

## import penetration
a measure of the importance of imports in the domestic economy, either by sector or overall, usually defined as the value of imports divided by the value of apparent consumption.

## import price index
price index of the goods that a country imports.

## import protection
see protection.

## import quota
see quota.

## import relief
usually refers to some form of restraint of imports in a particular sector, in order to assist domestic producers and with the connotation that these producers have been suffering from the competition with imports. If done formally under existing statutes, it is administered protection, but it may also be done informally using a VER.

## import substitute
a good produced on the domestic market that competes with imports, either as a perfect substitute or as a differentiated product.

## import substituting industrialisation
a strategy for economic development, based on replacing imports with domestic production. (ISI)

## import substitution
a strategy for economic development that replaces imports with domestic production. It may be motivated by the infant industry argument or simply by the desire to mimic the industrial structure of advanced countries. Contrasts with export promotion.

■ **import surcharge**
a tax levied uniformly on most or all imports, in addition to already-existing tariffs.

■ **import surveillance**
the monitoring of imports, usually by means of automatic licensing.

■ **import-competing**
refers to an industry that competes with imports. That is, in a two-good model with trade, one good is the export good and the other is the import-competing goods.

■ **imports**
goods or services that were produced abroad.

■ **import-weighted average tariff**
see **trade weighted average tariff**.

■ **impossibility theorem**
one of a class of theorems following Arrow (1951), showing that social welfare functions cannot have certain collections of desirable attributes in common.

■ **improve the terms of trade**
to increase the terms of trade, that is, to increase the relative price of exports compared to imports. Because it represents an increase in what the country gets in return for what it gives up, this is associated with an improvement in the country's welfare, although whether that actually occurs depends on the reason prices changed.

■ **improve the trade balance**
this conventionally refers to a increase in exports relative to imports, which thus causes the balance of trade to become large if positive or smaller if negative. The terminology ignore that exports drain resource while imports satisfy domestic needs and reflects instead the association of exports with either accumulation of wealth or jobs.

■ **impulse response function**
consider a shock to a system. graph of the response of the system over time after the shock an impulse response function graph. One use is in models of monetary systems. One graphs, for example, the percentage deviation in output or consumption over time after a one-time, one percent increase in the money stock.

■ **in kind**
referring to a payment made with goods instead of money.

■ **Inada conditions**
a function f() satisfies the Inada conditions if: f(0) = 0, f'(0) = infinity and f'(infinity) = 0. f() usually a production function in this context.

■ **inadmissibility**
a possible action by a player in game may be said to be inadmissible if it is dominated by another feasible actions.

■ **income**
money that comes into a personal, business or government account. Income can be generated in a number of different ways including trading your work for wages and selling a product.

■ **income disparity**
inequality of income, usually referring to differences in average per capita incomes across countries.

■ **income distribution**
a description of the fractions of a population that are at various levels of income. The larger are the differences in income, the 'worse' the income distribution is usually said to be, the smaller the 'better.' International trade and factor movements can alter countries' income distributions by changing prices of low- and high-paid factors.

■ **income effect**
1. the effect of a change in income on the quantity of a good or service consumed.
2. that portion of the effect of price on quantity demanded that reflects the change in real income due to the price change. Contrasts with substitution effect.

■ **income elasticity**
1. normally the income elasticity of demand, that is, the elasticity of demand with respect to income.

2. the percentage change in quantity demanded divided by the percentage change in income.

■ **income redistribution argument for a tariff**
the argument that tariffs should be used in order to redistribute income towards the poor. In a rich country, where unskilled labour is the scarce factor, this can make sense as explained in the Stolper-Samuelson Theorem, but it is a second-best argument.

■ **incomplete specialisation**
production of goods that compete with imports.

■ **increasing opportunity cost**
the characteristic of an economy that the opportunity cost of a good rises as it produces more of it, resulting in a transformation curve that is concave to the origin. In the HO Model, this happens even with CRTS if sectors have different factor intensities.

■ **Increasing Returns To Scale (IRS, IRTS)**
a property of a production function such that changing all inputs by the same proportion changes output more than in proportion. Common forms include homogeneous of degree greater than one and production with constant marginal cost but positive fixed cost. Also called economies of scale, scale economies and simply, increasing returns.

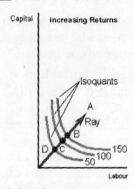

tion is true and zero if it is false.

# ■ indifference curve

1. a curve showing all possible combinations of two goods among which the consumer is indifferent.

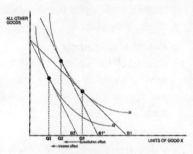

*Indifference Curve*

2. a means of representing the preferences and well being of consumers. Formally, it is a curve representing the combinations of arguments in a utility function, that yield a given level of utility.

# ■ indifference theory

the analysis of consumer demand using indifference curves and an income constraint, to demonstrate the reason for the inverse relationship between price and quantity demand. An alternative to the older marginal utility explanation of this phenomenon.

# ■ indirect taxes

taxes levied on a producer which the producer then passes on to the consumer as part of the price of a good. Distinguished from direct taxes, such as sales taxes which are visible to the person who pays them.

# ■ indebtedness

the amount that is owed, thus the amount of an entity's (individual, firm or government's) financial obligations to creditors.

# ■ indemnity payment

a kind of insurance, in which payment is made (often in previously determined amounts) for injuries suffered, not for the costs of recovery. The indemnity payment is designed not to be a dependent on anything the patient can control. From the point of view of the insurer, the indemnity mechanism avoids the moral hazard problem of victim spending too much in recovery.

# ■ independent random variables

two random variables X and Y are statistically independent if and only if their joint density (pdf) is the product of their marginal densities, that is if $f(x,y)=f_x(x)f_y(y)$.

# ■ indicator variable

in a regression, an indicator variable is a variable that is one if a condi-

- **indirect utility function**
denoted $v(p, m)$ where p is a vector of prices for goods and m is a budget in the same units as the prices. The indirect utility function takes the value of the maximum utility that can be achieved by spending the budget m on the consumption goods with prices p.

- **individually rational allocation**
an allocation is individually rational if no agent is worse off in that allocation than with his endowment.

- **induction**
a process of reasoning ('generalising') leading from the observation and recording of particular cases to general conclusions or 'laws'.

- **inductive reasoning**
characterises a reasoning process of generalising from facts, instances or examples.

- **industrial concentration**
the extent to which a small number of firms dominate an industry, often measured by the four-firm concentration ratio. Concentration is, in effect, the opposite of competition, though in an open economy imports complicate the relationship.

- **industrial district**
a localised network of producers bound together in a social division of labour, in necessary association with a local labour market.

- **industrial inertia**
tendency to continue to invest and reinvest at an already existing location even if such a location would be non-optimal for a new location decision. The concept appears to have its roots in Allan Rogers' investigation of the US steel industry and the effects of basing-point pricing and freight absorption on the location pattern of this industry.

- **industrial park**
a well demarcated, often governmentally encouraged and subsidised industrial real estate development, providing basic industrial infrastructure facilities, developed sites which can be purchased or buildings which can be leased, designed to attract industrial job providers to locations separate from, yet accessible to residential areas.

- **industrial policy**
government policy to influence which industries expand and, perhaps implicitly, which contract, via subsidies, tax breaks and other aids for favoured industries. The purpose, aside from political favour, may be to foster competitive advantage where there are beneficial externalities and/or scale economies.

- **industrialisation**
a historical phase and experience. Industrialisation is the overall change in circumstances accom-

panying a society's movement population and resources from farm production to manufacturing production and associated services.

■ **industrialisation economies**
a type of agglomeration economies or external economies, resulting from the spatial concentration of industrial activities, as different from or overlapping with: localisation economies or urbanisation economies.

■ **industry**
a group of firms producing similar products. Hence, the auto industry or the steel industry.

■ **industry-mix effect**
in shift/share analysis. See **proportionality effect**

■ **indwelling**
a term M. Polanyi used to suggest that 'human beings create knowledge by involving themselves with objects, that is, through self-involvement and commitment...'

■ **inelastic**
having an elasticity less than one. For a price elasticity of demand, this means that expenditure falls as price falls. For an income elasticity, it means that expenditure share falls with income. Contrasts with elastic and unit elastic.

■ **inelastic offer curve**
an offer curve with inelastic demand for imports. That inelasticity implies that exports decline as imports increase and it therefore means that the offer curve is backward bending. Strictly speaking, the natural definition of an offer curve's elasticity would be negative in this case, not just less than one, but that definition is seldom used.

■ **inequality**
differences in per capita income or household income across populations within a country or across countries.

■ **infant industry**
an industry at an early stage of its development. Concept often related to the need for tariff protection or agglomeration economies during and (for some time) after 'incubation'.

■ **infant industry argument**
the theoretical rationale for infant industry protection.

■ **infant industry protection**
protection of a newly established domestic industry that is less productive than foreign producers. If productivity will rise with experience enough to pass Mill's and Bastable's tests, there is a second-best argument for protection. The term is very old, but a classic treatment may be found in Baldwin (1969).

■ **inferior good**
1. a good for which the demand decreases when income increases. When a household's income goes up, it will buy a smaller quantity

of such a good.

2. a good the demand for which falls as income rises. The income elasticity of demand is therefore negative.

3. a good that has the property that when a person's income rises the demand for the inferior good falls.

■ **inflation**

a general increase in prices usually attributed to a situation in which there is too much money chasing too few goods, thus driving up the price of all goods by driving down the value of money. There are two major ways of calculating inflation. Price inflation is based on the Consumer Price Index (CPI), a monthly measure of how much the price of goods changes. Income inflation is based on the change in wages and based on measures such as the Average Industrial Wage.

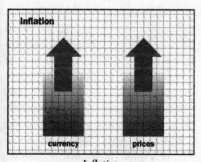

*Inflation*

■ **inflation adjusted**

adjusted for inflation.

■ **inflation rate**

the percentage increase in the price level per year. See **inflation**.

■ **informal economy**

a reference to those parts of the economy which operate without official recognition or with only ambiguous or tenuous ties to governmental institutions. Activities operating outside the regulatory and often also outside the taxation system.

■ **information impactedness**

a derivative condition that arises mainly because of uncertainty and opportunism, though bounded rationality is involved as well. It exists when true underlying circumstances relevant to the transaction or related set of transactions, are known to one or more parties but cannot be costlessly discerned by or displayed for others. Particularly significant when there are sellers, buyers and intermediaries.

■ **information literacy**

implicit in a full understanding of information literacy is the realisation that several conditions must be simultaneously present. First, someone must desire to know, use analytic skills to formulate questions, identify research methodologies and utilise critical skills to evaluate experimental (and experiential) results. Second, the person must possess the skills to search for answers to those questions in increasingly diverse and complex ways. Third, once a person has identified what is sought, be able to access it.

■ **informational cascades**
economic actors improve on their limited private information by observing and mimicking the actions of others.

■ **infrastructure**
1. the network of goods that make up the physical structure that support other forms of economic and social activity such as roads, water treatment plants, airports and canals. There is also a social infrastructure of institutions and relationships.
2. the facilities that must be in place in order for a country or area to function as an economy and as a state, including the capital needed for transportation, communication and provision of water and power and the institutions needed for security, health and education.

■ **Initial Public Offering (IPO)**
selling corporate stock to the public for the first time. First, stocks are sold in the primary market at an offering price determined by the syndicate, thereafter the shares are traded in the secondary market or what is called the aftermarket.

■ **injury**
harm to an industry's owners and/or workers. Import protection under the safeguards, AD and CVD provisions of the GATT require a finding of serious (for safeguards) or material (for AD/CVD) injury (as determined by, in the US, the ITC). Known as the injury test.

■ **innovation**
the setting up of a new production function. Innovation combines factors in a new way or carries out new combinations.

■ **input-output**
refers to the structure of intermediate transactions among industries, in which one industry's output is an input to another or even to itself.

■ **input-output table**
a table of all inputs and outputs of an economy's industries, including intermediate transactions, primary inputs and sales to final users. As developed by Wassily Leontief, the table can be used to calculate gross outputs and primary factor inputs needed to produce specified net outputs. Leontief (1954) used this to find the factor content of US trade, generating the Leontief Paradox

■ **institutional thickness**
a reference to the institutional structure and qualities of institutions of a region, more specifically the presence, interaction, collective action (lack of inter-institutional conflict) and legitimacy of institutions in a region.
1. an economic variable that is controlled by policy makers and can be used to influence other variables, called targets. Examples are monetary and fiscal policies used

to achieve external and internal balance.

2. see **financial instrument**.

■ **insurance**
a financial product that insures against risk. Insurance is available for many risks including death, disability, fire, health care and theft. Insurance costs a certain amount each month or year. It is always important to find out the coverage and limitations of any insurance plan.

■ **Integrated World Economy (IWE)**
a hypothetical, theoretical benchmark in which both goods and factors move costlessly between countries. The IWE is associated with a retangular diagram depicting allocation of factors to countries, showing conditions for FPE. The name was coined by Dixit and Norman (1980), but the concept and technique was introduced by Travis (1964).

■ **integration**
economic integration refers to reducing barriers among countries to transactions and to movements of goods, capital and labour, including harmonisation of laws, regulations and standards. Common forms include FTAs, customs unions and common markets. Sometimes classified as shallow integration vs. deep integration.

■ **Intellectual Property (IP)**
products of the mind, such as inventions, works of art, music, writing, film, etc.

■ **intellectual property protection**
laws that establish and maintain ownership rights to intellectual property. The principal forms of IP protection are patents, trademarks and copyrights.

■ **intellectual property right**
the right to control and derive the benefits from something one has invented, discovered or created.

■ **intelligent enterprise**
such enterprises are 'converting intellectual resources into a chain of service outputs and integrating these into a form most useful for certain customers.'

■ **intensity of land use**
factor inputs (capital, labour, fertiliser, etc.) per unit area of land, generally yielding high returns per unit area of land, as, e.g., in 'intensive agriculture' (as different from 'extensive land use' and 'extensive agriculture')

■ **intensive**
of production, using a relatively large input of an input. See factor intensity.

■ **intensive agriculture**
system of farming characterised by relatively high levels of factor inputs (capital [including fertiliser] and/or labour] per unit of land.

■ **interbank rate**
the rate of interest charged by a

bank on a loan to another bank. See **LIBOR**.

■ **interest**
the payment made for the use of funds to create capital goods with.

■ **interest parity**
equality of returns on otherwise identical financial assets denominated in different currencies. May be uncovered, with returns including expected changes in exchange rates or covered, with returns including the forward premium or discount. Also called interest rate parity.

■ **interest rate**
1. the percentage rate which must be paid for the use of investable funds.

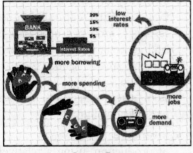

*Interest Rate*

2. the rate of return on bonds, loans or deposits. When one speaks of 'the' interest rate, it is usually in a model where there is only one.

■ **interest**
the cost of borrowing money. Interest rates are the amount that the person borrowing the money is charged, usually a percentage of

how much she has borrowed. Prime interest rates refer to the amount set by the Bank of Canada. Other banks usually decide their interest rate as prime plus a certain percentage.

■ **interindustry trade**
trade in which a country's exports and imports are in different industries. Typical of models of comparative advantage, such as the Ricardian Model and Heckscher-Ohlin Model. Contrasts with intraindustry trade.

■ **intermediate good**
same as intermediate input.

■ **intermediate input**
an input to production that has itself been produced and that, unlike capital, is used up in production. As an input, it is in contrast to a primary input and as an output it is in contrast to a final good. A very large portion of international trade is in intermediate inputs.

■ **intermediate transaction**
the sale of a product by one firm to another, presumably to be used as an intermediate input.

■ **intermittant dumping**
dumping that occurs for short periods of time, presumably to dispose of temporary surpluses of goods and not intended to eliminate competition. Same as sporadic dumping.

■ **internal balance**
a target level for domestic aggregate economic activity, such as a level of GDP that minimises unemployment without being inflationary. Contrasts with external balance.

■ **internal economies of scale**
economies of scale that are internal to a firm, that is, the firm's average costs fall as its own output rises. Likely to be inconsistent with perfect competition. Contrasts with external economies of scale.

■ **internalise**
to cause, usually by a tax or subsidy, an external cost or benefit of someone's actions to be experienced by them directly, so that they will take it into account in their decisions.

■ **international adjustment process**
1. any mechanism for change in international markets.
2. the mechanism by which payments imbalances diminish under pegged exchange rates and nonsterilisation. Similar to the specie flow mechanism, exchange-market intervention causes money supplies of surplus countries to expand and vice versa, leading to price and interest rate changes that correct the current and capital account imbalances.

■ **International Bank for Reconstruction & Development (IBRD)**
the largest of the five institutions that comprise the World Bank Group, IBRD provides loans and development assistance to middle-income countries and creditworthy poorer countries.

■ **International Centre for Settlement of Investment Disputes (ICSID)**
one of the five institutions that comprise the World Bank Group, ICSID provides facilities for the settlement - by conciliation or arbitration - of investment disputes between foreign investors and their host countries.

■ **International Cocoa Organisation**
an intergovernmental organisation set up in 1973 to administer the International Cocoa Agreement, the most recent version of which was negotiated in 1993. See **International Commodity Agreement**.

■ **International Coffee Organisation**
an intergovernmental organisation set up in 1963 that administers the International Coffee Agreement. See **International Commodity Agreement**.

■ **International Commodity Agreement (ICA)**
an agreement among producing and consuming countries to im-

prove the functioning of the global market for a commodity. May be administrative, providing information or economic, influencing world price, usually using a buffer stock to stabilise it. ICAs are overseen by UNCTAD.

■ **International Cotton Advisory Committee**
an association of governments dealing with cotton. It grew out of an International Cotton Meeting in 1939. See **International Commodity Agreement**.

■ **International Development Association**
one of the five institutions that comprise the World Bank Group, IDA provides interest free loans and other services to the poorest countries.

■ **international exhaustion**
see **exhaustion**.

■ **international factor movement**
the international movement of any factor of production, including primarily labour and capital. Thus it includes migration and foreign direct investment. Also, it may include the movement of financial capital in the form of international borrowing and lending.

■ **international finance**
the monetary side of international economics, in contrast to the real side or real trade. Often called international monetary economics or international macroeconomics,

each term has a slightly different meaning and none seems entirely right for the entire field. 'International finance' is best for the study of international financial markets including exchange rates.

■ **International Finance Corporation (IFC)**
one of the five institutions that comprise the World Bank Group, IFC promotes growth in the developing world by financing private sector investments and providing technical assistance and advice to governments and businesses.

■ **International Grains Council**
an intergovernment organisation concerned with grains trade that administers the Grains Trade Convention of 1995. See **International Commodity Agreement**.

■ **International Jute Organisation**
the organisation set up in 1984 to implement the International Agreement on Jute and Jute Products, 1982. See **International Commodity Agreement**.

■ **International Labour Organisation (ILO)**
a United Nations specialised agency that establishes and monitors compliance with international standards for human and labour rights.

■ **International Lead and Zinc Study Group**
the international organisation formed in 1959 to share information about lead and zinc. See **International Commodity Agreement**.

■ **international macroeconomics**
Same as international finance, but with more emphasis on the international determination of macroeconomic variables such as national income and the price level.

■ **International Monetary Fund (IMF)**
an organisation formed originally to help countries to stabilise exchange rates, but today pursuing a broader agenda of financial stability and assistance. As of July 2000, it had 182 member countries.

■ **International Olive Oil Council**
the intergovernmental organisation in charge of administering the International Olive Oil Agreement, which originated in 1956. See **International Commodity Agreement**.

■ **international reserves**
the assets denominated in foreign currency, plus gold, held by a central bank, sometimes for the purpose of intervening in the exchange market to influence or peg the exchange rate. Usually includes foreign currencies themselves (especially US dol-

lars), other assets denominated in foreign currencies, gold and a small amount of SDRs.

■ **International Rubber Study Group**
an intergovernmental organisation, founded in 1944, that provides a forum for the discussion of matters affecting the supply and demand for both synthetic and natural rubber. See **International Commodity Agreement**.

■ **International Sugar Organisation**
an intergovernmental body that administers the International Sugar Agreement of 1992. See **International Commodity Agreement**.

■ **International Trade Administration (ITA)**
a part of the United States Department of Commerce, the ITA acts on behalf of U.S. businesses in its global competition. In trade policy, its Import Administration has the duty of determining whether imports are dumped or subsidised.

■ **International Trade Commission (ITC)**
an independent, quasi-judicial federal agency of the US government that provides information and expertise to the legislative and executive branches of government and directs actions against unfair trade practices. In trade policy, its commissioners assess injury in cases filed under the escape clause, antidumping and countervailing duty

statutes.

# International Trade Organisation (ITO)

conceived as a complement to the Bretton Woods institutions — the IMF and World Bank — the ITO was to provide international discipline in the uses of trade policies. The Havana Charter for the ITO was not approved by the United States Congress, however and the initiative died, replaced by the continuing and growing importance of the GATT.

# interoperability

ability of diverse intelligent devices to communicate with one another in performing meaningful tasks.

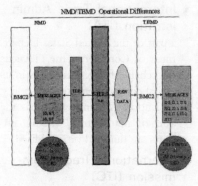

*Interoperability*

# intra-firm (international) trade

flow of imports and exports of goods and services across national boundaries between different components of a corporate network (e.g. between home-country parent firms and their foreign affiliates).

# Intraindustry trade (IIT)

trade in which a country exports and imports in the same industry, in contrast to interindustry trade. Ubiquitous in the data, much IIT is due to aggregation. Can be horizontal or vertical. Grubel and Lloyd (1975) wrote the book on IIT.

# intra-mediate trade

another term for fragmentation. Used by Antweiler and Trefler (2002).

# intra-product specialisation

another term for fragmentation. Used by Arndt (1997).

# inventories

stocks of goods in the hands of producers. These stocks are included in the definition of capital and an increase in inventories is considered to be investment.

# invertible

said of a matrix if its inverse exists. That is, a matrix A is invertible if there exists another matrix B such that BA=I, where I is the identity matrix.

# invest/investment

to invest essentially means to put the valuable things you own into a form in which they will earn more money or other benefit. Putting money in the bank is an investment because it earns interest in the form of money. Buying a house is also an investment because it gives you the use of the house and because houses generally increase in monetary value over the years. Bonds, GICs and houses are fairly low-risk investments. Stocks or shares in certain companies are high-risk investments because you never know how well the company will do. Some people earn a lot on stocks, others lose a lot. While people generally talk about monetary investments there are other kinds. Love is a way of investing in people. Reading is an investment in educating yourself.

■ **investing**
creating capital goods. Acquiring or producing structures, machinery and equipment or inventories.

■ **investment spending**
the total amount of spending during some period of time on capital goods.

■ **invisible**
in referring to international trade, used as a synonym for 'service'. 'Invisibles trade' is trade in services. Contrasts with visible.

■ **invisible hand**
the force Adam Smith believed would guide free market economics, ensuring that prosperity would come to all. See also **laissez faire economics**.

■ **invisible trade (imports or exports of a region or country)**
trade in non-commodity services

such as finance (banking, insurance etc.), communications, transportation or tourism.

■ **invoice**
the itemised bill for a transaction, stating the nature of the transaction and its cost. In international trade, the invoice price is often the preferred basis for levying an ad valorem tariff.

■ **involuntary unemployment**
unemployment caused by a deficiency in aggregate demand.

■ **IPRs**
Intellectual Property Rights

■ **Irrelevance of Independent Alternatives (IIA)**
an assumption in a model. In a discrete choice setting, the multinomial logit model is appropriate only if the introduction or removal of a choice has no effect on the proportion of probability assigned to each of the other choices.

■ **IS-Curve**
in the **IS-LM model**, the curve representing the combinations of national income and interest rate at which aggregate demand equals supply for all goods. It is normally downward sloping because a rise in income increases output by more than aggregate demand (through consumption), while a rise in the interest rate reduces aggregate demand through investment.

■ **ISI**

Import Substituting Industriali-sation

■ **IS-LM model**

a Keynesian macroeconomic model, popular especially in the 1960s, in which national income and the interest rate were deter-mined by the intersection of two curves, the IS-curve and the LM-curve.

■ **IS-LM-BP model**

a particular version of the Mundell-Fleming Model that extends the IS-LM model by including in the dia-gram a third curve, the BP-curve, representing the balance of pay-ments and/or the exchange mar-ket.

■ **isocost curve**

also called iso-outlay line. A line (curve) representing the different combinations of factor inputs (such as labour and capital) that can be purchased given the prices of these inputs and the total outlays. Super-imposing the relevant isocost curve on the map of isoquants, we can determine which combination of our inputs will maximise the output for the given outlays.

■ **isocost line**

a line along with the cost of some-thing — usually a combination of two factors of production — is constant. Since these are usually drawn for given prices, which are therefore constant along the line, an isocost line is usually a straight line, with slope equal to the ratio of the (factor) prices.

■ **isodapane**

points of equal additional trans-port costs around the minimum-total-transport-cost point.

■ **iso-price curve**

a curve along which price is (or prices are) constant, most com-monly in factor-price space where it shows the combinations of prices of factors consistent with zero profit in producing a good at a specified price of the good.

■ **isoquant**

a curve representing the combi-nations of factor inputs that yield a given level of output in a pro-duction function.

■ **isostante**

term used by Tord Palander (fol-lowing Schilling) to refer to the boundary between two market areas served by two market cen-tres with varying prices and trans-port costs. The isostante specifies the points with equal delivered prices from both centres.

■ **Israel-US Free Trade Area**

a free trade area between the United States and Israel that was initiated in 1985.

■ **J-curve**

the dynamic path followed by the balance of trade in response to a devaluation, which typically causes the trade balance to worsen be-fore it improves, tracing a path that looks like the letter 'J'.

# Jensen's Inequality

if X is a real-valued random variable with $E(|X|)$ finite and the function g() is convex, then $E[g(X)] >= g(E[X])$.

Jensen's inequality is the inequality one can refer to when showing that an investor with a concave utility function prefers a certain return to the same expected return with uncertainty.

# Jevons, William Stanley (1835-1882)

an English philosopher and scientist instrumental in developing the marginal utility theory of consumer choice. He demonstrated that consumers will purchase increasing quantities of goods until the marginal utility derived from the last penny's worth of one good is equal to the marginal worth of every other good. His major work was *The Theory of Political Economy* published in 1871.

# Jigyobusei (jp)

multidivisional     system     of organisation.

# job lock

describes the situation of a person with a US job who is not free to leave for another job because the first job has medical benefits associated with it that the person needs and the second one would not, perhaps because 'pre-existing conditions' are often not covered under US health insurance.

# Joint Venture (JV)

an undertaking by two parties for a specific purpose and duration, taking any of several legal forms. Two corporations, for example, perhaps from two different countries, may undertake to provide a product or service that is distinct, in kind or location, from what the companies do on their own.

# journals

in context of research economics, journals are academic periodicals, usually with peer-reviewed contents.

# just-in-time

an organisational system of production designed to minimise the time and thereby associated cost between different stages of production as well as between initial expressions of demand and the delivery of goods or services. Just-in-time principles and methods were first applied by Japanese car manufacturers but have found wide application in other activities.

# k percent rule

a monetary policy rule of keeping the growth of money at a fixed rate of k percent a year. This phrase is often used as stated, without specifying the percentage.

# Kaldor-Hicks criterion

the criterion that, for a change in policy or policy regime to be viewed as beneficial, the gainers should be able to compensate the losers and still be better off. The criterion does not require that the compensation actually be paid, which, if it did, would make this the same as the **Pareto criterion**.

■ **keiretsu system**

the framework of relationships in post-war Japan's big banks and big firms. Related companies organised around a big bank (like Mitsui, Mitsubishi and Sumitomo) which own a lot of equity in one another and in the bank and do much business with one another. The keiretsu system has the virtue of maintaining long term business relationships and stability in suppliers and customers. The keiretsu system has the disadvantage of reacting slowly to outside events since the players are partly protected from the external market.

■ **kernel estimation**

the estimation of a regression function or probability density function. Such estimators are consistent and asymptotically normal if as the number of observations n goes to infinity, the bandwidth (window width) h goes to zero and the product nh goes to infinity.

■ **kernel function**

a weighting function used in non-parametric function estimation. It gives the weights of the nearby data points in making an estimate. In practice, kernel functions are piecewise continuous, bounded, symmetric around zero, concave at zero, real valued and for convenience often integrate to one. They can be probability density functions. Often, they have a bounded domain like [-1,1].

■ **Keynes effect**

as prices fall, a given nominal amount of money will be a larger real amount. Consequently, the interest rate would fall and investment demanded rise. This *Keynes effect* disappears in the liquidity trap. Contrast the Keynes effect with the Pigou effect.

■ **Keynes, John Maynard (1883-1946).**

the most important economist of the 20th century. Keynes first came to prominence with his attack on the 1919 treaty with Germany (*The Economic Consequences of the Peace*, 1919). During the 1920s he became dissatisfied with the mainstream economics based on the tradition established by Alfred Marshall. The conventional analysis of individual markets appeared inadequate to explain the economic problems then being experienced in England. Keynes became convinced that deflationary policies were the cause of the difficulties and published several works on money, notably a two volume work, *The Treatise on Money*. From this, he went on to develop the analysis subsequently elaborated in *The General Theory of Employment, Interest and Money*, 1936.

- **Keynesian growth models**
  models in which a long run growth path for an economy is traced out by the relations between saving, investing and the level of output.

- **Keynesian macroeconomics**
  the theory that shows how a market-based capitalist economy may reach equilibrium with large scale unemployment and how government spending may be used to raise it out of this to a new equilibrium at the full-employment level of output.

- **kitchen sink regression**
  a regression where the regressors are not in the opinion of the writer thoroughly 'justified' by an argument or a theory. Often used pejoratively, at other times it describes an exploratory regression.

- **k-nearest-neighbour estimator**
  a kind of nonparametric estimator of a function. Given a data set $\{X_i, Y_i\}$, it estimates values of Y for X's other than those in the sample. The process is to choose the k values of $X_i$ nearest the X for which one seeks an estimate and average their Y values. Here, k is a parameter to the estimator. The average could be weighted, e.g. with the closest neighbour having the most impact on the estimate.

- **knightian uncertainty**
  unmeasurable risk.

- **knots**
  if a regression will be run to estimates different linear slopes for different ranges of the independent variables, it's a spline regression and the endpoints of the ranges are called knots.

- **Kruskal's theorem**
  let X be a set of regressors, y be a vector of dependent variables and the model be: $y=Xb+e$ where $E[ee']$ is the matrix OMEGA. The theorem is that if the column space of (OMEGA)X is the same as the column space of X, that is, that there is heteroskedasticity but not cross-correlation, then the GLS estimator of b is the same as the OLS estimator of b.

- **kurtosis**
  an attribute of a distribution, describing 'peakedness'. Kurtosis is calculated as $E[(x-mu)^4]/s^4$ where mu is the mean and s is the standard deviation.

- **Kuznets curve**
  a graph with measures of increased economic development (presumed to correlate with time) on the horizontal axis and measures of income inequality on the vertical axis hypothesised by Kuznets (1955) to have an inverted-U-shape. That is, Kuznets made the proposition when an economy is primarily agricultural, it has a low level of income inequality, that during early industrialisation income inequality in-

creases over time, then at some critical point it starts to decrease over time. Kuznets (1955) showed evidence for this.

## ■ L¹

the set of Lebesgue-integrable real-valued functions on [0,1].

## ■ L²

a Hilbert space with inner product $(x,y) = $ integral of $x(t)y(t)$ dt. Equivalently, $L^2$ is the space of real-valued random variables that have variances. This is an infinite dimensional space.

## ■ labeling

a requirement to label imported goods with information about how they were produced. This is often suggested as an alternative to trade restrictions as a means to pursue particular trade-related objectives involving, for example, environment or labour standards.

## ■ labour

the economically productive capabilities of humans, their physical and mental talents as applied to the production of goods and services.

*Labour*

## ■ labour abundant

a country is labour abundant if its endowment of labour is large compared to other countries. Relative labour abundance can be defined by either the quantity definition or the price definition.

## ■ labour augmenting

said of a technological change or technological difference if one production function produces the same as if it were the other, but with a larger quantity of labour. Same as factor augmenting with labour as the augmented factor. Also called Harrod neutral.

## ■ labour intensive

describing an industry or sector of the economy that relies relatively heavily on inputs of labour, usually relative to capital but sometimes to human capital or skilled labour, compared to other industries or sectors. See **factor intensity**.

## ■ labour market outcomes

shorthand for worker (never employer) variables that are often considered endogenous in a labour market regression. Such variables, which often appear on the right side of such regressions: wage rates, employment dummies or employment rates.

## ■ labour productivity

the value of output per unit of labour input. The reciprocal of the unit labour requirement.

■ **labour right**
see **labour standard**.

■ **labour scarce**
a country is labour scarce if its endowment of labour is small compared to other countries. Relative labour scarcity can be defined by either the quantity definition or the price definition.

■ **labour standard**
any of many conditions of workers in the workplace that are viewed as important for their well being and minimum levels of which are advocated by labour rights activists and have been agreed to by many of the countries that are members of the ILO.

■ **labour standards argument for protection**
the view that trade restrictions (trade sanctions) should be used as a tool to improve labour standards, limiting imports, for example, from countries that do not enforce such labour rights as freedom of association and collective bargaining.

■ **labour theory of value**
both Ricardo and Marx say that the value of every commodity is (in perfect equilibrium and perfect competition) proportional to the quantity of labour contained in the commodity, provided this labour is in accordance with the existing standard of efficiency of production (the 'socially necessary quantity of labour'). Both measure this quantity in hours of work and use the same method in order to reduce different qualities of work to a single standard.

■ **labour theory of value**
the theory that the value of any produced good or service is equal to the amount of labour used, directly and indirectly, to produce it. Sometimes said to underlie the Ricardian Model of international trade.

■ **labour-augmenting**
one of the ways in which an effectiveness variable could be included in a production function in a Solow model. If effectiveness A is multiplied by labour L but not by capital K, then we say the effectiveness variable is labour-augmenting.

■ **labour-saving**
a technological change or technological difference that is biased in favour of using less labour, compared to some definition of neutrality.

■ **labour-using**
a technological change or technological difference that is biased in favour of using more labour, compared to some definition of neutrality.

■ **lag operator**
denoted by L, a lag operator operates on an expression by moving the subscripts on a time series back one period, so:

■ **lag polynomial**
a polynomial expression in lag operators.

■ **lagging indicator**
a measurable economic variable that varies over the business cycle, reaching peaks and troughs somewhat later than other macroeconomic variables such as GDP and unemployment. Contrasts with leading indicator.

■ **Lagrangian**
a function constructed in solving economic models that include maximisation of a function (the 'objective function') subject to constraints. It equals the objective function minus, for each constraint, a variable 'Lagrange multiplier' times the amount by which the constraint is violated.

■ **Lagrangian Multiplier**
an algebraic term that arises in the context of problems of mathematical optimisation subject to constraints, which in economics contexts is sometimes called a shadow price.

■ **laissez faire**
free enterprise. The doctrine or system of government non-interference in the economy except as necessary to maintain economic freedom. Includes free trade.

■ **laissez faire economics**
a school of economics inspired by Adam Smith who believed that if we would just let the market be, competition would create order and eventually prosperity for all. See also **invisible hand**.

■ **land**
all natural resources. The 'gifts of nature' which are economically useful.

■ **large country**
a country that is large enough for its international transactions to affect economic variables abroad, usually for its trade to matter for world prices. Contrasts with a small open economy.

■ **large sample size**
usually a synonym for 'asymptotic' rather than a reference to an actual sample magnitude.

■ **Laspeyres Index**
a price index following a particular algorithm.

■ **Latin American Free Trade Association (LAFTA)**
a group of Latin American countries formed in 1960 with the aim of establishing a free trade area. This aim was never achieved and LAFTA was replaced in 1980 with the Latin American Integration Association.

■ **Latin American Integration Association (LAIA)**
an organisation of Latin American countries that replaced the failed LAFTA. LAIA has the more limited goal of encouraging free trade but with no timetable for achieving it.

# Launhardt, Wilhelm (1832-1918)

professor of Engineering in Hanover (Germany). He made important contributions to transportation economics, location theory, market area analysis and price theory. A major concept in Launhardt's analysis is the 'funnel' which relates transport costs to distance (outwardly extending wall of the funnel) around a production location with production costs (central shaft of funnel).

# Laursen-Metzler Effect

see **Harberger-Laursen-Metzler Effect**.

# law of comparative advantage

the principle that, given the freedom to respond to market forces, countries will tend to export goods for which they have comparative advantage and import goods for which they have comparative disadvantage and that they will experience gains from trade by doing so.

# law of demand

the inverse relationship between price and quantity of a good or service demanded.

# law of diminishing marginal utility

as a person increases her consumption of a good or service (other consumption being held constant), the marginal utility of the good or service eventually will tend to decline.

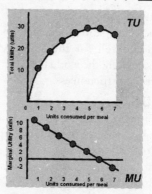

*Law of Diminishing Marginal Utility*

# ■ law of diminishing returns

the principle that, in any production function, as the input of one factor rises holding other factors fixed, the marginal product of that factor must eventually decline.

*Law of Diminishing Returns*

# ■ law of iterated expectations

often exemplified by $E_t E_{t+1}(.) = E_t(.)$ That is, 'one cannot use limited information (at time t) to predict the forecast error one would make if one had superior information (at t+1).'

■ **law of one price**

the principle that identical goods should sell for the same price throughout the world if trade were free and frictionless.

■ **LDC**

for many years, the acronym LDC has stood for Less Developed Country, which was more or less the same as developing country. However, in recent years LDC has also been used for Least Developed Country, which has a narrower and more formal definition.

■ **leading indicator**

a measurable economic variable that varies over the business cycle, reaching peaks and troughs somewhat earlier than other macroeconomic variables such as GDP and unemployment and therefore useful for forecasting them. Contrasts with lagging indicator.

■ **lean manufacturing/ production**

a reference to the transition from a mass production system to a system which emphasises quality and speedy responses to changing market conditions using new technologies organisational forms and labour contracts and achieving significant productivity increases.

■ **learning by doing**

refers to the improvement in technology that takes place in some industries, early in their history, as they learn by experience so that average cost falls as accumulated output rises. See **infant industry protection, dynamic economies of scale.**

■ **learning curve**

a relationship representing either average cost or average product as a function of the accumulated output produced. Usually reflecting learning by doing, the learning curve shows cost falling or average product rising.

■ **learning curve effects**

cost reductions resulting from skill improvements based on repetitive (usually production related) experiences.

■ **learning objective**

a written statement describing measurable achievements you hope can be accomplished during your class experience or any other definable learning activity.

■ **learning organisation**

an organisation that is continually expanding its capacity to create its future. A learning organisation is not merely trying to survive, i.e engage in adaptive learning, but i adds 'generative learning'.

■ **learning web**

an integrated system of Internet based, hypertextually organised course or program materials, resources, links to resources and communication opportunities designed to facilitate learning environments and processes.

## least developed country

a country designated by the UN as least developed based on criteria of low per capita GDP, weak human resources (life expectancy, calorie intake, etc.) and a low level of economic diversification (share of manufacturing and other measures). As of 2002 there are 49 LDCs.

## least squares learning

the kind of learning that an agent **in a model** exhibits by adapting to past data, by running least squares on it to estimate a hypothesised parameter and behaving as if that parameter were correct.

## Leibenstein, Harvey (1922- )

an American economist, born in 1922. Leibenstein taught at the University of California Berkeley in the 1950s and 60s and subsequently at Harvard. He has published widely in area of economic growth and development, but remains best known for his theory of X-efficiency, which postulates that individuals are non-maximisers when there is little pressure on them and that convention plays a large part in determining the amount of effort they put into their work.

## leisure

in some models, individuals spend some time working and the rest is lumped into a category called leisure, the details of which are usually left out.

## Lemons Model

describes models like that of Akerlof's 1970 paper, in which the fact that a good is available suggests that it is of low quality. For example, why are used cars for sale? In many cases, because they are 'lemons,' that is, they were problematic to their previous owners.

## lender of last resort

the function whereby central banks stand ready to make cash advances to commercial banks in the event they misjudge their cash reserve requirements.

## Lenin (Vladimir Il'ich Ul'ianov) (1870-1924)

a Russian-born intellectual who masterminded the formation of the Russian Communist Party and successfully seised power with the revolutionary uprising of November 7, 1917. Although he produced a considerable volume of writing, ranging from polemical tracts to serious scholarly works (notably a history of capitalism in Russia), Lenin (the name he began using while living in exile in Germany) was above all else a master politician who succeeded in welding the disputatious radical factions in Russia together to create a well-disciplined political machine. His adaptation of the principles of Karl Marx to the situation in Russia was built on the idea of using the Party as the instrument for forging a revolutionary working class.

*Lenin*

■ **Leontief composite**

a composite of two or more goods or factors that includes them in fixed proportions, analogous to the Leontief technology.

■ **Leontief inverse matrix (& coefficients)**

as applied to regional interindustry or input-output analysis, the values in this matrix (Leontief coefficients) represent the total direct and indirect (and, possibly 'induced') requirements of any industry j (typically in columns) supplied by other industries (i) within the region in order for industry j to be able to deliver $1 worth of output to final demand.

■ **Leontief paradox**

the finding of Leontief (1954) that US imports embodied a higher ratio of capital to labour than US exports. This was surprising because it was thought that the US was capital abundant and the Heckscher-Ohlin Theorem would

then predict that U.S. exports would be relatively capital intensive.

■ **Leontief Production Function**

has the form $q=\min\{x1,x2\}$, where q is a quantity of output and x1 and x2 are quantities of inputs or functions of the quantities of inputs.

■ **Leontief technology**

a production function in which no substitution between inputs is possible: $F(V) = \min_i(Vi/ai)$, where V is a vector of inputs Vi and ai are the constant per unit input requirements. Isoquants are L-shaped.

■ **leptokurtic**

an adjective describing a distribution with high kurtosis. 'High' means the fourth central moment is more than three times the second central moment, such a distribution has greater kurtosis than a normal distribution. This term is used in Bollerslev-Hodrick 1992 to characterise stock price returns.

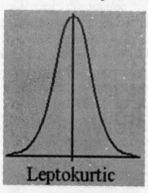

*Leptokurlic*

■ **Lerman Ratio**

a government benefit to the underemployed that will presumably reduce their hours of work. The ratio of the actual increase in income to the benefit is the Lerman ratio, which is ordinarily between zero and one. Moffitt (1992) estimates it in regard to the US AFDC program at about .625.

■ **Lerner Diagram**

this diagram, drawn for given prices and technology, uses unit-value isoquants of two or more goods to deduce patterns of specialisation and factor prices as they depend on factor endowments. Due originally to Lerner (1952) and popularised by Findlay and Grubert (1959).

■ **Lerner Index**

a measure of the profitability of a firm that sells a good: (price - marginal cost) / price.

■ **Lerner paradox**

the possibility, identified by Lerner (1936), that a tariff might worsen a country's terms of trade. This can happen only if the country spends a disproportionately large fraction of the tariff revenue on the imported good and it will not happen (from a stable equilibrium) if the tariff revenue is redistributed. See **offer curve diagram**.

■ **Lerner Symmetry Theorem**

the proposition that a tax on all imports has the same effect as an equal tax on all exports, if the revenue is spent in the same way. The result depends critically on balanced trade, as in a real model, so that a change in imports leads to an equal change in the value of exports. Due to Lerner (1936).

■ **Lerner, Abba P. (1903-1982)**

an American academic economist, born in Russia and educated largely in England, Lerner was one of the first and most enthusiastic converts to Keynesian economics. He subsequently taught at a number of different universities in the US including Michigan State and UCLA Berkeley. His major publication was *The Economics of Control* (1944) which combined Keynesian principles with welfare economics to produce a complete system of economic management equally applicable to capitalist or socialist economies.

■ **Lerner-Pearce Diagram**

this name is sometimes given to the Lerner Diagram. In fact, Pearce's (1952) diagram uses unit isoquants rather than unit value isoquants and is much more cumbersome.

■ **less developed country**

any country whose per capita income is low by world standards. Same as developing country.

■ **level playing field**

the objective of those who advocate protection on the grounds that the foreign firms have an unfair advantage. A level playing field would remove such advantages, although it is not usually clear what sorts of advantage (including comparative advantage) would be permitted to remain. See **fairness argument for protection.**

■ **leverage ratio**
often, the ratio of debts to total assets. Can also be the ratio of debts (or long-term debts in particular, excluding for example accounts payable) to equity.

■ **Leveraged Buy-Out (LBO)**
the act of taking a public company private by buying it with revenues from bonds and using the revenues of the company to pay off the bonds.

■ **leviathan**
the all-powerful kind of state that Hobbes thought 'was necessary to solve the problem of social order.'

■ **levy**
1. to impose and collect a tax or tariff.
2. a tax or tariff.

■ **liabilities**
1. in general, debts owed by individuals or firms.

*Liabilities*

2. in the case of commercial banks, their liabilities are largely in the form of what they owe their customers, that is, the total amount of deposits held.

■ **licensing**
1. the requirement that importers and/or exporters get government approval prior to importing or exporting. Licensing may be automatic or it may be discretionary, based on a quota, a performance requirement or some other criterion.
2. granting of permission, in return for a licensing fee, to use a technology. When done by firms in one country to firms in another, it is a form of technology transfer. See compulsory licensing.

■ **life cycle**
see **product cycle**.

■ **likelihood function**
in maximum likelihood estimation, the likelihood function (often denoted L()) is the joint probability function of the sample, given the probability distributions that are assumed for the errors. That function is constructed by multiplying the pdf of each of the data points together.

■ **Likert Scale**
measures the extent to which a person agrees or disagrees with the question in a survey (e.g. 1=strongly disagree, 2=disagree, 3=not sure, 4=agree and 5=strongly agree).

■ **limited dependent variable**
a dependent variable in a model is limited if it is discrete (can take on only a countable number of values) or if it is not always observed because it is truncated or censored.

■ **linear function**
1. a function whose graph is a straight line.
2. graph (example)
3. a "function" is a relation in which each element in the domain is matched with only one element of the range
4. f y = f(x) we call y the dependent variable and x the independent variable.
5. a function can be specified:
a. numerically: by means of a table
b. algebraically: by means of a formula
c. graphically: by means of a graph

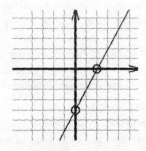

■ **linear model / linear econometric model**
an econometric model is linear if it is expressed in an equation which the parameters enter linearly, whether or not the data require nonlinear transformations to get to that equation.

■ **linear pricing schedule**
say the number of units or quantity, paid for is denoted q and the total paid is denoted T(q), following the notation of Tirole. A linear pricing schedule is one that can be characterised by T(q)=pq for some price-per-unit p.

■ **linear probability models**
are econometric models in which the dependent variable is a probability between zero and one. These are easier to estimate than probit or logit models but usually have the problem that some predictions will not be in the range of zero to one.

■ **linear transport cost function**
a reference to a theoretical, linear mathematical function, usually involving the variables like the total transport costs and the distance. The function would be linear if it is suggested that the increase in transport cost is proportional to the increase in distance. Linearity may exist with or without terminal (or distance-fixed) cost. The latter would result in a curvi-linear, downward sloping average transport-cost function.

■ **linearly homogeneous**
homogeneous of degree 1. Sometimes called linear homogeneous.

■ **linking scheme**
a requirement that, in order to get an import license, the importer must buy a certain amount of the

same product from local producers.

■ **liquid**
a liquid market is one in which it is not difficult or costly to buy or sell.

■ **liquidity**
refers to how quickly and cheaply an asset can be converted into cash. Money (in the form of cash) is the most liquid asset. Assets that generally can only be sold after a long exhaustive search for a buyer are known as illiquid.

■ **liquidity**
the capacity to turn assets into cash or the amount of assets in a portfolio that have that capacity. Cash itself (i.e., money) is the most liquid asset.

■ **liquidity constraint**
many households, e.g. young ones, cannot borrow to consume or invest as much as they would want, but are constrained to current income by imperfect capital markets.

■ **liquidity crisis**
a financial crisis that occurs due to lack of liquidity. In international finance, it usually means that a government of central bank runs short of international reserves needed to peg its exchange rate and/or to service its foreign loans.

■ **liquidity trap**
1. a Keynesian idea. When expected returns from investments in securities or real plant and equipment are low, investment falls, a recession begins and cash holdings in banks rise. People and businesses then continue to hold cash because they expect spending and investment to be low. This is a self-fulfilling trap.
2. a situation in which expansionary monetary policy fails to stimulate the economy. As used by Keynes (1936), this meant interest rates so low that expectations of their increase made people unwilling to hold bonds. Today it usually means a nominal interest rate so near zero that lowering it further is impossible or ineffective.

■ **little giants**
a reference to those medium-sised firms which are technologically and organisationally particularly innovative and forward-looking in terms of employee relations. In contrast to corporate giants, such medium-sised firms are more entrepreneurial, less bureaucratic, with fewer managerial layers.

■ **living wage**
as defined by the 'Job Gap Study', a wage that allows families to meet their basic needs without resorting to public assistance and provides them some ability to deal with emergencies and plan ahead. It is not a poverty wage.

■ **Ljung-Box Test**
the same as the portmanteau test.

# LM-Curve
in the IS-LM model, the curve representing combinations of income and interest rate at which demand for money equals the money supply in the domestic money market. It is normally upward sloping because an increase in income increases demand for money while an increase in the interest rate reduces the demand for money.

# $L^n$
the set of continuous bounded functions with domain $R^N$.

# local content requirement
see domestic content requirement.

# local optimum
an allocation that by some criterion is better than all those in its neighbourhood.

# locality
localisation economies or external economies of localisation. Agglomeration economies (benefits, cost reductions) resulting from the concentration of the same or similar activities: eg. benefits resulting from the local access to a specialised work force or the specialised reputation of a locality (to which some but maybe not all of these specialised activities contribute). See also product localisation.

# Locally Asymptotically Normal (LAN)
a characteristic of many ('a family of') distributions.

# locally identified
linear models are either globally identified or there are an infinite number of observably equivalent ones. But for models that are nonlinear in parameters, 'we can only talk about local properties.' Thus the idea of locally identified models, which can be distinguished in data from any other 'close by' model. 'A sufficient condition for local identification is that' a certain Jacobian matrix is of full column rank.

# locally nonsatiated / local nonsatiation
an agent's preferences are locally nonsatiated if they are continuous and strictly increasing in all goods.

# location decisions and locational decision-making
decisions and behaviours related to locational choices.

# location quotient
a measure of the relative significance of a phenomenon (e.g. employment in software activities) in a region (Redmond) compared with its significance in a larger ('benchmark') region. A high location quotient for a specific activity implies specialisation and the export of the goods or services produced by the activity.

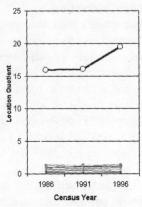

*Location Quotient*

# location rent

generally considered a special form of economic (land) rent. Benefits accruing to (factor) land due to the relative or comparative advantage associated with its location.

# locational advantage

any reason for a firm to locate production or a stage of production in a particular place, such as availability of a natural resource, transport cost or barriers to trade. May explain why a country's firms succeed in trade or why a multinational firm locates there.

# locational triangle

the triangle was devised and used by Wilhelm Launhardt and Alfred Weber to construct their basic locational model. This model was used to demonstrate the impact of the forces of attraction of three (in a polygon more) reference locations (originally 2 raw material locations and one market) vis-a-vis the (dependent) optimal (=least-transport-cost) location of a processing plant. Subsequently, the triangle was used by Isard and Moses to demonstrate the impact of substitution between distances and/or materials and by Beyers and Krumme substitution between products (outputs) on optimal locations.

# locomotive effect

the effect that economic expansion in one large country can have on other parts of the world economy, causing them to expand as well, as the large country demands more of their exports.

# log concavity

a function $f(w)$ is said to be log-concave if its natural log, $\ln(f(w))$ is a concave function, that is, assuming $f$ is differentiable, $f''(w)/f(w) - f'(w)^2 <= 0$. Since log is a strictly concave function, any concave function is also log-concave.

# log convexity

a random variable is said to be log-convex if its density function is log-concave. Pareto distributions with finite means and variances have this property and so do gamma densities with a coefficient of variation greater than one.

# log or natural log

in economics, log always means 'natural log', that is $\log_e$, where e is the natural constant that is approximately 2.718281828. So $x = \log y$ <=> $e^x = y$.

■ **log utility**

a utility function. Some versions of this are used often in finance.

■ **logical omniscience**

an assumption underlying the information facets of most microeconomic models: If an agent has knowledge of a phenomenon, he/she also has perfect knowledge of all its implications.

■ **logistic distribution**

a logistic distribution has the cdf
$F(x) = 1/(1+e^{-x})$
This distribution is quicker to calculate than the normal distribution but is very similar. Another advantage over the normal distribution is that it has a closed form cdf. pdf is $f(x) = e^x(1+e^x)^{-2} = F(x)F(-x)$

■ **logit model**

a univariate binary model. That is, for dependent variable $y_i$ that can be only one or zero and a continuous indepdendent variable $x_i$, that:
$Pr(y_i=1)=F(x_i'b)$
Here b is a parameter to be estimated and F is the **logistic** cdf. The probit model is the same but with a different cdf for F.

■ **lognormal distribution**

let X be a random variable with a standard normal distribution. Then the variable $Y=e^X$ has a lognormal distribution. Example: Yearly incomes in the United States are roughly log-normally distributed.

■ **Lomé Convention**

an agreement originally signed in 1975 committing the EU to programs of assistance and preferential treatment for the ACP Countries. The Lomé Convention was replaced by the Cotonou Agreement in June 2000.

■ **London Interbank Offered Rate (LIBOR)**

the interest rate that the largest international banks charge each other for loans, usually of Eurodollars. In fact, LIBOR includes rates quoted each day for many currencies, excluding the euro, but it is the rate for dollar loans that is used as a benchmark for other transactions.

■ **long run**

in the context of the theory of the firm, the long run is a period of time that is long enough for the firm to vary the quantities of all the inputs it is using, including its physical plant.

■ **long run average costs**

total costs divided by the number of units of output. The long run average cost curve plots the relationship between output and the lowest possible average total cost when all inputs can be varied.

■ **long run costs**

production costs when the firm is using its economically most efficient size of plant.

■ **longitudinal data**

a synonym for panel data.

■ **long-term capital**

in the capital account of the balance of payments, long-term capital movements include FDI and movements of financial capital with maturity of more than one year (including equities).

■ **Lorenz curve**

1. a curve showing the cumulative percentage of income plotted against the cumulative percentage of population.

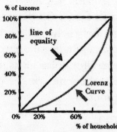

A Lorenz Curve illustrates inequality

2. the graph of the percent of income owned by the poorest x percent of the population, for all x. Provides a picture of the income distribution within the population and is used to construct the Gini Coefficient.

■ **Louvre Accord**

an agreement reached in 1987 among the central banks of France, Germany, Japan, US and UK to stop the decline in the value of the US dollar that they had initiated at the Plaza Accord.

■ **love of variety**

preference for variety.

■ **Lowry Model**

a very influential and widely used urban model (developed originally in the 1960s) which combines the economic base multiplier model and the gravity model to accomplish the spatial allocation of the indirect and induced effects of (exogenous) economic stimuli (such as export activities).

■ **loyal opposition firms**

medium-sised or small firms operating in the shadow of large corporations. These smaller firms try to be competitive in regional or product-oriented niche markets, as subcontractors or even as direct competitors without wanting or be able to challenge the larger firm in any major market.

■ **lump sum**

a tax or subsidy that does not distort behaviour. By using a tax (or subsidy) in an amount (the lump sum) independent of any aspect of the payer's or recipient's behaviour, it does not alter behaviour. Nondistorting lump sum taxes and subsidies do not exist, but are a convenient fiction for theoretical analysis, especially of gains from trade.

■ **lump sum taxes**

a tax of a fixed amount that has to be paid by everyone regardless of the level of his or her income. Lump sum taxes are considered efficient taxes because they do not influence a person's decision on how much to work.

# M1 Money Supply
a measure of total money supply. M1 includes only checkable demand deposits.

# M2 Money Supply
a measure of total money supply. M2 includes everything in M1 and also savings and other time deposits.

# Maastricht Treaty
the 1991 treaty among members of the EU to work towards a monetary union or common currency. This ultimately resulted in adoption of the euro in 1999.

# macroeconomics
the branch of economic theory concerned with the economy as a whole. It deals with large aggregates such as total output, rather than with the behaviour of individual consumers and firms.

# made-to-measure tariff
a tariff set so as to raise the price of an imported good to the domestic price, so as to leave domestic producers unaffected. Also called a scientific tariff.

# magnification effect
the property of the Heckscher-Ohlin Model that changes in certain exogenous variables lead to magnified changes in the corresponding endogenous variables: goods prices as they affect factor prices in the Stolper-Samuelson Theorem, factor endowments as they affect outputs in the Rybczynski Theorem. Due to Jones (1965).

# majority goods
goods which are generally available to consumers because they can be mass produced in whatever quantities there is a demand for. Fast food and consumer electronics are good examples.

# Malthus, Thomas (1766-1834)
born the son of an eccentric country gentleman-scholar, Malthus was educated at Cambridge, studying mainly social studies and mathematics in preparation for his intended career as a cleric. He wrote widely on economic issues of his day, maintaining a close correspondence with David Ricardo. His most famous work, however, was on the subject of population. His recognition of what subsequently came to be called the 'principle of diminishing returns' underlay his famous proposition that production of the means of subsistence increases as an arithmetic progression (1,2,3,4, etc.) whereas human population has a tendency to increase geometrically (2,4,16, etc.).

# managed float
an exchange rate regime in which the rate is allowed to be determined in the exchange market without an announced par value as the goal of intervention, but the authorities do nonetheless intervene at their discretion to influence the rate.

■ **Management Buy-Out /**
**Management by Objectives**
**(MBO)**
the purchase of a company by its
management. Sometimes means
Management By Objectives, a
goal-oriented personnel evaluation
approach.

■ **mantissa**
the fractional part of a real number.

■ **manufactured good**
a good that is produced by manufacturing.

■ **manufacturing**
comprises the establishments that
are engaged in the mechanical,
physical or chemical transformation of materials, substances or
components into new products.

■ **manufacturing**
production of goods primarily
by the application of labour and
capital to raw materials and
other intermediate inputs, in
contrast to agriculture, mining,
forestry, fishing and services.

■ **Maquiladora**
this is a program for the temporary
importation of goods into Mexico
without duty, under the condition
that they contribute — through further processing, transformation or
repair — to exports. The program
was established in 1965 and expanded in 1989. The purchase of
a company by its management.
Sometimes means Management by
Objectives, a goal-oriented person-

nel evaluation approach.

■ **marginal analysis**
an analytical technique which fo-
cuses attention on incremental
changes in total values, such as the
*last* unit of a good consumed or
the *increase* in total cost.

■ **marginal benefit**
the increase in total benefit consequent upon a one unit increase
in the production of a good.

■ **marginal cost**
the increase in total cost consequent upon a one unit increase in
the production of a good.

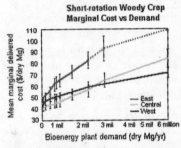

**Short-rotation Woody Crop
Marginal Cost vs Demand**

■ **marginal physical product**
the change in total product measured in physical terms caused by
a one unit increase in a variable
input.

■ **marginal principle**
to maximise the net benefits, the
strategic or action variable should
be increased until MB = MC, i.e.
marginal benefits equal marginal
costs

■ **marginal propensity to**
**consume**
the part of the last rupee of dis-

posable income that would be spent on additional consumption.

## marginal propensity to import

the increase in expenditure on imports per unit increase in (disposable) income.

## marginal propensity to save

1. the part of the last rupee of disposable income that would be saved.
2. the increase in saving per unit increase in (disposable) income.

## marginal rate of substitution

1. generally referring to the rate at which the consumer is willing to substitute one good for another (without loss or gain of satisfaction) see also indifference curve.
2. the rate at which factor inputs can be exchanged in a production process without a change in the production (output) level. See also isoquant

## marginal rate of transformation

the increase in output of one good made possible by a one-unit decrease in the output of another, given the technology and factor endowments of a country, thus the absolute value of the slope of the transformation curve.

## marginal revenue

the addition to total revenue resulting from the sale of one additional unit of output.

## marginal revenue product

1. the change in total revenue that results from employing one more unit of a factor.
2. the additional revenue generated by the extra output from employing one more unit of a factor of production. In a competitive industry this equals the marginal value product, but with imperfect competition it is smaller, due to the implied price reduction. Determines factor prices in competitive factor markets.

## marginal value product

the value of the marginal product of a factor in an industry, that is, the price of the good produced times the marginal product. Determines factor prices when all markets are competitive.

## market access

the ability of firms from one country to sell in another.

## market capitalisation

the total number of shares times the market price of each. May be said of a firm's shares or of all the shares on an equity market.

## market clearing

equality of supply and demand. A market-clearing condition is an equation (or other representation) stating that supply equals demand.

## market demand

the relationship between the total quantity of a good demanded and its price.

■ **market economy**
a country in which most economic decisions are left up to individual consumers and firms interacting through markets. Contrasts with central planning and non-market economy.

■ **market equilibrium**
equality of supply and demand. See **equilibrium**.

■ **market exchange**
exchange of scarce goods or services, at a price determined by a market mechanism.

■ **market failure**
instances of a free market being unable to achieve an optimum allocation of resources.

■ **market failure**
1. a situation, usually discussed in a model not in the real world, in which the behaviour of optimising agents in a market would not produce a Pareto optimal allocation.
2. any departure from the ideal benchmark of perfect competition, especially the complete absence of a market due to incomplete or asymmetric information.

■ **market for corporate control**
shares of public firms are traded and in large enough blocks, this means control over corporations is traded. That puts some pressure on managers to perform, otherwise their corporation can be taken over.

■ **market forces**
the stimuli and influences affecting the supply and demand of goods and services and thereby determining the allocation of resources and the relative prices of goods, services and assets in a market economy.

■ **market power**
1. the power held by a firm over price and the power to subdue competitors.
2. a continuum from *perfectly competitive* to monopsony and there's an extensive practice/industry/science of measuring the degree of market power.

■ **market power theory of advertising**
the theory of advertising is that established firms use advertising as a barrier to entry through product differentiation. Such a firm's use of advertising differentiates its brand from other brands to a degree that consumers see its brand as a slightly different product, not perfectly substituted by existing or potential competitors. This makes it hard for new competitors to gain consumer acceptance.

■ **market price**
the price at which a market clears.

■ **market price of risk**
is a synonym for the Sharpe ratio.

■ **market rate**
the interest rate or exchange rate at which a market clears.

# market structure

the way that suppliers and demanders in an industry interact to determine price and quantity. There are four main idealised market structures that have been used in trade theory: perfect competition, monopoly, oligopoly and monopolistic competition.

# market value

see factor cost.

# marketing

analysis, planning, implementation and control of carefully formulated programs designed to bring about voluntary exchanges of values with target markets for the purpose of achieving organisational objectives.

# marketing board

a form of state trading enterprise, a marketing board typically buys up the domestic supply of a good and sells it on the international market.

# markets

any coming together of buyers and sellers of produced goods and services or the services of productive factors.

# Markov Chain

a stochastic process is a Markov chain if:

1. time is discrete, meaning that the time index t has a finite or countably infinite number of values.

2. the set of possible values of the process at each time is finite or countably infinite.

3. it has the Markov property of memorylessness.

# Markov Process

a stochastic process where all the values are drawn from a discrete set. In a first-order Markov process, only the most recent draw affects the distribution of the next one. All such processes can be represented by a Markov transition density matrix. A Markov process can be periodic only if it is of higher than first order.

# Markov Property

a property that a set of stochastic processes may have. The system has the Markov property if the present state predicts future states as well as the whole history of past and present states does — that is, the process is memoryless.

# Markov Strategy

in a game, a Markov strategy is one that does not depend at all on state variables that are functions of the history of the game except those that affect payoffs.

# Markov Transition Matrix

a square matrix describing the probabilities of moving from one state to another in a dynamic system. In each row are the probabilities of moving from the state represented by that row, to the other states. Thus the rows of a Markov transition matrix each add to one. Sometimes such a matrix is denoted something like $Q(x' \mid x)$ which can be understood this way:

that Q is a matrix, x is the existing state, x' is a possible future state and for any x and x' in the model, the probability of going to x' given that the existing state is x, are in Q.

- **Markov's Inequality**

if Y is a nonnegative random variable, that is, if $Pr(Y<0)=0$ and k is any positive constant, then $E(Y) = kPr(Y = k)$.

- **markup**

1. the ratio of price to marginal cost. Can be used as a measure of market power across firms, industries or economies.
2. the amount (percentage) by which price exceeds marginal cost. A profit-maximising seller facing a price elasticity of demand, h will set a markup equal to $(p-c)/p=1/h$. One effect of international trade that increases competition is to reduce markups.

- **Marshall, Alfred (1842-1924)**

one of the great synthesisers of economic theory, who also developed and refined many of the most useful analytical tools of the discipline. His famous student at Cambridge, John Maynard Keynes, called him the greatest economist of the 19th century. His influential textbook, *Principles of Economics*, first published in 1890, served for more than a quarter of a century as the standard reference on the subject. In it, he set out clearly such basic concepts as price elasticity of demand, competitive short-run and long-run equilibrium of the firm, consumer surplus, increasing and decreasing cost industries and economies of scale. Trained in mathematics, Marshall relegated the mathematical expression of his principles to footnotes.

- **Marshallian Demand Function**

denoted x(p,m), it is the amount of a factor of production that is demanded by a producer given that it costs p per unit and the budget limit that can be spent on all factors is m. p and x can be vectors.

- **Marshall-Lerner condition**

the condition that sum of the elasticities of demand for exports and imports exceed one (in absolute value), that is, $hX + hM > 1$, where hX, hM are the demand elasticities for a country's exports and imports respectively, both defined to be positive for downward sloping demands. Under certain assumptions, this is the condition for a depreciation to improve the trade balance, for the exchange market to be stable and for international barter exchange to be stable.

- **Marx, Karl (1818-83)**

one of the most influential social philosophers in history, Marx lived a life of almost constant conflict and adversity. Despite a Ph.D. in philosophy from the University of Jena, he was unable to secure a university teaching position and his involvement in revolutionary political activity led to his expulsion from Germany. He was also subsequently forced to leave Belgium and France before finally settling in London where he made a meagre living by journalism (serving as a correspondent for the *New York Herald-Tribune*). While continuing to involve himself in radical political affairs, he devoted as much time as he could to an extraordinary scholarly undertaking, which was nothing less than an attempt to synthesise all human knowledge since the time of Aristotle. The fruits of this labour, much of it pursued in the Reading Room of the British Museum, was eventually published in his massive work, *Das Kapital* which established the intellectual foundation of the Marxist interpretation of history and which posited the coming of a new world order following the inevitable collapse of capitalism.

■ **mass production**
a production system characterised by mechanisation, high wages, low prices and large-volume output.

■ **matching pennies**
a zero-sum game with two players. Each shows either heads or tails from a coin. If both are heads or both are tails, then player One wins, otherwise Two wins. The payoff matrix is at right.

■ **material injury**
the injury requirement of the AD and CVD statutes, understood to be less stringent than serious injury but otherwise apparently not rigorously defined.

■ **Matlab**
a matrix programming language and programming environment. Used more by engineers but increasingly by economists.

■ **matrix multiplications**
the multiplication of matrices or vectors is 'commutative', i.e. the order of the multiplicand and the multiplier cannot be reversed as is the case in regular multiplications. The process of multiplication of matrices proceeds by multiplying (more exactly: 'post-multiplying') horizontal vectors by vertical vectors. The sum of the products of this multiplication of corresponding numbers of the respective vectors results in a number which is placed in the position of the resulting matrix (or vector) where the two vectors would intersect (overlap).

■ **maturity date**
the maturity date of a financial asset is the date at which that asset is converted into a specified amount of money or physical assets.

■ **maximin/minimax strategy**
see **uncertainty** or **game theory**.

■ **maximum price system**

similar to a minimum price system, except that the price specified is the highest, rather than the lowest, permitted for an imported good.

■ **maximum revenue tariff**

a tariff set to collect the largest possible revenue for the government.

■ **Meade Geometry**

the geometric technique introduced by Meade (1952), of deriving a country's offer curve from its transformation curve and community indifference curves by first constructing a set of trade indifference curves.

■ **mean**

the arithmetic average of the values of an economic or statistical variable. For a variable x with values xi, i=1,...,n, the mean is mean(x) = Si=1...n(xi/n).

■ **mean square error**

a criterion for an estimator: the choice is the one that minimises the sum of squared errors due to bias and due to variance.

■ **mechanism design problems**

a certain class of principal-agent problems are called mechanism design problems. In these, a principal would like to condition her own actions on the private information of agents. The principal must offer incentives for the agents to reveal information.

■ **median voter theorem**

the proposition that political parties will tend to adopt moderate policies to appeal to voters near the middle of the political spectrum.

■ **medium of exchange**

a distinguishing characteristic of money is that it is taken as a medium of exchange, that is, the same is taken by anybody in exchange for any commodity, without hesitation.

■ **meet**

given a space of possible events, the meet is the finest common coarsening of the information sets of all the players. The meet is the finest partition of the space of possible events such that all players have beliefs about the probabilities of the elements of the partition.

■ **mental models**

one of Senge's five learning disciplines for the learning organisation: 'reflecting upon and continually clarifying and improving our internal pictures of the world and seeing how they shape our actions and decisions.'

■ **mercantilism**

a body of policy recommendations designed to promote the development of the early nation states of western Europe in the 17th and 18th centuries. The emphasis was on utilising trade to increase national wealth at the expense of the countries being traded with through fostering a 'favourable balance of trade', by which was meant an excess of exports over imports.

■ **merchandise trade**
exports and imports of goods. Contrasts with trade in services.

■ **MERCOSUR**
a common market among Argentina, Brazil, Paraguay and Uruguay, known as the 'Common Market of the South' ('Mercado Comun del Sur'). It was created by the Treaty of Asunción on March 26, 1991 and added Chile and Bolivia as associate members in 1996 and 1997.

■ **mesokurtic**
an adjective describing a distribution with kurtosis of 3, like the normal distribution. See by contrast leptokurtic and platykurtic.

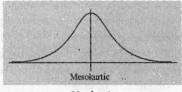
Mesokurtic

*Mesokurtic*

■ **m-estimators**
estimators that maximise a sample average. The 'm' means 'maximum-likelihood-like'.

■ **metatheorem**
an informal term for a proposition that can be proved in a class of economic model environments.

■ **method of moments estimation**
a way of generating estimators: set

the distribution moments equal to the sample moments and solve the resulting equations for the parameters of the distribution.

■ **Metzler paradox**
the possibility, identified by Metzler (1949), that a tariff may lower the domestic relative price of the imported good. This will happen if it drives the world price down by even more than the size of the tariff, as it may do if the foreign demand for the importing country's export good is inelastic.

■ **MFN status**
the status given by the US to some non-members of the GATT/WTO whereby they are charged MFN tariffs even though they are eligible for higher tariffs.

■ **MFN tariff**
the tariff level that a member of the GATT/WTO charges on a good to other members.

■ **micro-micro theory**
concerned with the 'study of what goes on inside the black box' (i.e. the artefact of classical micro-economic theory of the firm).

■ **middle product**
a good that has undergone some processing and that requires further processing before going to final consumers, an intermediate good. Sanyal and Jones (1982) introduced the term, observing that almost all international trade is of middle products and they provided a model based on that assumption.

- **migration**

  the permanent relocation of people from one country to another. See **emigration, immigration**.

- **milestones**

  subprojects into which a project is broken up, to be able to monitor development progress and adhere to deadlines.

- **milieu**

  used by economic geographers in a variety of contexts to refer to the particular local or regional business or entrepreneurial climate or innovate atmosphere.

- **millennium round**

  the name suggested by the European Union for the trade round that they and others hoped would be initiated at the Seattle Ministerial in 1999. That ministerial ended without agreement to start a new round.

- **Mill's test**

  one of two conditions needed for infant industry protection to be welfare-improving, this requires that the protected industry become, over time, able to compete internationally without protection.

- **minimum efficient scale**

  the smallest output of a firm consistent with minimum average cost. In small countries, in some industries the level of demand in autarky is not sufficient to support minimum efficient scale.

- **minimum import price**

  see minimum price system.

- **minimum price system**

  specification of the lowest price permitted for an import. Prices below the minimum may trigger a tariff, hence a variable levy or quota. See maximum price system. These have several names: basic import price, minimum import price, reference.

- **Ministry of Economy, Trade and Industry (METI)**

  the Japanese government ministry that deals with economic issues, including the vitality of the private sector, external economic relations, energy policy and industrial development.

- **Ministry of International Trade and Industry (MITI)**

  the Japanese government ministry that deals with trade and industrial policies. Established in 1949 as the Ministry of Commerce and Industry, MITI was renamed METI as of January 6, 2000.

- **minority goods**

  goods which have a very low elasticity of supply. That is, even large increases in their price can call forth little, if any, additional supply, which means that only the very wealthy can afford them. Large, secluded waterfront properties might be an example.

■ **Mishan, Ezra Joshua (1917-)**

born in Manchester England, Mishan taught at the London School of Economics from 1956 to 1977. He published a large number of articles in professional journals and several books, the best known of which is *The Costs of Economic Growth*, 1967. In later years, he has been a frequent contributor to more popular journals writing on variety of issues, including what he has referred to as 'the pretensions of economists.'

■ **missing trade**

see **mystery of the missing trade.**

■ **mixed economy**

an economy in which some production is done by the private sector and some by the state, in state-owned enterprises.

■ **mixing regulation**

1. specification of the proportion of domestically produced content in products sold on the domestic market.
2. specification of an amount of domestically produced product that must be bought by an importer for given quantities of imports, under a linking scheme.

■ **mobile and immobile factors of production ('factor mobility')**

the mobility between different uses or occupations of factors of production (land, labour, capital, etc.).

■ **modality**

method or procedure. WTO documents speak of modalities of negotiations, i.e., how the negotiations are to be conducted.

■ **mode of supply**

the method by which suppliers of internationally traded services deliver their service to buyers. The four modes usually identified are: cross-border supply, consumer movement, producer presence and movement of natural persons.

■ **model**

a stylised simplification of reality in which behaviour is represented by variables and assumptions about how they are determined and interact. Models enable one to think consistently and logically about complex issues, to work out how changes in an economic system matter and (sometimes) to make predictions about economic performance.

■ **monetarism**

a view that market economies are inherently self-stabilising and that variations in the quantity of money are the main cause of fluctuations in the level of aggregate demand.

■ **monetarist view**

in extreme form, the monetarist view is the view that only the quantity of money matters by way of aggregate demand policy. Relevant only in an overheated economy.

■ **monetary base**
the same as high-powered money. It refers to the cash in commercial banks, plus cash in circulation and deposits of the commercial bank at the central bank.

■ **monetary policy**
the use of the central bank's power to control the domestic money supply to influence the supply of credit, interest rates and ultimately the level of real economic activity.

■ **money**
anything generally acceptable in exchange. Money serves a number of functions: it is a medium of exchange, it is used as a unit of account and it can be used as a store of value. In its latter use, it is an alternative to holding value in the form of goods or other types of financial assets such as stocks or bonds.

*Money*

■ **money income**
nominal income. Contrasts with real income.

■ **money market**
the money market, in macroeconomics and international finance, refers to the equilibration of demand for a country's domestic money to its money supply. Both refer to the quantity of money that people in the country hold (a stock), not to the quantity that people both in and out of the country choose to acquire during a period in the exchange market, mostly for the purpose of then using it to buy something else.

■ **money overhang**
a money supply that is larger than people want to hold at prevailing prices. This was said to be a major cause of inflation in Russia after the fall of the Soviet Union, which left an excess of money in circulation.

■ **money supply**
there are several formal definitions, but all include the quantity of currency in circulation plus the amount of demand deposits. The money supply, together with the amount of real economic activity in a country, is an important determinant of its price level and its exchange rate.

■ **monopolistic competition**
essentially the same as imperfect competition. A market situation in which one or more firms may be capable of influencing the price of the product. It is characterised by product differentiation, often established through advertising.

# monopoly

strictly defined as a market situation in which there is a single supplier of a good or service, but often used to suggest any situation in which a firm has considerable power over the market price.

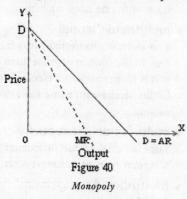

Figure 40
*Monopoly*

# monopoly argument

the monopoly argument for a tariff is the same as the optimal tariff argument. It gets its name from the fact that a country using a tariff to improve the terms of trade is acting much like a monopoly firm, restricting its sales to get a better price.

# monopsonistic firm

a firm which is the sole buyer of a good or service, most likely of labour in a particular market.

# monopsony

a state in which demand comes from one source. If there is only one customer for a certain good, that customer has a monopsony in the market for that good. Analogous to monopoly, but on the demand side not the supply side. A common theoretical implication is that the price of the good is pushed down near the cost of production. The price is not predicted to go to zero because if it went below where the suppliers are willing to produce, they won't produce.

# Monte Carlo Simulations

the data obtained by simulating a statistical model in which all parameters are numerically specified.

# moral hazard

the tendency of individuals, firms and governments, once insured against some contingency, to behave so as to make that contingency more likely. A pervasive problem in the insurance industry, it also arises internationally when international financial institutions assist countries in financial trouble.

# morbidity

an incidence of ill health. It is measured in various ways, often by the probability that a randomly selected individual in a population at some date and location would become seriously ill in some period of time. Contrast to mortality.

# mortality

the incidence of death in a population. It is measured in various ways, often by the probability that a randomly selected individual in a population at some date and location would die in some period of time. Contrast to morbidity.

# ■ Most Favoured Nation (MFN)

the principle, fundamental to the GATT, of treating imports from a country on the same basis as that given to the most favored other nation. That is and with some exceptions, every country gets the lowest tariff that any country gets and reductions in tariffs to one country are provided also to others.

# ■ mothballing

the preservation of a production facility without using it to produce, but keeping the machinery in working order and supplies available. This may be preferable — if the facility's operating costs are high and the aim is to have it available in time of war — to having it produce in peacetime under a subsidy or import protection. See **national defence argument**.

# ■ movement of natural persons

one of four modes of supply under the GATS, this involves the temporary movement across national borders of natural persons employed by or associated with a firm in order to participate in the firm's business. Also called temporary producer movement.

# ■ multi-cone equilibrium

a free-trade equilibrium in the Heckscher-Ohlin Model in which prices are such that all goods cannot be produced within a single country and instead there are multiple diversification cones. This or a two cone equilibrium, will arise if countries' factor endowments are sufficiently dissimilar compared to factor intensities of industries. Contrasts with one cone equilibrium.

# ■ multifactor model

a model with more than two factors. In the context of trade theory, this is likely to mean a Heckscher-Ohlin Model with more than two factors.

# ■ multi-factor productivity

same as total factor productivity, a certain type of Solow residual.

# ■ Multifiber Arrangement (MFA)

an agreement (OMA) among developed country importers and developing country exporters of textiles and apparel, to regulate and restrict the quantities traded. It was negotiated in 1973 under GATT auspices as a temporary exception to the rules that would otherwise apply and was superceded in 1995 by the ATC.

# ■ multifunctionality

the purposes that an industry may serve in addition to producing its output. Most often applied to agriculture by countries that wish to subsidise it, who argue that subsidies are needed to serve these other purposes, such as rural viability, land conservation, cultural heritage, etc.

■ **multilateral**

among a large number of countries. Contrasts with bilateral and plurilateral.

■ **multilateral agreement**

an agreement among a large number of countries.

■ **Multilateral Agreement on Investment (MAI)**

an agreement to liberalise rules on international direct investment that was negotiated in the OECD but never completed or adopted because of adverse public reaction to it. Preliminary text of the agreement was leaked to the Internet in April 1997, where many groups opposed it. Negotiations were discontinued in November 1998.

■ **Multilateral Investment Guarantee Agency (MIGA)**

one of the five institutions that comprise the World Bank Group, MIGA helps encourage foreign investment in developing countries.

■ **Multinational Corporation (MNC)**

a corporation that operates in two or more countries. Since it is headquartered in only one country but has production or marketing facilities in others, it is the result of previous FDI.

■ **Multinational Enterprise (MNE)**

a firm, usually a corporation, that operates in two or more countries. In practice the term is used interchangeably with multinational corporation.

■ **multiplier**

1. a numerical coefficient which relates the change of a component of aggregate demand (such as the export demand for a region's products) to a consequent change in income (or employment).
2. in Keynesian macroeconomic models, the ratio of the change in an endogenous variable to the change in an exogenous variable. Usually means the multiplier for government spending on income. In the simplest Keynesian model of a closed economy, this is $1/s$, where $s$ is the marginal propensity to save. See **open economy multiplier**.

■ **multiplier effect**

the tendency for a change in aggregate spending to cause a more than proportionate change in the level of real national income.

■ **multistage production**

another term for fragmentation. Used by Dixit and Grossman (1982).

■ **multivariate discrete choice model**

a discrete choice model. The choice that is made from a set with more than one dimension is said to be a multivariate discrete choice model.

■ **Mun, Thomas**

a British mercantilist writer of the 17th century.

■ **Mundell-Fleming Model**

an open-economy version of the IS-LM model that allows for international trade and international capital flows. Due to Mundell (1962,63) and Fleming (1962).

■ **Mundell-Tobin Effect**

states that nominal interest rates would rise less than one-for-one with inflation because in response to inflation, the public would hold less in money balances and more in other assets, which would drive interest rates down.

■ **mutatis mutandis**

the necessary changes having been made, substituting new terms.

■ **mutual recognition**

the acceptance by one country of another country's certification that a satisfactory standard has been met for ability, performance, safety, etc.

■ **mystery of the missing trade**

the empirical observation, by Trefler (1995), that the amount of trade is far less than predicted by the HOV version of the Heckscher-Ohlin Model. More precisely, the factor content of trade is far less than the differences between countries in their factor endowments.

■ **NAICS**

North American Industry Classification System.

■ **Nash**

used as an adjective applied to a strategy in a game, this means that it is part of a Nash equilibrium.

■ **Nash equilibrium**

an equilibrium in game theory in which each player's action is optimal given the actions of the other players. E.g., in a tariff-and-retaliation game, with each country able to improve its terms of trade with a tariff, zero tariffs are not Nash, since each can do better by raising its tariff. A Nash equilibrium, with positive tariffs, is likely to be inferior to free trade for both.

■ **nation**

as used in international economics, a nation is almost invariably a country or occasionally a similar entity (e.g., Hong Kong) with a single, usually independent government.

■ **national**

1. of, relating to or belonging to a nation.

2. a person who is a citizen or long-term resident of a nation.

■ **National Bureau of Economic Research (NBER)**

a nonprofit, nonpartisan organisation based in Cambridge, MA, that assembles economic data and sponsors economic research. Its Business Cycle Dating Committee also is traditionally responsible for identifying the beginnings and ends of recessions.

■ **National defence argument for protection**

the argument that imports should be restricted in order to sustain a domestic industry so that it will be available in case of trade disruption due to war. This is a second best argument, since there are a variety of ways of providing for defence at lower economic cost, including production subsidies, mothballing and stockpiling.

■ **national exhaustion**

see **exhaustion**.

■ **national income**

1. the general term used to refer to the total value of a country's output of goods and services in some accounting period without specifying the formal accounting concept such as Gross Domestic Product.

2. the income generated by a country's production and therefore the total income of its factors of production. Except for some adjustments that don't usually enter theoretical models, NI is the same as GDP.

■ **national income (GDP) deflator**

a general way of referring to the price index which measures the average level of the prices of all the goods and services comprising the national income or GDP.

■ **national sovereignty**

see **sovereignty**.

■ **national treatment**

the principle of providing foreign producers and sellers the same treatment provided to domestic firms.

■ **natural increase**

growth of the population due to an excess of births over deaths.

■ **natural monopoly**

a market situation in which economies of scale are such that a single firm of efficient size is able to supply the entire market demand.

■ **natural person**

this term appears in the GATS where it deals with the international movement of employees of firms that are providing services in another country. Persons are called 'natural' to distinguish them from 'juridical persons,' such as partnerships or corporations, that are given certain rights of persons under the law.

■ **natural rate of unemployment**

the rate of unemployment that would exist when the economy is operating at full capacity. It would be equal to the amount of frictional unemployment in the system.

■ **natural resource**

anything that is provided by nature, such as deposits of minerals, quality of land, old-growth forests, fish populations, etc. The availability of particular natural resources is an important determinant of comparative advantage and trade in products that depend on them. Natural resources constitute one of the primary factors of production.

■ **natural trade**
trade that is either free or restricted, but that is not artificially encouraged by subsidies or other stimulants.

■ **necessity test**
a procedure to determine whether a trade restriction intended to serve some purpose is necessary for that purpose.

■ **negative externality**
a harmful externality, that is, a harmful effect of one economic agent's actions on another. Considered a distortion because the first agent has inadequate incentive to curtail their action. Examples are pollution from factories (a production externality) and smoke from cigarettes (a consumption externality).

■ **negative introspection**
implicit assumption of most decision models: If an agent does not know something than he/she, however, knows that he/she does not know it.

■ **negative list**
in an international agreement, a list of those items, entities, products, etc. to which the agreement will not apply, the commitment being to apply the agreement to everything else. Contrasts with positive list.

■ **neighbourhood production structure**
a structure of technology for a general equilibrium model due to Jones and Kierzkowski (1986). With an arbitrary but equal number of goods and factors, each factor produces two (different) goods, each good uses two (different) factors, in a way that yields more unambiguous results than one normally finds in high-dimension trade models without specific factors.

■ **neighbourhood**
in mathematical Euclidean space, a small set of points surrounding and including a particular point. Thus, for an economic variable, such as an allocation, the neighbourhood of a particular allocation includes all those allocations that are sufficiently similar to it.

■ **Nemawashi (jp)**
a Japanese term which refers to the practice of broad consultation before taking action.

■ **neoclassical**
a collection of assumptions customarily made by mainstream economists starting in the late 19th century, including profit maximisation by firms, utility maximisation by consumers and market equilibrium, with corresponding implications for determination of factor prices and the distribution of income. Contrasts

with classical, Keynesian and Marxist.

## neoclassical economics

most of modern, mainstream economics based on neoclassical assumptions. Tends to ascribe inevitability, if not necessarily desirability, to market outcomes.

## neoclassical growth model

a model of economic growth in which income arises from neoclassical production functions in one or more sectors displaying diminishing returns to saving and capital accumulation. Due to Solow (1956) and Swan (1956).

## neoclassical production function

a production function with the properties of constant returns to scale and smoothly diminishing returns to individual factors.

## neoliberalism

a view of the world that favours social justice while also emphasising economic growth, efficiency and the benefits of free markets.

## Net Domestic Product (NDP)

gross domestic product minus depreciation. This is the most complete measure of productive activity within the borders of a country, though its accuracy suffers from the difficulty of measuring depreciation.

## ■ net exports

the total value of goods and services exported during the accounting period minus the total value of goods and services imported.

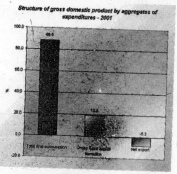

Net Exports

## ■ net foreign asset position

the value of the assets that a country owns abroad, minus the value of the domestic assets owned by foreigners. Equals balance of indebtedness.

## ■ net immigration

the total number of people leaving the country to take up permanent residence abroad minus the number of people entering the country for the purpose of taking up permanent residence.

## ■ net investment

total investment during some accounting period minus the amount of depreciation during the same period.

## ■ Net National Product (NNP)

gross national product minus depreciation. This is the most complete measure of productive activity by a country's nationals, though its accuracy suffers from the difficulty of measuring depreciation.

■ **net output**

the output of a product that is available for final users, after deducting amounts of it used up as an intermediate input in producing itself and other products. Contrasts with gross output.

■ **net present value**

same as present value, being sure to include (negative) payments as well as (positive) receipts.

■ **neutral**

1. said of a technological change or technological difference if it is not biased in favour of using more or less of one factor than another. This can be defined in several different ways that are not normally equivalent: Hicks-neutral, Harrod-neutral and Solow-neutral.

2. said of economic growth if it expands actual or potential output of all goods at the same rate, not being biased in favour of one over another. In the Heckscher-Ohlin Model neutral growth will occur all factor endowments grow at the same rate or if there is Hicks Neutral technological progress at the same rate in all industries.

3. said of a trade regime if the structure of protection favours neither exportables nor importables. See **bias**.

■ **new bancor**

a proposed new non-national world currency to be used for payment and reserve purposes, to be issued by the IMF and intended to maintain a fixed purchasing power in the dollar and euro countries.

■ **new economic geography**

the study of the location of economic activity across space, particularly a strand of literature begun by Krugman (1991a) using agglomeration economies to help explain why industries cluster within particular countries and regions.

■ **new economy**

this term was used in the late 1990's to suggest that globalisation and/or innovations in information technology had changed the way that the world economy works. Conjectures included changes in productivity, the inflation-unemployment tradeoff, the business cycle and the valuation of enterprises.

■ **New Trade Theory**

models of trade that, especially in the 1980s, incorporated aspects of imperfect competition, increasing returns and product differentiation into both general equilibrium and partial equilibrium models of trade and trade policy. Many contributed to this literature, but the most prominent was Krugman starting with Krugman (1979).

- **Newly Industrialising Country (NIC)**
  a group of countries previously regarded as LDCs that have recently achieved high rates and levels of economic growth.

- **Newly Industrialising Economy (NIE)**
  newly industrialising country.

- **news**
  unexpected information. In an efficient market, as the exchange market is supposed to be, price reflects all available information. It can change, therefore, only in response to news.

- **Niskanen, William Arthur (1933- )**
  an American economist born in Oregon who studied economics at both Harvard and Chicago. Niskanen has held various posts in government (US Department of Defense) and business (Ford Motor Co.) He was a pioneer in the economic theory of bureaucracy. His best-known book is *Bureaucracy and Representative Government*, 1971.

- **nominal**
  1. in the form most directly observed or named, in contrast to a form that has been adjusted or modified in some fashion.
  2. as measured in terms of money, usually in contrast to real.

- **nominal exchange rate**
  the actual exchange rate at which currencies are exchanged on an exchange market. Contrasts with real exchange rate.

- **nominal interest rate**
  the interest rate actually observed in the market, in contrast to the real interest rate.

- **nominal rate of protection**
  the protection afforded by an industry directly by the tariff and/or NTB on its output, ignoring effects of other trade barriers on the industry's inputs. Contrasts with the ERP.

- **nominal tariff**
  the nominal protection provided by a tariff, that is, the tariff itself. Contrasts with effective tariff.

- **non-actionable subsidy**
  a subsidy that is permitted by the rules of the WTO, thus not subject to countervailing duties. These include non-specific subsidies, subsidies for industrial research, regional aids and some environmental subsidies.

- **non-automatic licensing**
  import licensing that is discretionary, based on an import quota or performance related.

- **nonconvexity**
  the property of an economic model or system that sets the representing technology, preferences or constraints as not mathematically convex. Because convexity is needed for proof that competitive equilibrium is efficient and well-behaved, nonconvexities may imply market failures.

■ **nondistorted**
without distortions. Many propositions in trade theory are strictly valid, often only implicitly, only in nondistorted economies.

■ **nondistorting lump sum**
redundant appellation for a lump sum tax or subsidy.

■ **noneconomic objectives argument for protection**
the view that a restriction on imports may serve a purpose outside of conventional economic models. Unless that purpose is itself the restriction of trade, then this is a second-best argument, since changes in output, consumption, etc. can be achieved at lower economic cost in other ways.

■ **Non-Governmental Organisation (NGO)**
a not-for-profit organisation that pursues an issue or issues of interest to its members by lobbying, persuasion and/or direct action. In the arena of international economics, NGOs play an increasing role defending human rights and the environment and fighting poverty.

■ **nonhomothetic**
any function that is not homothetic, but usually applied to consumer preferences that include goods whose shares of expenditure rise (and others that fall) with income.

■ **non-market economy**
a country in which most major economic decisions are imposed by government and by central planning rather than by free use of markets. Contrasts with a market economy.

■ **nonproduction worker**
a worker not directly engaged in production. In empirical studies of skilled and unskilled labour, data on nonproduction workers are often taken to represent skilled labour.

■ **non-specific subsidy**
a subsidy that is available to more than a single specific industry and is therefore non-actionable under WTO rules.

■ **nonsterilisation**
the exchange market intervention that is done without sterilising its effects on the domestic money supply.

■ **Nontariff Barrier (NTB)**
any policy that interferes with exports or imports other than a simple tariff, prominently including quotas and VERs.

■ **nontariff measure**
any policy or official practice that alters the conditions of international trade, including ones that act to increase trade as well as those that restrict it. The term is therefore broader than nontariff barrier, although the two are usually used interchangeably.

■ **nontradable good**
a good that, by its nature, cannot be traded internationally.

- **nontraded good**
  a good that is not traded, either because it cannot be or because trade barriers are too high. Except when services are being distinguished from goods, they are often mentioned as examples of nontraded goods or at least they were until it became common to speak of trade in services.

- **nonviolation**
  in WTO terminology, this is shorthand for a complaint that a country's action, though not a violation of WTO rules, has nullified or impaired a member's expected benefits from the agreement.

- **normal good**
  any good for which the demand increases as the incomes increases.

- **normal value**
  price charged for a product on the domestic market of the producer. Used to compare with export price in determining dumping.

- **normative**
  the value judgments as to 'what ought to be,' in contrast to positive which is about 'what is'.

- **normative theory**
  the theory which depends on underlying values, not on facts. It identifies 'what ought to be' if such values are adhered to.

- **North American Free Trade Agreement (NAFTA)**
  the agreement to form a free trade area among the United States,

Canada and Mexico that went into effect on January 1, 1994.

- **nullification**
  see **nonviolation**

- **numeraire**
  the unit in which prices are measured. This may be a currency, but in real models, such as most trade models, the numeraire is usually one of the goods, whose price is then set at one. The numeraire can also be defined implicitly by, for example, the requirement that prices sum to some constant.

- **offer curve**
  a curve showing, for a two-good model, the quantity of one good that a country will export (or 'offer') for each quantity of the other that it imports. Also called the reciprocal demand curve, it is convenient for representing both exports and imports in the same curve and can be used for analysing tariffs and other changes.

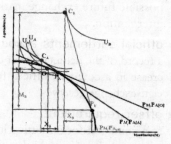

*Offer Curve*

- **offer curve diagram**
  a diagram that combines the offer curves of two countries (or one country and the rest of world)

to determine equilibrium relative prices.

■ **official rate**

the par value of a pegged exchange rates.

■ **official reserve transactions**

transactions by a central bank that cause changes in its official reserves. These are usually purchases or sales of its own currency in the exchange market in exchange for foreign currencies or other foreign-currency-denominated assets. In the balance of payments, a purchase of its own currency is a credit (+) and a sale is a debit (-).

■ **official reserves**

the reserves of foreign-currency-denominated assets (and also gold and SDRs) that a central bank holds, sometimes as backing for its own currency, but usually only for the purpose of possible future exchange market intervention.

■ **official settlements account**

a record of the net increase or decrease in a country's official foreign exchange reserves.

■ **offset requirement**

as a condition for importing into a country, a requirement that foreign exporters purchase domestic products and/or invest in the importing country.

■ **offsets**

side payments or other commitments made by countries or corporations to secure export orders. In the aerospace industry, companies often have to subcontract parts production and/or to transfer technology in order to receive a purchase order. However, offsets can take many other forms, including barter trade.

■ **Ohlin definition**

the price definition of factor abundance. In contrast to the quantity definition, the price definition incorporates differences in demands as well as supplies. Due to Ohlin (1933).

■ **OLI Paradigm**

represents a mix of three different FDI theories = O + L + I, each with a different focus or question:

O: Ownership Advantages (Firm Specific Advantages) address the why question.

L: Location Advantages (Country Specific Advantages) focus on the where question.

I: Internalisation Advantages refer to the how or organisational question.

■ **oligopoly**

a market structure in which there are a small number of sellers, at least some of whose individual decisions about price or quantity matter to the others.

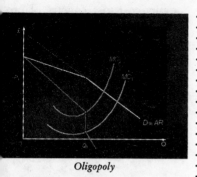

*Oligopoly*

# oligopsony
a market structure in which there are a small number of buyers.

# one cone equilibrium
a free-trade equilibrium in the Heckscher-Ohlin Model in which prices are such that all goods can be produced within a single country and there is only one diversification cone. This will arise if countries' factor endowments are sufficiently similar compared to factor intensities of industries. Contrasts with multi-cone equilibrium.

# one-way arbitrage
the use, by a potential supplier or demander in a market, of a different market or markets to accomplish the same purpose, taking advantage of a discrepancy among their prices. With transaction costs, this enforces smaller price discrepancies than would be permitted by conventional arbitrage. Due to Deardorff (1979).

# one-way option
the situation of a speculator on an exchange market with a pegged exchange rate. If there is doubt about the viability of the peg, the speculator can sell the currency short, knowing that there is only one direction (one way) that the currency is likely to move. Therefore, there is little risk associated with such speculation.

# open economy
an economy that permits transactions with the outside world, at least including trade of some goods. Contrasts with closed economy.

# Open Market Operation (OMO)
the sale or purchase of government bonds by a central bank, in exchange for domestic currency or central-bank deposits. This changes the monetary base and therefore the domestic money supply, contracting it with a bond sale and expanding it with a bond purchase.

# open position
an obligation to take or make delivery of an asset or currency in the future without cover, that is, without a matching obligation in the other direction that protects them from effects of change in the price of the asset or currency. Aside from simple ownership and debt, an open position can be acquired or avoided using the forward market.

# open regionalism
regional economic integration that is not discriminatory against out-

side countries, typically, a group of countries that agrees to reduce trade barriers on an MFN basis. Adopted as a fundamental principle, but not defined, by APEC in 1989. Bergsten (1997) offers five definitions, ranging from open membership to global liberalisation and trade facilitation.

■ **open space land**
land within or outside an urban area to be set aside, maintained or cleared for recreation or beautification.

■ **open-economy multiplier**
the simple Keynesian multiplier for a small open economy. Equals 1/(s+m), where s is the marginal propensity to save and m is the marginal propensity to import.

■ **openness**
the extent to which an economy is open, often measured by the ratio of its trade (exports plus imports) to GDP.

■ **opportunism**
the suggestion (widely associated with transaction cost analysis) that a decision-maker may unconditionally seek his/her self-interests and that such behaviour cannot necessarily be predicted. This proposition extends the simple self-interest seeking assumption to include 'self-interest seeking with guile' thereby making allowance for strategic behaviour.

■ **opportunity cost**
the cost of something in terms of opportunity foregone. The opportunity cost to a country of producing a unit more of a good, such as for export or to replace an import, is the quantity of some other good that could have been produced instead.

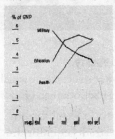

**Fig. 2 Industrialized countries spending more on health and education, less on military**

■ **optimal currency area**
the optimal grouping of regions or countries within which exchange rates should be held fixed. First defined (as 'optimum currency areas') by Mundell (1961).

■ **optimal tariff**
the level of a tariff that maximises a country's welfare. In a nondistorted small open economy the optimal tariff is zero. In a large country it is positive, due to its effect on the terms of trade.

■ **optimal tariff argument**
an argument in favour of levying a tariff in order to improve the terms of trade. The argument is valid only in a large country and then only if other countries do not retaliate by raising tariffs themselves. Even then, this is a beggarthy neighbour policy, since it lowers welfare abroad.

■ **optimum**

the best. Usually refers to a most preferred choice by consumers subject to a budget constraint, a profit maximising choice by firms or industry subject to a technological constraint or in general equilibrium, a complete allocation of factors and goods that in some sense maximises welfare.

■ **optimum optimorum**

the best of the best or the global optimum. This term is used, when there are several allocations each of which is locally optimal, to refer to the best among these.

■ **option**

a contract which gives the holder of the contract the right to buy or sell a commodity or financial asset for a given price before a specified date.

■ **Orderly Marketing Arrangement (OMA)**

an agreement among a group of exporting and importing countries to restrict the quantities traded of a good or group of goods. Since the impetus normally comes from the importers protecting their domestic industry, an OMA is effectively a multi-country VER.

■ **Organisation for Economic Cooperation and Development (OECD)**

an international organisation of developed countries that 'provides governments a setting in which to discuss, develop and perfect economic and social policy.' As of July 2002, it had 30 member countries.

■ **Organisation for European Economic Cooperation (OEEC)**

an international organisation established in 1948 as the recipient instituion of aid through the Marshall Plan. In 1961, it was replaced by the OECD.

■ **Organisation of Petroleum Exporting Countries (OPEC)**

a group of countries that includes many, but not all, of the largest exporters of oil. Its major purpose is to regulate the supply of petroleum and thereby to stabilise (often raise) its price. The international oil cartel. As of July 2002, it had 11 member countries.

■ **origin rule**

see **rules of origin**.

■ **output augmenting**

said of a technological change or technological difference if one production function produces a scalar multiple of the other. Also called Hicks neutral.

■ **outsourcing**

1. performance of a production activity that was previously done inside a firm or plant outside that firm or plant.

2. manufacture of inputs to a production process or a part of a process, in another location, especially in another country.

3. another term for fragmentation.

- **outward oriented strategy**
  see **export promotion**.

- **overhang**
  see **debt overhang** and **money overhang**.

- **over-invoicing**
  the provision of an invoice that reports the price as higher than is actually being paid.

- **overshooting**
  see **exchange rate overshooting**.

- **over-valued currency**
  the situation of a currency whose value on the exchange market is higher than is believed to be sustainable. This may be due to a pegged or managed rate that is above the market-clearing rate or, under a floating rate, it may be due to speculative capital inflows. Contrasts with under-valued currency.

- **panel**
  a three-person committee assembled by the **WTO** to hear evidence in disputes between members, as part of the WTO dispute settlement mechanism. Panels are also used to settle disputes under NAFTA.

- **par**
  1. equality. See **at par**.

- **par value**
  the central value of a pegged exchange rate, around which the actual rate is permitted to fluctuate within set bounds.

- **para tariff**
  a charge on imports that is not in-

cluded in a country's tariff schedule, such as a statistical tax, stamp fee, etc.

- **paradox**
  as used in economics, it seems to mean something unexpected, rather than the more extreme normal meaning of something seemingly impossible. Some paradoxes are just theoretical results that go against what one thinks of as normal. Others, like the Leontief paradox, are empirical findings that seem to contradict theoretical predictions.

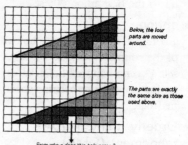

How can this be true?

Below, the four parts are moved around.

The parts are exactly the same size as those used above.

From where does this hole come?

*Paradox*

- **parallel import**
  trade that is made possible when the owner of intellectual property causes the same product to be sold in different countries for different prices. If someone else imports the low-price good into the high-price country, that is a parallel import.

- **para-tariff**
  a charge on an imported good instead of or in addition to, a tariff.

■ **Pareto criterion**

the criterion that for change in an economy to be viewed as socially beneficial it should be Pareto-improving.

■ **Pareto optimality**

the condition which exists when it is impossible to make any individual better off without making any other individual worse off.

■ **Pareto, Vilfredo (1848-1923)**

born in Paris of French and Italian parents, Pareto was educated in Italy where he was trained in mathematics and engineering. After working as an engineer for some years, he inherited a fortune and devoted himself to his broadranging interests in mathematics, sociology and religion. He was active in the turbulent politics of turn-of-the-century Europe. He also held an academic appointment at Lausanne where he lectured in economics and sociology. In 1906, he retired to his estate near Celigny on Lake Geneva and occupied himself developing a rather peculiar system of sociology. When the fascists came to power in Italy, Mussolini appointed him a Senator, presumably because of his professed hatred of democrats. His major contributions to economics were the indifference curve analysis which he had adapted from the work of Francis Edgeworth, a British economist and which was in turn picked up and developed by J.R. Hicks.

■ **Pareto-improving**

making no one worse off and making at least one person better off.

■ **Pareto-optimal**

a situation in which no Pareto-improving change is possible.

■ **parity**

equality. Same as **par**. See also **interest parity** and **purchasing power parity**.

■ **partial equilibrium**

equality of supply and demand in only a subset of an economy's markets, usually just one, taking variables from other markets as given. Partial equilibrium models are appropriate for products that constitute only a negligibly small part of the economy. They are used routinely (not always appropriately) for analysis of trade policies in single industries. Contrasts with **general equilibrium**.

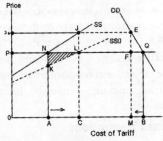

*Partial Equilibrium*

■ **partnership**

an unincorporated business owned by two or more people.

■ **pass-through**
the extent to which an exchange rate change is reflected in the prices of imported goods. With full pass-through, a currency depreciation, which increases the price of foreign currency, would increase the prices of imported goods by the same amount and vice versa. With no pass-through, prices of imports remain constant. See **pricing to market**.

■ **patent**
the legal right to the proceeds from and control over the use of an invented product or process, granted for a fixed period of time, usually 20 years.

■ **path dependency**
reference to effects of past commitments or acquired knowledge on subsequent actions and decisions. Recognising that 'history matters' for a future course of action or development, such past commitments or learning activities could entail previous investments, e.g. in transaction-specific assets, contracts, research & development or the pool of (usually locally) learned behaviours and organisational routines which constrain (including spatially) future activities.

■ **path dependent**
the property that where you get to depends on how you got there. That is, if the equilibrium that will ultimately be reached by a system depends on the values of variables taken on away from equilibrium, then the equilibrium is path dependent.

■ **patriotism argument for protection**
the view that one is helping one's country by buying domestically produced goods instead of imports. In a nondistorted economy, this is not correct, since the country can do better producing where it has a comparative advantage rather than using scarce resources where it does not.

■ **pattern of specialisation**
what all goods a country produces and which it does not produce.

■ **pattern of trade**
see **trade pattern**.

■ **Pauper labour argument**
the view that a country loses by importing from another country that has low wages, presumably by lowering wages at home. This view ignores the fact that low wages are due to low productivity and that the high-wage home country, with high productivity, will have comparative advantage in some products and will gain from trade.

■ **payments imbalance**
imbalance in the balance of payments, normally including both current and capital accounts.

■ **peak**
the point in the business cycle when an economic expansion

**reaches** its highest point before turning down. Contrasts with **trough**.

# ■ pedagogy (pedagogical)

the study and science of teaching and teaching methods

*Pedagogy*

# ■ pegged exchange rate

a regime in which the government or central bank announces an official (par value) of its currency and then maintains the actual market rate within a narrow band above and below that by means of exchange market intervention.

# ■ per capita

per person.

# ■ per capita income

income per person, usually measured as GDP divided by population.

# ■ perfect capital mobility

1. the absence of any barriers to international capital movements.
2. the requirement that, in equilibrium, rates of return on capital (interest rates) must be the same in different countries.

# ■ perfect competition

an idealised market structure in which there are large numbers of both buyers and sellers, all of them small, so that they act as price takers. Perfect competition also assumes homogeneous products, free entry and exit and complete information. Most international trade theory prior to the New Trade Theory assumed perfect competition.

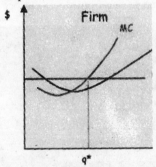

*Perfect Competition*

# ■ perfect foresight

exact knowledge of the future. Under perfect foresight, for example, the forward rate would exactly equal the spot rate that later prevails when the forward contract matures.

# ■ perfect substitute

a good that is regarded by its demanders as identical to another good, so that the elasticity of substitution between them is infinite.

# ■ perfectly competitive

refers to an economic agent (firm

or consumer), group of agents (industry), model or analysis that is characterised by perfect competition. Contrasts with imperfectly competitive.

■ **perfectly elastic**
refers to a supply or demand curve with a price elasticity of infinity, implying that the supply or demand curve as usually drawn is horizontal. A small open economy faces perfectly elastic demand for its exports and supply of its imports and a foreign offer curve that is a straight line from the origin.

*Perfectly Elastic*

■ **perfectly mobile capital**
perfect capital mobility.

■ **performance requirement**
a requirement that an importer or exporter achieve some level of performance, in terms of exporting, domestic content, etc., in order to obtain an import or export license.

■ **performance zoning**
an alternative to traditional zoning. It provides greater flexibility by requiring that any development meet specified performance standards, rather than meeting detailed requirements as to allowed uses and the characteristics of those uses. The flexibility allowed by performance zoning should allow greater opportunity for market forces to affect land use and thus provide for greater economic efficiency.

■ **periodic market**
markets which meet at designated locations in periodic intervals. The periodicity tends to be fixed and (as has been frequently suggested) is based on the traders' need to tap a large market in order fulfil threshold conditions and the consumers' unwillingness/ inability to travel long distances and bridge the intervals between market days.

■ **Permanent Normal Trading Relations (PNTR)**
the granting of permanent MFN status to a country that is not a member of the WTO. It is 'normal' in the sense that most countries are WTO members and therefore have MFN status (or better) automatically.

■ **permatemps**
workers arbitrarily classified as 'temporary' by employers while they perform regular jobs and work over extended periods of time with other workers who are given regular employee status. Permatemps tend to receive lower wages and less benefits.

■ **personal distribution**
the distribution of income on the basis of income groups. For example, by dividing all income recipients into ten groups (deciles) and showing the share each of these groups had of the total income.

■ **personal mastery**
one of Senge's 5 principles for the learning organisation: 'learning to expand our personal capacity to create the results we most desire and creating an organisational environment which encourages all its members to develop themselves toward the goals and purposes they choose.'

■ **pessimum distance**
reference to the (possibly) disadvantageous location of a smaller city relative to a larger one.

■ **petrodollar**
the profits made by oil exporting countries when the price rose during the 1970s and their preference for holding these profits in U.S. dollar-denominated assets, either in the US or in Europe as Eurodollars. A portion of these were in turn lent by banks to oil-importing developing countries who used them to buy oil.

■ **physical capital**
the same as capital, without any adjective, in the sense of plant and equipment. The word 'physical' is used only to distinguish it from human capital.

■ **phytosanitary**
pertaining to the health of plants.

■ **piecemeal tariff reform**
the reduction of only one tariff (or a subset of tariffs) by a country that has additional tariffs on other products.

■ **Pittsburgh Plus**
a form of spatial price discrimination based on oligopolistic collusion. The mill price at one location determines the delivered price at all locations regardless of the location of the plant from which delivery is actually made.

■ **place**
a relatively small part of geographical space occupied by a person or small segment of society. Often, 'place' is used to signify certain relationships or ties between people and this specific space.

■ **place utility**
the utility (benefits, satisfaction) associated with or derived from the attributes of a place or location.

■ **Planned Unit Development (PUD)**
a land development project comprehensively planned as an entity via a unitary site plan which permits flexibility in building setting, mixtures of housing types and land uses, usable open spaces and the preservation of significant natural features.

■ **planning curve**

the long run average cost curve.

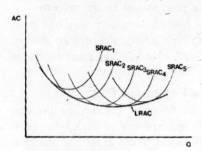

*Planning Curve*

■ **plasticity**

resources and investments are called 'plastic', to indicate that there is a wide range of discretionary, legitimate decisions within which the user may choose.

■ **Plaza Accord**

an agreement reached in 1985 among the central banks of France, Germany, Japan, US and UK to bring down the value of the US dollar, which had appreciated substantially since 1980. By the time of the Louvre Accord, two years later, the dollar had fallen 30%.

■ **plurilateral**

among several countries — more than two, which would be bilateral, but not a great many, which would be multilateral.

■ **plurilateral agreement**

the plurilateral agreements of the WTO contrast with the larger multilateral agreements in that the former are signed onto by only those member countries that choose to do so, while all members are party to the multilateral agreements.

■ **point elasticity**

see elasticity

■ **political economy**

1. early name for the discipline of economics.
2. a field within economics encompassing several alternatives to neoclassical economics, including Marxist economics. Also called radical political economy.
3. a field within economics that concerns the interactions between political processes and economic variables, especially economic policies.

■ **political economy of protection**

the study of reasons, especially political ones, that countries choose to use protection. Includes models of voting, lobbying and campaign contributions as these lead policy makers to erect tariffs.

■ **poll tax**

a tax that must be paid by every member of the community regardless of their income. With a poll tax, each person has to pay the same amount of money.

■ **pollution haven**

a country that, because of its weak or poorly enforced environmental regulations, attracts industries that pollute the environment.

■ **population density**
population within an areal unit (usually one square kilometre or square mile)

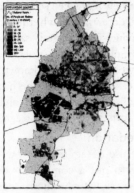

*Population Density*

■ **portal**
a Web site that has become an individual's primary entry point to the Internet.

■ **portfolio**
1. the entire collection of financial assets held by an investor.
2. the entirety of the financial assets (and usually also liabilities) that an economic agent or group of agents owns.

■ **portfolio approach**
an approach to explaining exchange rates that stresses their role in changing the proportions of different currency-denominated assets in portfolios. The exchange rate adjusts to equate these proportions to desired levels.

■ **portfolio capital**
financial assets, including stocks, bonds, deposits and currencies.

■ **portfolio flow**
the sale or purchase of financial assets across countries.

■ **portfolio investment**
the acquisition of portfolio capital. Usually refers to such transactions across national borders and/or across currencies.

■ **portfolio theory**
the analysis of how an investor can maximise the expected return from a 'portfolio' of various kinds of financial assets having given degrees of risk and uncertainty associated with them (or minimise the risk involved in realising some given expected return).

■ **positional goods**
goods which are at least in part demanded because their possession or consumption implies social or other status of those acquiring them.

■ **positive**
refers to 'what is,' in contrast to normative which involves value judgments as to 'what ought to be.' The word is not, in this use, the opposite of either 'negative' or 'harmful.'

■ **positive externality**
a beneficial externality, that is, a beneficial effect of one economic agent's actions on another. Considered a distortion because the first agent has inadequate incentive to act. Examples are the attractiveness of well-kept farms for the tourism industry (a pro-

duction externality) and reduced contagion of disease due to vaccines (a consumption externality).

■ **positive list**
in an international agreement, a list of those items, entities, products, etc. to which the agreement will apply, with no commitment to apply the agreement to anything else. Contrasts with negative list.

■ **Posner, Richard A. (1939- )**
an American lawyer, economist and jurist, educated at Yale and Harvard. Posner lectured at the University of Chicago Law School in the 1980s and was appointed to the US Court of Appeals during the Reagan administration. His major work in economics has been concerned with the economic analysis of law. He has published several important articles and three major books, *Economic Analysis of Law*, 1973, *Antitrust Law: An Economic Perspective*, 1976 and *The Economics of Justice*, 1981.

■ **postmodernism**
a still tenuous attempt to lend identity to a new era beginning in the early 1970s which is associated with changes from and reaction to certain attributes of modernity or modernism.

■ **Prebisch-Singer Hypothesis**
the idea that the relative prices of primary products would decline over the long term and therefore that developing countries that were led by comparative advantage to specialise in them would find their prospects for development diminished. Due to Prebisch (1950) and Singer (1950).

■ **precautionary principle**
the view that when science has not yet determined whether a new product or process is safe or unsafe, policy should prohibit or restrict its use until it is known to be safe. Applied to trade, this has been used as the basis for prohibiting imports of GMOs, for example.

■ **predation**
the use of aggressive (low) pricing to put a competitor out of business, with the intent, once they are gone, of raising prices to gain monopoly profits.

■ **predatory dumping**
dumping for the purpose of driving competitors out of business and then raising price. This is the one motivation for dumping that most economists agree is undesirable, like predatory pricing (predation) in other contexts.

■ **predatory pricing**
a company engages in predatory pricing when it sets the price of its goods very low in order to eliminate its competitors and prevent new companies from entering into the marketplace.

■ **preference for variety**
the increased utility that people experience when they have access to a larger number of differentiated product varieties. In reality, this may reflect their ability to find

products more closely suited to their own particular needs, but as modelled in the Dixit-Stiglitz utility function, they are better off consuming small quantities of each of a larger number of products.

## preferences

1. in trade policy, this refers to special advantages, such as lower-than-MFN tariffs, accorded to another country's exports, usually in order to promote that country's development. See GSP.

2. in trade theory, this refers to the attitudes of consumers toward different goods, as represented by a utility function. Some propositions in trade theory use the assumption of identical and/or homothetic preferences.

## preferential trading arrangement

a group of countries that levies lower (or zero) tariffs against imports from members than outsiders. Includes FTAs, customs unions and common markets. Encouragement to use this term instead of the more misleading FTA has come from Jagdish Bhagwati, as in Bhagwati and Panagariya (1996).

## present value

the value today of a stream of payments and/or receipts over time in the future and/or the past, converted to the present using an interest rate. If $X_t$ is the amount

in period t and r the interest rate, then present value at time $t=0$ is $V = S_t (X_t)/(1+r)^t$.

## preshipment inspection

certification of the value, quality and/or identity of traded goods done in the exporting country by specialised agencies or firms on behalf of the importing country. Traditionally used as a means to prevent over- or under-invoicing, it is now being used also as a security measure.

## price

the value of the goods or money that must be given up to acquire a good or service.

## price ceiling

a government-imposed upper limit on the price that may be charged for a product. If that limit is binding, it implies a situation of excess demand and shortage.

## price definition

a method of defining relative factor abundance based on ratios of factor prices in autarky: Compared to country B, country A is abundant in factor X relative to factor Y, iff $wXA/wYA < wXB/wYB$, where $wIJ$ is the autarky price of factor I in country J, $I=X,Y$, $J=A,B$.

## price discrimination

the sale by a firm to buyers at two different prices. When this occurs internationally and the lower price is charged for export, it is regarded as dumping.

- **price elasticity**
  the elasticity of supply or demand with respect to price.

- **price elasticity of demand**
  change in the quantity demanded of a good or service in response to a change in price.

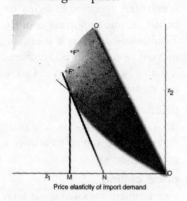
Price elasticity of import demand

- **price floor**
  a government-imposed lower limit on the price that may be charged for a product. If that limit is binding, it implies a situation of excess supply, which the government may need to purchase itself to keep the price from falling.

- **price index**
  a measure of the average prices of a group of goods relative to a base year. A typical price index for a vector of quantities q and prices pb, pg in the base and given years respectively would be I = 100 Spgq / Spbq.

- **price inelastic**
  having a price elasticity of less than one (in absolute value).

- **price level**
  the overall level of prices in a country, as usually measured empirically by a price index, but often captured in theoretical models by a single variable.

- **price line**
  a straight line representing the combinations of variables, usually two goods, that cost the same at some given prices. The slope of a price line measures relative prices and changes in prices can therefore be represented by changing the slope of or rotating, a price line. A steeper line means a higher relative price of the good measured on the horizontal axis.

- **price support**
  government action to increase the price of a product, usually by buying it. May be associated with a price floor.

- **price taker**
  an economic entity that is too small relative to a market to affect its price and that therefore must take that price as given in making its own decisions. Applies to all buyers and sellers in markets that are perfectly competitive. Applies also to a country if it is a small open economy.

- **price undertaking**
  a commitment by an exporting firm to raise its price in an importing-country market, as a means of settling an anti-dumping suit

and preventing an anti-dumping duty.

## pricing to market
the practice of an exporting firm holding fixed (or not fully adjusting) the price it charges in the export market when its costs or exchange rate change. See **pass-through**.

## primary budget surplus
the primary budget surplus (or deficit) of a government is the surplus excluding interest payments on its outstanding debt.

## primary commodity
primary product.

## primary factor
an input that exists as a stock providing service that contributes to production. The stock is not used up in production, although it may deteriorate with use, providing a smaller flow of services later. The major primary factors are labour, capital, human capital (or skilled labour), land and sometimes natural resources.

## primary input
same as **primary factor**.

## primary product
a good that has not been processed and is therefore in its natural state, specifically products of agriculture, forestry, fishing and mining.

## primary sector
a generally accepted reference to agricultural and livestock production, fishing, hunting and forestry (at times also including mineral extraction).

## primate city
a country's leading city (economically, culturally & politically) disproportionately larger than the next largest ones in the country's city size distribution.

## prime rate
1. the prime rate of interest is a rate of interest that serves as a benchmark for most other loans in a country. The precise definition of prime rate differs from country to country.
2. the interest rate that a country's largest banks announce for loans to their best customers. In practice, their most creditworthy customers get a rate lower than this.

## principal supplier
the country that has the largest share of imports of a good into a particular importing country, among those exporters subject to MFN tariffs. It is customary in tariff negotiations and to some extent mandated by WTO rules, that countries negotiate with their principal suppliers.

## principle of diminishing marginal utility
the proposition that the satisfaction derived from consuming an additional unit of a good or service declines as additional units are acquired.

■ **principle of diminishing returns**

the proposition that the marginal product of the last unit of labour employed declines as additional units of labour are employed.

■ **Prisoners' dilemma**

a strategic interaction in which two players both gain individually by not cooperating, leading to a Nash equilibrium in which both are worse off than if they cooperated. Important especially for explaining why countries may choose protection even though all lose as a result.

Prisoners' Dilemma

|  |  | Prisoner A | |
|---|---|---|---|
|  |  | Cooperation | Defect |
| Prisoner B | Coop | A + 5 B + 5 | A + 10 B - 10 |
|  | Defect | A - 10 B + 10 | A 0 B 0 |

■ **private benefit**

the benefit to an individual economic agent, such as a consumer or firm, from an event, action or policy change. Contrasts with social benefit.

■ **private cost**

the cost to an individual economic agent, such as a consumer or firm, from an event, action or policy change. Contrasts with social cost.

■ **private goods**

a good which cannot be consumed without paying for it and the supply of which is reduced when it is consumed by a particular user of it.

■ **private sector**

private sector companies are one that are not owned by the government. This is opposed to the public sector that consists of industries such as education and unemployment insurance.

■ **privatisation**

occurs when the government sell a government owned business to private interests. This is usually the first step in creating a competitive market for the good or service that the government owned business previously had a monopoly on.

■ **probability density**

for a continuous random variable a function whose integral over any set is the probability of the variable being in that set.

■ **probability distribution**

a specification of the probabilities for each possible value of a random variable.

■ **processed good**

a good that has been transformed in some way by a production activity, in contrast to a raw material.

■ **producer presence**

a mode of supply of a traded service in which the producer establishes a presence in the buyer country by FDI and/or permanent relocation of workers.

■ **producer subsidy equivalent**

1. producer support estimate.
2. this ought logically to measure

the extent to which existing policies serve to subsidise producers, defined as the ad valorem subsidy that, if paid directly to producers per unit of production, would lead to the same level of output as existing policies.

■ **Producer Support Estimate (PSE)**
introduced by the OECD to quantify support in agriculture, it measures 'transfers from consumers and taxpayers to agricultural producers as a result of measures (of) support,' expressed as a percentage of gross farm receipts. Also called producer subsidy equivalent.

■ **producer surplus**
the difference between the revenue of producers and production cost, measured as the area above the supply (or marginal cost) curve and below price, out to the quantity supplied and net of fixed cost and losses at low output. If input prices are constant, this is profit, if not, it includes gains to input suppliers, such as labour. Normally useful only as the change in producer surplus.

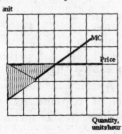
*Producer Surplus*

■ **product**
a good or service that is produced.

■ **product cycle**
1. associated with observed regularities in the way in which the production and marketing of products change during the life of a product and thereby change their interaction with and demands on their environment.
2. the life cycle of a new product, which first can be produced only in the country where it was developed, then as it becomes standardised and more familiar, can be produced in other countries and exported back to where it started. Due to Vernon (1966).

■ **product differentiation**
causing buyers to believe that a particular version of a product is superior to that being offered by competitors.

■ **product life cycle**
see **product cycle**.

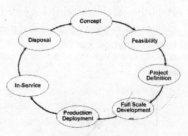
*Product Cycle*

■ **product localisation**
modifying and adapting foreign-made products/services to render them suitable for a new market.

■ **production externality**
an externality arising from production.

■ **production function**
a function that specifies the output in an industry for all combinations of inputs.

■ **production possibilities**
levels of output which are within the range of possibilities for a particular economy.

■ **Production Possibility Curve (PPC)**
points describing alternative combinations of output levels for two different products to be produced by given resources. At the macro level, the curve describes a schedule of trade-offs for a two commodity society.

■ **Production Possibility Frontier (PPF)**
a diagram showing the maximum output possible for one good for various outputs of another (or several others), given technology and factor endowments. Also called the transformation curve.

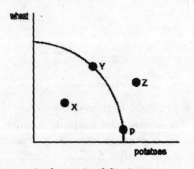

*Production Possibility Frontier*

■ **production worker**
a worker directly engaged in production. In empirical studies of skilled and unskilled labour, data on production workers are often taken to represent unskilled labour.

■ **productivity**
output per unit of input, usually measured either by labour productivity or by total factor productivity.

■ **productivity of labour**
see **labour productivity**.

■ **profit**
when a firm's revenues exceed its costs, profit is the difference between the two.

■ **profit centre**
semiautonomous, independently accounting corporate unit responsible for its own operations, profits and losses.

■ **profit maximising**
the level of a variable or behaviour that maximises the profit of a firm.

■ **profit shifting**
the use of government policies to alter the outcome of international oligopolistic competition so as to increase the profits of domestic firms at the expense of foreign firms. This is a key element of strategic trade policy.

■ **progressive tax**
a tax on income in which the proportion of tax paid relative to income increases as income increases.

- **prohibited subsidy**
  a subsidy that is prohibited under the rules of the WTO. These include subsidies that are specifically designed to distort international trade, such as export subsidies or subsidies that require use of domestic rather than imported inputs.

- **prohibition**
  denial of the right to import or export, applying to particular products and/or particular countries. Includes embargo.

- **prohibitive tariff**
  a tariff that reduces imports to zero.

- **proportional tax**
  a tax on income where the proportion of tax paid relative to income does not change as income changes.

- **proportionality effect**
  in shift & share analysis, that part of the total 'regional shift' which is attributable to the (compositional) structure ('mix' of activities) of the region in combination with the general, usually national development of individual industries.

- **prospective analysis**
  see **ex ante analysis**.

- **prosumer**
  a reference to the 'reunification of producers and consumers'.

- **protection**
  1. without any adjective or as 'import protection,' this refers to restriction of imports by means of tariffs and/or NTBs and thereby to insulate domestic producers from competition with imported goods.
  2. as 'IP protection,' or 'intellectual property protection', this refers to enforcement of intellectual property rights by granting patents, copyrights and trademarks and by prosecuting those who violate them.

- **protectionism**
  advocacy of protection. The word has a negative connotation and few advocates of protection in particular situations will acknowledge being protectionists.

- **protocol of accession**
  legal document specifying the procedures for a country to join an international agreement or organisation, including the rights and responsibilities that accompany such accession.

- **public goods**
  a good which can only be supplied to all if it is supplied to one and the availability of which is not diminished by any one consumer's use of it.

- **public interest**
  the notion that there is some kind of general interest of the community as a whole which can be affected by the actions of governments or private agents.

■ **public procurement**
government procurement.

■ **punitive tariff**
a high tariff the purpose of which is to inflict harm on a foreign exporter as punishment for some previous behaviour.

■ **purchasing power**
the amount of goods that money will buy, usually measured (inversely) by the CPI.

■ **Purchasing Power Parity (PPP)**
1. the equality of the prices of a bundle of goods (usually the CPI) in two countries when valued at the prevailing exchange rate. Called absolute PPP.
2. the equality of the rates of change over time in the prices of a bundle of goods in two countries when valued at the prevailing exchange rate. Called relative PPP. Implies that the rate of depreciation of a currency must equal the difference between its inflation rate and the inflation rate in the currency to which it is being compared.

■ **purchasing power parity exchange rate**
an exchange rate calculated to yield absolute purchasing power parity. Useful for making comparisons of real values (wages, GDP) across countries with different currencies. Since the purchasing power parity theory is rarely correct, this contrasts with the nominal exchange rate.

■ **purchasing power parity theory**
a theory of the exchange rate that the rate will adjust to achieve purchasing power parity, in either its absolute or its relative form.

■ **push-pull factors**
push factors act to drive people or goods and services away from a place whereas pull factors draw them to a new location.

■ **quad**
refers both to the Quadrilateral Meetings and to the participants in those meetings, the US, Canada, EU and Japan.

■ **quadrilateral meetings**
meetings that occur occasionally involving the trade ministers of the US, Canada, EU and Japan to discuss trade policy issues.

■ **quality multiplier**
secondary effects resulting from learning, innovative activities and quality improvements of existing products or technologies.

■ **Quantitative Restriction (QR)**
a restriction on trade, usually imports, limiting the quantity of the good or service that is traded. A quota is the most common example, but VERs usually take the form of QRs. QRs on traded services are more likely to restrict the number or activities of foreign service providers than the ser-

vices themselves, since the latter are hard to monitor and measure.

# quantity definition

a method of defining relative factor abundance based on ratios of factor quantities: Compared to country B, country A is abundant in factor X relative to factor Y iff $XA/YA > XB/YB$, where IJ is the quantity of factor I with which country J is endowed, I=X,Y, J=A,B.

# quantity quota

a quota specifying quantity in units, weight, volume, etc. of a good.

# quantity theory of money

the idea that there is a direct link between the quantity of money in the economy and the price level.

# quarter

one of the four three-month periods into which the calendar year is divided for the reporting of economic data.

# quartile

one of four segments of a distribution that has been divided into quarters. For example, the second-from-the-bottom quartile of an income distribution is those whose income exceeds the incomes of from 25% to 50% of the population.

# quasi-linear utility

a utility function of the form $U(x0,x1,...,xn) = x0 + Siui(xi)$, where $ui(\times)$ are strictly concave functions. This is useful for generating demand functions for goods xi that depend only on their own prices in terms of the numeraire x0.

# quaternary & quinary (economic) activities

a further disaggregation of that part of the service sector (business services) which is information oriented into quaternary activities (referring to activities which involve the collection, recording, arranging, storage, retrieval, exchange and dissemination of information) and quinary activities which emphasise the creation, rearrangement and interpretation of new and old ideas and information as well as innovation of methods in data interpretation.

# quid pro quo FDI

FDI in response to the threat of protection. Done by a firm that exports into the domestic market, the motive is to create jobs there and lessen the threat that its exports will be restricted. Due to Bhagwati (1985).

# quintile

one of five segments of a distribution that has been divided into fifths. For example, the second-from-the-bottom quintile of an income distribution is those whose income exceeds the incomes of from 20% to 40% of the population.

- **quota**

  a limitation on the amount of a good that can be produced or offered for sale domestically or internationally.

- **quota by country**

  a quota that specifies the total amount to be imported (or exported) and also assigns specific amounts to each exporting (or importing) country.

- **quota rent**

  the economic rent received by the holder of the right (or license) to

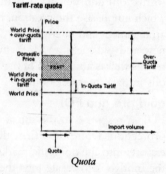

*Quota*

import under a quota. Equals the domestic price of the imported good, net of any tariff, minus the world price, times the quantity of imports.

- **radical political economy**

  see **political economy**.

- **random variable**

  an economic or statistical variable that takes on multiple (or a continuum of) values, each with some probability that is specified by a probability distribution (or probability density function).

- **range**

  usually used in the context of the 'outer range' of a good. This range refers to the maximum distance over which a product can be sold at a given FOB price.

- **ration**

  1. in the presence of excess demand (for a good, etc.), to allocate among demanders by some means other than the price they are willing to pay.
  2. the quantity of a rationed good allocated to one demander.

- **ration foreign exchange**

  to ration access to scarce foreign currency under a pegged exchange rate with an over-valued currency. Usually done by means of import licensing. See **exchange control.**

- **raw material**

  a good that has not been transformed by production, a primary product.

- **reaction coefficient**

  terms used as a relatively general reference to the manner in which a dependent subsystem is (structurally) linked to another subsystem within a larger systems model. The coefficient specifies the impact of a change in one variable (representing the independent subsystem) on another variable (representing the dependent subsystem). Input-output coefficients, 'propensities to consume locally' (pcl) and probabilities in transition matrices represent examples.

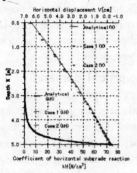

*Reaction Coefficient*

■ **reaction curve**
the graph of a **reaction function**.

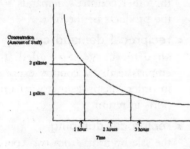

*Reaction Curve*

■ **reaction function**
the function specifying the choice of a strategic variable by one economic agent as a function of the choice of another agent. Most familiar specifying output choices of firms in a Cournot duopoly.

■ **real**
1. adjusted for inflation.
2. referring only to real economic variables as opposed to nominal or monetary ones, as in real models.

3. used with 'appreciation' or 'depreciation,' refers to the real exchange rate. Thus, a real appreciation means that the nominal value of a country's currency has increased by more than its relative price level may have decreased, so that the prices of its goods relative to foreign goods have increased.

■ **real balance effect**
the influence that a change in the quantity of real money has on the quantity of real national income demanded.

■ **Real Estate Investment Trust (REIT)**
a trust (corporation) that pools the capital of different investors to acquire (or provide financing for) all forms of real estate. A REIT functions like a mutual fund for real estate.

■ **real exchange rate**
1. the nominal exchange rate adjusted for inflation. Unlike most other real variables, this adjustment requires accounting for price levels in two currencies. The real exchange rate is: $R = EP^*/P$ where E is the nominal domestic-currency price of foreign currency, P is the domestic price level and $P^*$ is the foreign price level.
2. the real price of foreign goods; i.e., the quantity of domestic goods needed to purchase a unit of foreign goods. Equals the reciprocal of the terms of trade. Equivalent

to definition 1.

3. the relative price of traded goods in terms of nontraded goods.

■ **real interest rate**
the nominal interest rate adjusted for inflation, to get the percentage yield an asset holder gets in terms of real resources. Equals the nominal interest rate minus the rate of inflation.

■ **real model**
an economic model without money. Most general equilibrium models of trade are real models. This includes the Ricardian Model, the Heckscher-Ohlin Model and the models of the New Trade Theory.

■ **real national income**
national income adjusted for inflation.

■ **real terms**
same as real. A 'wage expressed in real terms' is just the real wage.

■ **real trade**
a shorthand term for most of the theory of international trade, which consists largely of real models. Contrasts with international finance.

■ **real wage**
the wage of labour or more generally, the price of any factor, relative to an appropriate price index for the goods and services that the worker (or factor owner) consumes.

■ **recession**
a not very well defined term that indicates a slowdown in economic activity. A particularly long-lasting and painful recession is known as a depression.

■ **reciprocal demand**
the concept that, in international trade, it is not just supply and demand that interact, but demand and demand. That is, a trading equilibrium is a reciprocal equilibrium in which one country's demand for another country's products (and willingness to pay for them with its own) matches with the other country's demands for the products of the first.

■ **reciprocal demand curve**
an offer curve. So called, to emphasise that a country exports in order, reciprocally, to get imports in return.

■ **reciprocal dumping**
the sale by firms from two countries into each others' markets for prices below what each charges at home. So called because the exports of both firms meet the price-discrimination definition of dumping.

■ **reciprocal trade agreement**
agreement between two countries to open their markets to each other's exports, usually by each reducing tariffs. Early trade rounds under the GATT consisted mostly of reciprocal trade agreements, extended to other contracting parties by the MFN requirement.

- **reciprocity**
  a principle that underlies GATT negotiations, that countries exchange comparable concessions.

- **red box**
  a category of subsidies that is forbidden under WTO rules. This terminology is used in the Agriculture Agreement, where however there is no red box. Presumably equivalent to prohibited subsidies.

- **redistributed tariff revenue**
  a common assumption that tariff revenue is given to consumers as transfer payments (not in proportion to what they paid by importing) to be spent like any other income. Since in general equilibrium the effects of a tariff depend on how the revenue is spent, this is a useful neutral assumption.

- **redistribution policy**
  measures taken by government to transfer income from some individuals to others.

- **redundant tariff**
  a tariff that, if changed, will not change the quantity of imports, either because the tariff is prohibitive or because some other policy such as a quota or an embargo is limiting quantity.

- **reexport**
  the export without further processing or transformation of a good that has been imported.

- **reference price**
  see **minimum price system**.

- **reflation**
  expansionary monetary or fiscal policy.

- **reflexivity**
  a post-structuralist concept increasingly used in industrial social geography to capture the ability of person to 'reflect on their own reflections' and to understand the foundations of one's own knowledge and understanding of one's local environment and context.

- **region**
  contiguous areas with common or complementary characteristics or linked by intensive interaction or flows.

- **regional aid**
  a subsidy directed at a geographic region of a country to assist its development. Such subsidies are non-actionable under WTO rules.

- **regional policy**
  in a trade context, this usually refers to a regional aid.

- **regionalism**
  the formation or proliferation of preferential trading arrangements.

- **regression analysis**
  the statistical technique of finding a straight line that approximates the information in a group of data points. Used throughout empirical economics, including in both international trade and finance.

- **regressive tax**
  a tax on income in which the proportion of tax paid relative to in-

come decreases as income increases.

■ **regulation school/theory**
a body of thought originating in French political economy focusing on structure and change of the capitalist economy. Rejecting market forces as allocative mechanisms, these theories suggest the dominance of the 'mode of regulation' (social norms, government rules and private practices) which motivate(s) individuals to achieve economic stability.

■ **Reilly's law of retail gravitation**
a statement related to the distribution of market share in hinterlands of competing cities or shopping centres.

■ **relative demand**
the ratio of the demand for one good to the demand for another, most useful in representing general equilibrium in a two-good economy, where relative price adjusts to equate relative supply and relative demand.

■ **relative location**
a position in space (location) defined on the basis of distances and relationships to other locations.

■ **relative price**
1. the price of one thing (usually a good) in terms of another, i.e., the ratio of two prices. The relative of good X in terms of good Y is $pX/pY$.
2. the relationship between the prices of different goods and services. May be thought of in terms of the amount of one good which can be had for a certain expenditure compared to the amount of another good which can be had for the same expenditure.

■ **relative supply**
the ratio of the supply of one good to the supply of another, most useful in representing general equilibrium in a two-good economy, where relative price adjusts to equate relative supply and relative demand.

■ **reliability**
the ability of a statistical instrument to come up with similar/consistent measurements/results over time.

■ **remedy**
a trade dispute in the WTO or other forum, the measure recommended by the dispute settlement panel to resolve the dispute, usually a measure that will bring the offending country into compliance with WTO (or other) rules.

■ **rent**
1. economic rent or the premium that the owner of a resource receives over and above its opportunity cost.
2. the payment to the owner of land or other property in return for its use.

■ **rent gradient**
2. a representation of the decline in rent with distance from a market or centre.

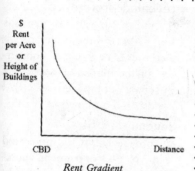

*Rent Gradient*

CBD          Distance

### rent seeking
the using up of real resources in an effort to secure the rights to economic rents that arise from government policies. In international economics the term usually refers to efforts to obtain quota rents.

### rental price
the payment per unit time for the services of a unit of a factor of production, such as land or capital.

### rentier
a person whose income comes mainly from rent on land or, more broadly, from assets rather than labour.

### rent-seeking
the activities of individuals or firms to obtain special privileges, such as monopoly power, which will enable them to increase their incomes. Using up resources to win such privileges from governments or their agencies.

### Research and Development (R&D)
the use of resources for the deliberate discovery of new information and ways of doing things, together with the application of that information in inventing new products or processes.

- **reserve asset**
  any asset that is used as international reserves, including a national currency, precious metal such as gold or SDRs.

- **reserve currency**
  a currency that is used as international reserves, often because it is an intervention currency.

- **reserves**
  international reserves.

- **resources**
  all those things which can be used to produce economic satisfaction.

- **restricted trade**
  trade that is restrained in some fashion by tariffs, transport costs or NTBs.

- **restrictive business practice**
  action by a firm or group of firms to restrict entry by other firms, that is, to prevent other firms from selling their product in their market. This is a restraint of competition and would normally be illegal under competition policy.

- **results-based trade policy**
  the use of trade policies targeted to specific indicators of economic performance. For example, in the early 1990s, the US insisted on achieving specified market shares in trade with Japan.

### ■ retaliation

1. the use of an increased trade barrier in response to another country increasing its trade barrier, either as a way of undoing the adverse effects of the latter's action or of punishing it.

2. the formal procedure permitted under the GATT, whereby a country may raise discriminatory tariffs above bound levels against a GATT member that has violated GATT rules and not provided compensation.

### ■ retrospective analysis

ex post analysis.

### ■ return to capital

same as the rental price of capital. Since capital can only be measured in monetary units, the rental price is, say, dollars per dollar's worth of capital per unit time and it therefore has the form of a rate of return like an interest rate.

### ■ returns to scale

same as **increasing returns to scale**.

### ■ Revealed Comparative Advantage (RCA)

Balassa's (1965) measure of relative export performance by country and industry, defined as a country's share of world exports of a good divided by its share of total world exports. The index for country i good j is $RCA_{ij} = 100(X_{ij} / X_{wj})/(X_{it} / X_{wt})$ where $X_{ab}$ is exports by country a (w=world) of good b (t=total for all goods).

### ■ revealed preference

the use of the value of expenditure to 'reveal' the preference of a consumer or group of consumers for the bundle of goods they purchase compared to other bundles of equal or smaller value.

### ■ revenue

referring to a tariff, the money collected by the government. Equals the size of the tariff times the quantity of imports. An analysis of the effects of a tariff needs to account for the revenue and in a general equilibrium model it must specify whether and how the revenue is spent.

### ■ revenue argument for a tariff

the use of a tariff to raise revenue for the government. Many other kinds of tax cause smaller distortions and are therefore preferable to tariffs for this purpose. However, a tariff is one of the easier taxes to collect and it is therefore common in the early stages of a country's development.

### ■ revenue seeking

the use of real resources in an effort to secure a share of the disposition of tariff revenues.

### ■ reverse engineering

the process of learning how a product is made by taking it apart and examining it.

### ■ Ricardian Model

the classic model of international trade introduced by David Ricardo to explain the pattern and the gains from trade in terms of comparative advantage. It assumes perfect competition and a single factor of production, labour, with constant requirements of labour per unit of output that differ across countries.

# Ricardo Point

on the world PPF of a two-country, 2-good Ricardian Model, the point at which each country is specialised in production of a different good, the kink of the world PPF.

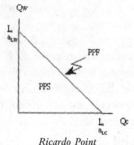

*Ricardo Point*

# Ricardo, David (1772-1823)

born in London, Ricardo had a successful financial career in the City. He developed a strong interest in the work of Adam Smith and other early contributors to economics such as Jeremy Bentham and Thomas Malthus. He had a life-long friendship with the latter, although their ideas were usually sharply conflicting. Ricardo wrote several influential pamphlets on economic issues of his day, particularly on taxation and commercial policy. In 1817, he published his major work, *Prin-*

*ciples of Political Economy and Taxation*. Smith, Malthus and Ricardo are generally regarded as the main members of the classical school of economics.

# Ricardo-Viner Model

the specific factors model, named after just two of the many who used this as the standard model of trade prior to the Heckscher-Ohlin Model. It extends the simple Ricardian Model by allowing the marginal product of labour to fall with output.

# Rio Summit

the United Nations Conference on Environment and Development, held 3-14 June 1992 in Rio de Janeiro, Brazil. 172 governments participated, including 108 heads of state. Also called the Earth Summit.

# risk

1. uncertainty associated with a transaction or an asset.
2. the probability of loss. Differs from definition 1, because 'uncertainty' includes probability of gain as well.

■ **risk aversion**
desire to avoid uncertainty. Risk aversion is usually quantified by the mathematical expected value that one is willing to forego in order to get greater certainty.

■ **risk premium**
1. the higher expected return (in the sense of mathematical expected value) that an uncertain asset must pay in order for risk averse investors to be willing to hold it.
2. the difference between the interest rate on a risky asset and that on a safe one.
3. in exchange markets the difference between the forward rate and the expected future spot rate.

■ **Robinson, Joan (1903-83)**
born in Surrey, England. A prominent Cambridge economist, Joan Robinson first attracted attention with her work on imperfect competition which became the basis of standard expositions in university textbooks on economic theory, but which she subsequently repudiated. She was a powerful advocate of Keynesian economics in the 1930s and 40s. After World War II, she sought to develop a dynamic version of the Keynesian model and her work was the basis for what is sometimes called 'neo-Keynesianism', a radical form of Keynesianism associated with a small group of economists at Cambridge.

■ **rollback**
1. the phasing out of measures that are not consistent with an agreement.
2. in the Uruguay Round, the agreement to remove all GATT-inconsistent trade-restricting and trade-distorting measures by the time negotiations were completed. See standstill.

■ **round**
see **trade round**.

■ **routine**
general term for all regular and predictable behavioural patterns of firms.

■ **rule of law**
a legal system in which rules are clear, well-understood and fairly enforced, including property rights and enforcement of contracts.

■ **Rules of Origin (ROO)**
rules included in a FTA specifying when a good will be regarded as produced within the FTA, so as to cross between members without tariff. Typical ROOs are based on per-

centage of value added or on changes in tariff heading.

## rules-based trade policy
institutional arrangements in which national trade policies are governed by internationally agreed-upon rules, as in the GATT and WTO.

## Rybczynski Theorem
the property of the Heckscher-Ohlin Model that, at constant prices, an increase in the endowment of one factor increases the output of the industry that uses that factor intensively and reduces the output of the other (or some other) industry. Due to Rybczynski (1955).

## sales tax
a tax levied on the sale of a good or service, which is usually proportional to the price of the good or service sold.

## sanction
1. to approve or give permission for an action, as when an international organisation sanctions the use of particular economic policies.

## Sanitary and phytosanitary regulations
government standards to protect health of humans, plants and animals. SPS measures are subject to rules in the WTO to prevent them from acting as NTBs.

## SAP
Structural Adjustment Program.

## satisficer, satisficing
references to behaviours which are constrained by limited information and 'bounded rationality'. Satisficers' behavioural objectives are associated with finding satisfactory solutions (instead of 'optimal' solutions) to problems which, in turn, are conditioned by the individual's 'aspiration levels'. The concept of satisficing originates with H.O.Simon (1950s).

## satisficing
seeking or achieving a satisfactory outcome, rather than the best possible. Contrasts with the optimising behavior usually assumed in economics and trade theory. Alternative models based on satisficing are spreading within economics, but not yet much in international.

## saving
the act of abstaining from consumption. In terms of the national accounts, the difference between personal income less taxes and total consumption spending.

## saving function
the relationship between saving and national income.

## scale economies
increasing returns to scale.

## scarce
available in small supply, opposite of abundant. Usually meaningful only in relative terms, compared to demand and/or to supply at another place or time. See **factor abundance, factor scarcity.**

## scarce factor
the factor in a country's endow-

ment with which it is least well endowed, relative to other factors, compared to other countries. May be defined by quantity or by price.

■ **scarcity**
the fact that human wants exceed the means of satisfying them.

■ **scarcity rent**
an economic rent that is due to something being scarce.

■ **schedule**
1. a table or list of values.
2. a graph ofa list of data, thus also a curve.

■ **schedule**
1. a list. See **tariff schedule**.

■ **Schengen Agreement**
an agreement (later, convention) signed in 1985 to remove all frontier controls and permit free movement of persons between the participating countries. In 1999 it was incorporated into the European Union. Currently (2001), the participants include all EU countries except Ireland and the UK, plus Iceland and Norway.

■ **Schumpeter, Joseph (1883-1950)**
an Austrian-born economist who had a broadly-based career as a lawyer, banker, teacher and senior civil servant in Austria before migrating to the US where he became a professor economics at Harvard in 1932. His scholarly writing ranges over topics as diverse as business cycles and the historical evolution of capitalism. He is perhaps best known today for his defence of monopoly, which he developed in conjunction with his view that the success of capitalism was largely attributable to the freedom it allowed for innovation and entrepreneurial activity.

*Schumpeter, Joseph*

■ **scientific tariff**
a made-to-measure tariff.

■ **Scitovszky indifference curve**
an indifference curve for a group of individuals representing the minimum needed to keep all of them at given levels of utility. A well-behaved family of such indifference curves is defined holding utilities of all but one individual constant and varying only the one These are useful in discussing the gains from trade. Due to Scitovszky (1942).

■ **SDR**
Special Drawing Right

■ **seasonal quota**
a restriction on the quantity of imports of a good for a specified period of the year.

■ **seasonal tariff**
a tariff that is levied at different rates at different times of the year, usually on agricultural products, being highest at the time of the domestic harvest.

■ **seasonal unemployment**
unemployment which occurs regularly because of seasonal changes in the demand for certain kinds of labour.

■ **second best**
refers to what is the optimal policy when the true optimum (the first best) is unavailable due to constraints on policy choice. The Theory of Second Best says that a policy that would be optimal without such constraints (such as a zero tariff in a small country) may not be second-best optimal if other policies are constrained.

■ **secondary tariffs**
any charges imposed on imports in addition to the statutory tariff, such as an import surcharge.

■ **second-best argument for protection**
1. any argument for protection that can be countered by pointing to a different and less distortionary policy that would achieve the same desired result at lower economic cost.
2. an argument for protection to partially correct an existing distortion in the economy when the first-best policy for that purpose is not available. For example, if domestic production generates a positive externality and a production subsidy to internalize it is not available, then a tariff may be second-best optimal.

■ **secular change**
change over a long period of time, such as a decade or more. Distinguished from cyclical change which occurs in shorter time periods such as a year.

■ **segmentation**
a segmented pattern of business organisations where every segment is 'conceived as a number of organisations, with similar characteristics which are both the cause and the effect of their membership of particular economic niches.'

■ **seigniorage**
the difference between what money can buy and its cost of production. Therefore, seigniorage is the benefit that a government or other monetary authority derives from the ability to create money. In international exchange, if one country's money is willingly held by another, the first country derives these seigniorage benefits. This is the case of a reserve currency.

■ **selective**
applied to a trade policy, this means one that affects only some

countries, not all, in contrast to MFN policy. Selectivity is an important concern in the use of safeguards, which countries often would prefer to make selective but are required by GATT Article XIX to be nondiscriminatory.

■ **selective closure**
a form of plant closure where the decision-maker has options between different plants and where the ultimate decision is based on relative (internal and/or external) locational merits. This type of closure is 'the most spatially specific type of closure'

■ **self-sufficiency**
provision by one's self of all of one's own needs. In international trade this means either not trading at all (autarky) or importing only non-necessities.

■ **self-sufficiency argument for protection**
the view that a country is better off providing for its own needs than depending on imports. It may be based on fear that war or foreign governments will interrupt imports. This is a second-best argument, since many policies could provide for that contingency without sacrificing all the gains from trade.

■ **sensitive**
in trade negotiations and agreements, countries often identify lists of particular sensitive products or sensitive sectors that they regard

as especially vulnerable to import competition and that they wish to exempt from trade liberalisation.

■ **serious injury**
the injury requirement of the escape clause, understood to be more stringent than material injury but otherwise apparently not rigorously defined.

■ **service**
a product that is not embodied in a physical good and that typically effects some change in another product, person or institution. Contrasts with good. Trade in services is the subject of the GATS.

■ **shadow price**
the implicit value or cost associated with a constraint. That is, the increased value that will be achieved by relaxing the constraint by one unit. When foreign exchange is rationed, the shadow price of foreign exchange becomes the relevant exchange rate decisions.

■ **shallow integration**
reduction or elimination of tariffs, quotas and other barriers to trade in goods at the border, such as trade-limiting customs procedures. Contrasts with deep integration.

■ **shared vision**
one of Senge's five learning disciplines for the learning organisation: 'building a sense of commitment in a group, by developing shared images of the future we seek to create and the principles and guid-

ing practices by which we hope to get there.'

■ **shareholder**

owner of some fraction of the stock issued by a corporation.

■ **shelf life**

the length of time that a good can be stored while still remaining useful enough to sell. Important for both perishable goods and goods that may become obsolete for reasons of technology or fashion. Relevant for international trade when, for example, customs procedures cause delays.

■ **Shimbel Index**

measure of the minimum number of links necessary to connect one node with all nodes in the network.

■ **Shitauke gaisha**

a Japanese term that refers to a subcontract(ed) company.

■ **shock**

1. an unexpected change.
2. any change in an exogenous variable (although strictly speaking, models often fail to deal adequately with the complications of an exogenous change being expected).

■ **short**

1. used with 'sell' or 'sale,' this means that the seller does not currently have the thing being sold, but intends to acquire it on the market prior to making delivery.
2. used by itself as a verb, it means

to sell short, as 'to short a currency', meaning to sell it forward in anticipation that its value on the spot market will fall.

■ **short run**

1. in the theory of the firm, a period of time which is too short for changes to be made in all inputs. For example, a period not long enough to permit the size of the physical plant to be altered.
2. referring to a short time horizon, usually one in which some aspects of behaviour that would vary over a longer time do not have time to do so. In trade models, it usually means that the employment of some factors of production is fixed. Contrasts with long run.

■ **Shrimp-Turtle Case**

a case filed in the WTO against the United States for restricting imports of shrimp from countries whose shrimp were caught by means that endangered sea turtles. The WTO ruled against the US, enraging many environmentalists.

■ **shuttle trade**

the trade accomplished by individuals and groups travelling to other countries, buying goods and bringing them home, often in their luggage, to resell. An important source of imports for Russia in 1990s, some people travelling abroad several times a month for this purpose.

- **silver standard**
  a monetary system in which the value of a currency is defined in terms of silver. If two currencies are both on a silver standard, then the exchange rate between them is approximately determined by their two prices in terms of silver.

- **simple money multiplier**
  the amount by which a change in the monetary base is multiplied to bring about the eventual change in the total money supply. It is called the simple money multiplier because it does not take into account possible offsets to the process, such as a rise in the amount of money individuals or households may choose to hold as cash when the money supply increases.

- **single market**
  removal of the remaining barriers among the countries of the European Union, permitting the free movement of goods, persons, services and capital. Also known as Europe 1992.

- **single proprietorship**
  a form of unincorporated business in which there is only one owner.

- **single undertaking**
  a term, in trade negotiations, for requiring participants to accept or reject the outcome of multiple negotiations in a single package, rather than selecting among them.

- **site**
  a reference to the physical attributes of a location ('absolute location').

- **situation**
  a reference to the 'relational' attributes of a location, i.e. to the location relative to (in relationships with) other key locations ('relative location').

- **size distribution of income**
  the distribution of income among groups of income recipients defined on the basis of the size of their incomes.

- **skill**
  the abilities acquired by workers through education, training and experience that permit them to be more productive. Essentially the same as human capital.

- **skill intensive**
  describing an industry or sector of the economy that relies relatively heavily on inputs of skilled labour, usually relative to unskilled labour, compared to other industries or sectors. See **factor intensity**.

- **skill-biased**
  a technological change or technological difference that is biased in favour of using more skilled labour, compared to some definition of neutrality.

- **skilled labour**
  labour with a high level of skill or human capital. Identified empirically as labour earning a high wage, with a high level of education or

in an occupational category associated with these. Sometimes crudely proxied as nonproduction workers.

# SMAC function

an acronym for the CES function based on the names of the four authors who introduced it in Arrow et al. (1961).

# small country assumption

the assumption in an economic model that a country is too small to affect world prices, incomes or interest rates.

# small open economy

an economy that is small enough compared to the world markets in which it participates that (as a good approximation) its policies do not alter world prices or incomes. The country is thus a price taker in world markets. The term is normally applied to a country as a whole, although it is sometimes used in the context of only a single product.

# Smith, Adam (1723-90)

generally regarded as the founder of modern economics, Adam Smith was born in 1723 in Kirkaldy, Scotland. Educated at Glasgow College and at Oxford, he eventually gained the chair of moral philosophy at the University of Edinburgh. He published his *Theory of Moral Sentiments* in 1759 and his great work, *An Inquiry into the Nature and Causes of the Wealth of Na-*

*tions* in 1776. The latter was an immediate success and its influence is still felt today. Perhaps, its most famous passage is that in which Smith elaborated on his notion that individuals are motivated not by altruism, but by self-interest. In pursing their own interests, however, they inadvertently advance the interest of society as a whole, led as it were by 'an invisible hand.'

# smuggle

to take a good across a national border illegally. If the good itself is legal, the purpose is usually to avoid paying a tariff or to circumvent some other trade barrier.

# social benefit

the benefit to society as a whole from an event, action or policy change. Includes externalities and deducts any benefits that are transfers from others, in contrast to private benefit.

# social cost

1. the real cost to society of having a good or service produced, which may be greater than the private costs incorporated by the producer in its market price.
2. the cost to society as a whole from an event, action or policy change. Includes negative externalities and does not count costs that are transfers to others, in contrast to private cost.

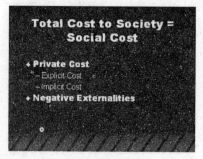

*Social Cost*

■ **Social Darwinists**
a disparate group of turn-of-the-century commentators on social issues who sought to utilise the Darwinian law of natural selection ('survival of the fittest') as a basis for social policy. The best-known of the social Darwinists was Herbert Spencer.

■ **social dumping**
export of a good from a country with weak or poorly enforced labour standards, reflecting the idea that the exporter has costs that are artificially lower than its competitors in higher-standards countries, constituting an unfair advantage in international trade.

■ **social indifference curve**
a curve showing the combinations of goods that, when available to a country, yield the same level of social welfare.

■ **social welfare function**
a function mapping levels of utility of the individuals in an economy to a level of welfare for the economy as a whole.

■ **SOE**
1. State-owned enterprise.
2. Small open economy.

■ **sole importing agency**
an entity, either private or government, that has been granted by government the exclusive right to import certain goods.

■ **Solow model**
the neoclassical growth model. Also called the Solow-Swan Model.

■ **Solow neutral**
a particular specification of technological change or technological difference that is capital augmenting.

■ **Solow residual**
a measure of technological progress equal to the difference between the rate of growth of output and the weighted average of the rates of growth of capital and labour, with factor income shares as weights. Due to Solow (1957). Also called the growth of total factor productivity. Used to compare sources of growth across countries.

■ **sound money**
a currency that is responsibly managed so as to avoid excessive inflation.

■ **source country**
see **FDI**.

■ **sovereignty**
a country or region's power and ability to rule itself and manage its own affairs. Some feel that

membership in international organisations such as the WTO are a threat to their sovereignty.

■ **space-cost curve**
expresses the spatial variability of total production costs of a firm with a given output level. Smith (1966) superimposed this spatial cost curve on the spatial revenue curve in order to determine the 'spatial margin of profitability'.

■ **spatial demand curve**
refers to the aggregate demand curve containing the individual demand of consumers located at different distances from the focal point of supply. In other words, demand is aggregated across space, as seen from the perspective of the supplier (and her fob prices), as if the delivered price of the good is increasing for the consumer with distance by the corresponding transport cost.

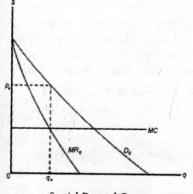

*Spatial Demand Curve*

■ **spatial entrapment**
a concept used to describe the situation of women restricted to distinctly female labour markets close to children and home in the urban periphery.

■ **spatial iso-outlay line**
this is a theoretical construct used to introduce space into micro-economic production theory. The curve represents the results of an optimisation process. Every point on the curve represents different locations but equal total production costs (outlays) based on varying (optimal) input combinations (and resulting varying transport costs for these inputs).

■ **spatial margin**
a line or boundary signifying the end of profitability or viability thus separating profitable from loss-making spaces.

■ **spatial margin of agricultural production**
the boundary of a region of profitability or positive rent. Beyond this boundary, transport costs outweigh net-returns leading to net losses.

■ **special and differential treatment**
the GATT principle that developing countries be accorded special privileges, exempting them from some requirements of developed countries. It also permits tariff preferences among developing

countries and by developed countries in favour of developing countries, as under the GSP.

- ### Special Drawing Right (SDR)
originally intended within the IMF as a sort of international money for use among central banks pegging their exchange rates, the SDR is a transferable right to acquire another country's currency. Defined in terms of a basket of currencies, today it plays the role in that form of a unit of international account.

- ### special economic zone
these exist in several countries, including especially China and their characteristics vary. Typically, they are regions designated for economic development oriented towards inward FDI and exports, both fostered by special policy incentives that may include being an EPZ.

- ### special entry procedure
an administrative procedure that is required as a condition of entry for an imported good, such as transport by the importing country's national fleet or entry through a specific port or customs station.

- ### specialisation
producing more than you need of some things and less of others, hence 'specialising' in the first. In international trade, this is just the opposite of self-sufficiency.

- ### specie
coins, normally including only those made of precious metal.

- ### specie flow mechanism
under the gold standard, the mechanism by which international payments would adjust. A country with high inflation would export less, import more and thus lose specie, i.e., gold. With the money supply fixed to the quantity of gold, the resulting monetary contraction would reduce prices. Due to David Hume.

- ### specific commitment
under the GATS, the identification of a category of services in which a country will apply national treatment and assure market access for foreign service providers.

- ### specific factor
a factor of production that is unable to move into or out of an industry. The term is used to describe both factors that would not be of any use in other industries and — more loosely — factors that could be used elsewhere but do not, in the short run, have the time or resources needed to move. See specific factors model. The term seems to come from Haberler (1937).

- ### specific factors model
a model in which some or all factors are specific factors. Must commonly, the specific factors model has one specific factor (often capital or land) in each industry plus another factor (often

labour) that is mobile between them. But an extreme form of the model can have all factors specific. See Ricardo-Viner Model.

■ **specific tariff**
a tariff specified as an amount of currency per unit of the good.

■ **specificity**
the property that a policy measure applies to one or a group of enterprises or industries, as opposed to all industries.

■ **specificity rule**
the principle that the optimal policy for correcting a distortion is one that deals most directly or specifically, with that distortion.

■ **speculation**
the purchase or sale of an asset (or acquisition otherwise of an open position) in hopes that its price will rise or fall respectively, in order to make a profit. See destabilising speculation and stabilising speculation.

■ **speculative attack**
in any asset market, the surge in sales of the asset that occurs when investors expect its price to fall. A common phenomenon in the exchange market, especially under an adjustable pegged exchange rate.

■ **speculator**
anyone who engages in speculation. May include those who transfer their assets into different forms (or currencies) in order to avoid a prospective capital loss.

■ **Spencer, Herbert (1820-1903)**
a British philosopher and early sociologist. Spencer was trained mainly in engineering, but he developed an early interest in social science. He became involved with several radical social movements and tried to develop an ambitious, but never fully coherent philosophical system he called "Synthetic Philosophy." He published three major books: *Social Statics*, 1850; *The Man versus the State*, 1884; and *The Principles of Ethics*, 1892-3. His social theories were founded on the conviction that the evolution of society from a state of brutal barbarism to modern industrial civilisation had depended on the subordination of the less capable members of society to their superiors. Any interventions which alleviated the circumstances of the less fit, Spencer contended, disrupted the operation of the benign natural processes which ensured progress by eliminating the idle, incompetent and unproductive members of society.

■ **splash page**

the entry page to a Website. The page uses flashy graphics to attract attention and often automatically refreshes into the actual home page or entry page to the substance of the site.

■ **splashing ('industrial splashing')**

a term used to refer to the establishment of multiple branch plants across the landscape (of Nigeria) by expatriate firms.

■ **splintering**

another term for fragmentation. Used by Bhagwati (1984).

■ **sporadic dumping**

intermittent dumping.

■ **spot**

on the spot market.

■ **spot market**

1. a market for exchange (of currencies, in the case of the exchange market) in the present (as opposed to a forward or futures market in which the exchange takes place in the future).
2. a market in which goods, services or financial assets are traded for immediate delivery. This differs from a futures market, where the delivery will be made at a future date.

■ **spot rate**

the exchange rate on the spot market. Also called the spot exchange rate.

■ **spread**

the difference between the price one must pay to buy something, such as a currency and the price one receives for selling it.

■ **stabilise**

to reduce the size of fluctuations in an economic variable, over time.

■ **stabilising speculation**

speculation that decreases the movements of the price in the market where the speculation occurs. See **destabilising speculation**. Freedman (1953) provided a classic argument that speculation on a floating exchange rate would be stabilising.

■ **stabilisation policy**

the use of monetary and fiscal policies to stabilise GDP, aggregate employment and prices.

■ **stable**

1. of an equilibrium, that the dynamic adjustment away from equilibrium converges to the equilibrium.
2. of an economic variable, not subject to large or erratic fluctuations.

■ **stakeholder**

all those claimants inside and outside the firm who have a vested interest in the organisation or any of its specific problems and solutions.

**stamp fee**

see **para tariff**.

**standard**

rule and/or procedure specifying characteristics that must be met for a product to be sold in a country's domestic market, typically to protect health and safety. When a standard puts foreign producers at a disadvantage, it may constitute an NTB.

**standard of living**

the concept has moved from a more or less strictly pecuniary interpretation of well-being to one which incorporates non-pecuniary components, thereby approaching the economist's concept of utility as expressed in a utility function. Dissatisfaction with using the simple measure of real per-capita GDP has lead to use of indicators which include length of life, level of education and access to jobs, infrastructure and amenities.

**standstill**

1. a commitment to refrain from introducing new measures that are not consistent with an agreement. 2. In the Uruguay Round, the agreement not to introduce new GATT-inconsistent trade-restricting and trade-distorting measures during the negotiations. See rollback.

**state trading enterprise**

an entity of government that is responsible for exporting and/or importing specified products. See **marketing board**.

**Stalin, Joseph Vissarionorich**

Lenin's disciple and successor as leader of the Soviet Union. Stalin reinforced the system of centralised state control after gaining power when Lenin died in 1924. Through systematic purging of dissenters from the Party apparatus, Stalin achieved supreme control and drove forward a massive program of industrial development and forced collectivisation of agriculture. As he once put it, "We lag behind the advanced countries by 50 to 100 years. We must make good this distance in ten years." Despite enormous losses due to famine in the 1930s and the devastation of World War II, by the time of his death Stalin had made the Soviet Union into a modern, industrial state, capable of challenging the United States for international economic, political and technological leadership.

**State-Owned Enterprise (SOE)**

a firm owned by government. Relations between SOEs and private firms on international markets raise special problems for GATT, since SOEs may not respond normally to market forces and their actions may reflect government policies.

**static gains from trade**

the economic benefits from trade that arise in static models, including the efficiency gains from exploiting comparative advantage, the reduced costs from scale economies, reduction in distortion from imperfect competition and increased product variety. Contrasts with dynamic gains from trade.

■ **static model**

an economic model that has no explicit time dimension. A static model abstracts from the process by which an equilibrium or an optimum might be reached only over time, as well as from the dependence of the variables in the model itself on a changing past or future. Contrasts with dynamic model.

■ **stationary state**

the economic condition envisioned by the classical writers once the growth of population had reached the point where output per capita was reduced to the subsistence level and the accumulation of capital had reduced the return to investment to zero. The economy would remain in equilibrium with no possibility of future increases in population or per capita incomes.

■ **statistical tax**

see **para tariff**.

■ **status quo**

the current situation. A preference for the status quo means a reluctance to change.

■ **steady state**

a type of equilibrium, especially in a neoclassical growth model, in which those variables that are not constant grow over time at a constant and common rate.

■ **sterilise**

to use offsetting open market operations to prevent an act of exchange market intervention from changing the monetary base. With sterilisation, any purchase of foreign exchange is accompanied by an equal-value sale of domestic bonds and vice versa.

■ **sticky place**

a concept used in industrial geography to refer to the geographic consequences of inertial forces which prevent hyper-mobility (in an increasingly 'slippery production space') from completely obliterating production assembles in space

■ **Stigler, George (1911- )**

Stigler was born and grew up in the western US and studied at the University of Washington, and Northwestern and Chicago. He subsequently taught at several universities in the American mid-west and at Columbia before settling down at the University of Chicago where he remained from 1958 until retirement in 1981. His published work covers a variety of topics in economic theory, including oligopoly, economies of scale and other aspects of industrial organisation. Some of his most original contributions have to do with the economics of information which he treated as a standard commodity subject to the usual influences of demand and supply and the economic theory of regulation.

*Stigler, George*

### stockpiling

the storage of something in order to have it available in the future if the need for it increases. In international economics, stockpiling occurs for speculative purposes, by governments to provide for national security and by central banks managing international reserves.

### stocks

a stock (also known as an equity or a share) is a portion of the ownership of a corporation. A share in a corporation gives the owner of the stock a stake in the company and its profits. If a corporation has issued 100 stocks in total, then each stock represents a 1% ownership in the company.

### ▪ Stolper-Samuelson Theorem

the proposition of the Heckscher-Ohlin Model that a rise in the relative price of a good raises the real wage of the factor used intensively in that industry and lowers the real wage of the other factor.

### ▪ straight-line PPF

the PPF that arises in the Ricardian Model or in the HO Model if the two sectors have the same factor intensity. It is a downward sloping straight line with, therefore, a constant marginal rate of transformation.

### ▪ strategic alliance

an agreement between companies for the purpose of achieving a common goal usually in the form of sharing complementary strengths, achieving cost efficiencies or adjusting to rapid technological or market changes.

### ▪ strategic decision-making

as different from programmed, routine decisions, strategic decisions tend to be relatively infrequent, not repetitive, involve the commitment of considerable resources (capital) and have long-time horizons with significant levels of uncertainty.

### ▪ strategic trade policy

the use of trade policies, including tariffs, subsidies and even export subsidies, in a context of imperfect competition and/or increasing returns to scale to alter the outcome of international competition in a country's favour, usually by allowing its firms to capture a larger share of industry profits. The seminal contribution was Brander and Spencer (1981).

■ **strategic variable**
an economic variable that is chosen with regard to and sometimes with a view to influencing, economic behaviour by someone else. Most frequently refers to the choice of firms in an oligopoly.

■ **strategy**
determination of the basic long-term goals and objectives of an enterprise and the adoption of courses of action and the allocation of resources necessary for carrying out these goals.

■ **structural adjustment**
the reallocation of resources (labour and capital) among sectors of the economy in response to changing economic circumstances, including trading conditions or changes in policy.

■ **structural adjustment program**
the list of budgetary and policy changes required by the IMF and World Bank in order for a developing country to qualify for a loan. This 'conditionality' typically includes reducing barriers to trade and capital flows, tax increases and cuts in government spending.

■ **stumbling block**
the term that Bhagwati (1991) used, together with building block, to address whether PTAs help move the world towards or away from multilateral free trade.

■ **subcontracting**
1. work contracted by a principal to a third-party 'subcontractor', who has to perform according to specifications.
2. delegation by one firm of a portion of its production process, under contract, to another firm, including in another country. An example of fragmentation.

■ **subsidy**
a payment by government, perhaps implicit, to the private sector in return for some activity that it wants to reward, encourage or assist. Under WTO rules, subsidies may be prohibited, actionable or non-actionable.

■ **subsistence agriculture**
an agricultural production system designed to satisfy the consumption needs of the farmer's household with no or little ability to produce a surplus.

■ **substitute goods**
goods which may be used in place of other goods.

■ **substitution effect**
1. the change in the quantity of a good demanded resulting from a change in its relative price, leaving aside any change in quantity demanded that can be attributable

to the associated change in the consumer's real income. It may also be thought of as a change in the quantity demanded as a result of a movement along a single indifference curve.

2. that portion of the effect of price on quantity demanded that reflects the changed tradeoff between the good and other alternatives. Contrasts with income effect.

### sunk costs

costs that are irrevocable and should not be used to influence current decisions.

### sunset clause

a provision within a piece of legislation providing for its demise on a specified date unless it is deliberately renewed.

### sunset industry argument

the argument, in contrast to the infant industry argument, that a mature industry should be provided protection, either to help it restore its competitiveness or to cushion its exit from the economy.

### superior good

a good the demand for which is elastic.

### supply

1. the act of offering a product for sale.
2. the total quantity of a good or service that is available for purchase at a given price.

### supply curve

the graph of quantity supplied as a function of price, normally upward sloping, straight or curved and drawn with quantity on the horizontal axis and price on the vertical axis. Supply curves for exports and for foreign exchange usually have the same qualitative properties as supply curves for labour, being potentially backward bending.

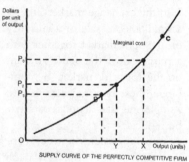

SUPPLY CURVE OF THE PERFECTLY COMPETITIVE FIRM

### ■ supply elasticity

the elasticity of a supply function, usually with respect to price.

### ■ supply price

the price at which a given quantity is supplied. The supply curve viewed from the perspective of price as a function of quantity.

### ■ surplus

in the balance of payments or in any category of international transactions within it, the surplus is the sum of credits minus the sum of debits. Also called simply the 'balance' for that category. Thus, the balance of trade is the same as the surplus on trade or the trade surplus and similarly for merchandise trade, current account and capital account.

■ **sustainable development**
1. a system of resource use that protects non-renewable resources and the environment.
2. economic development that is achieved without undermining the incomes, resources or environment of future generations.

■ **swap**
1. in the exchange markets, this is a simultaneous sale of a currency on the spot market together with a purchase of the same amount on the forward market. By combining these two transactions into a single one, transactions costs may be reduced.
2. an arrangement between central banks whereby they each agree to lend their currency to the other.

■ **swap rate**
the difference between the spot and forward exchange rates. Thus the price of a swap.

■ **systems thinking**
the last of Senge's five learning disciplines of his learning organisation: 'A way of thinking about and a language for describing and understanding, the forces and interrelationships that shape the behaviour of systems, helps us to see how to change systems more effectively and to act more in tune with the larger processes of the natural and economic world.'

■ **Systems, Applications, Programs (SAP)**
a presently hugely popular German Management Organisation System and software.

■ **tacit knowledge**
a reference to types of knowledge which cannot be stated explicitly and therefore cannot be easily communicated and transferred. It therefore contrasts with 'codified' or 'explicit' knowledge. Personal skills are frequently cited as an important example of tacit knowledge.

■ **target**
1. any objective of economic policy.
2. the value of an economic variable that policy makers regard as ideal and use as the basis for setting policy. Contrasts with instrument.
3. the level of an exchange rate that guides exchange market intervention by a central bank or exchange stabilisation fund.

■ **tariff**
1. a tax imposed on an imported good.
2. a tax on trade, usually an import tariff but sometimes used to denote an export tax. Tariffs may be ad valorem or specific.

■ **tariff binding**
a commitment, under the GATT by a country not to raise the tariff on an item above a specified level, called the bound rate.

**tariff classification**
see **tariff heading**.

**tariff equivalent**
the level of tariff that would be the same, in terms of its effect, usually on the quantity of imports, as a given NTB.

**tariff escalation**
in a country's tariff schedule, the tendency for tariffs to be higher on processed goods than on the raw materials from which they are produced. This causes the effective rate of protection on these goods to be higher than the nominal rate and puts LDC producers of primary products at a disadvantage.

**tariff factory**
a production facility established by a foreign firm through FDI in a country in spite of its higher production costs, in order to serve its market without paying a tariff.

**tariff heading**
the descriptive name attached to a tariff line, indicating the product to which it applies. Same as **tariff classification**.

**tariff jumping**
the establishment of a production facility within a foreign country, through FDI or licensing, in order to avoid a tariff.

**tariff line**
a single item in a country's tariff schedule.

**tariff peak**
in a tariff schedule, a single tariff or a small group of tariffs that are particularly high, often defined as greater than three times the average nominal tariff.

**tariff preference**
a lower (or zero) tariff on a product from one country than is applied to imports from most countries. This violation of the MFN principle is permitted in special cases, including some preferential trade arrangements and the GSP.

**tariff quota**
a tariff rate quota.

**Tariff Rate Quota (TRQ)**
a combination of an import tariff and an import quota in which imports below a specified quantity enter at a low (or zero) tariff and imports above that quantity enter at a higher tariff. Also called a tariff quota.

**tariff redundancy**
see **redundant tariff**.

**tariff revenue**
see **revenue**.

**tariff schedule**
the list of all of a country's tariffs organised by product.

**Tariff Schedule of the United States (TSUS)**
the official product nomenclature for specifying tariffs in the United States used until 1988, when it was replaced with the harmonised system.

■ **tariff wall**
a tariff, presumably a high one, perhaps in lots of industries. The term is used to highlight the difficulty foreign sellers have in getting their products past the tariff, often in the context of the incentive therefore provided for FDI. See **foreign investment argument for protection**.

■ **tariff-and-retaliation game**
the game of countries setting tariffs knowing that by doing so they alter the terms of trade to their own advantage. This is one very specific form of trade war.

■ **tariffication**
conversion of NTBs to ad valorem tariffs at the level of their tariff equivalents. In the Uruguay Round, developed country agricultural NTBs were tariffied and bound, the purpose being to replace unwieldy NTBs with tariffs that can then become the subject of negotiation.

■ **tariffs and retaliation**
the process of one country raising its tariff to secure some advantage, to which another country responds by raising its tariff, the first raises its tariff still further, etc. See retaliation, trade war. Classic treatment is Johnson (1954).

■ **task environment**
those elements or inputs in an organisation's environment which bear potentially on goal setting and on goal attainment within an organisation .

■ **tastes**
the preferences of consumers.

■ **tax base**
the amount on which a taxpayer pays taxes, as for example their taxable income in the case of an income tax or the taxable value of their property in the case of a property tax.

■ **tax break**
any provision of the tax code, such as a tax credit or tax deduction, that reduces the amount of tax that a firm or individual will pay, perhaps in return for behaviour that the government wishes to encourage.

■ **tax credit**
a provision of the tax code that specifies an amount by which a taxpayer's taxes will be reduced in return for some behaviour.

■ **tax deduction**
a provision of the tax code that specifies an amount by which a taxpayer's tax base will be reduced in return for some behaviour, resulting in a lowering of the amount of tax paid that depends on their tax rate.

■ **tax increment financing**
is used to facilitate the financing of larger development projects by capturing the property tax revenue stream projected for the development and investing it into improvements associated with the project.

■ **taxes, income taxes**
money the government collects from individuals and corporations to fund the services it provides. Personal income tax is paid by individuals while corporate income tax is paid by corporations and businesses. There are two categories of taxes. **Progressive taxes** serve to redistribute wealth within a country by ensuring that the wealthiest people pay a higher percentage of taxes. Income taxes are progressive taxes. In contrast, **regressive taxes** charge everyone the same percentage of tax, no matter what their income level. The GST is a good example of a regressive tax.

■ **team**
any group of people who need each other to accomplish a result.

■ **team learning**
one of Senge's five learning disciplines for his 'learning organisation': transforming conversational and collective thinking skills, so that groups of people can reliably develop intelligence and ability greater than the sum of individual members' talents.'

■ **Technical Barrier to Trade (TBT)**
a technical regulation or other requirement (for testing, labelling, packaging, marketing, certification, etc.) applied to imports in a way that restricts trade.

■ **technical coefficient**
in input-output analysis, identifies the percentage or portion of the total inputs of a sector required to be purchased from another sector irrespective of the geographic origin of this purchase. Technical (input) coefficients represent direct backward linkages of an industry to other industries and constitute the 'recipe' for production of that industry. See also **regional coefficient**.

■ **technical inefficiency**
see **X-efficiency**.

■ **technical progress**
same as technological progress.

■ **technical regulation**
a requirement of characteristics (such as dimensions, quality, performance or safety) that a product must meet in order to be sold on a country's market. See **standards**.

■ **technique**
1. a specific method of production, using a particular combination of inputs.
2. a point on an isoquant.

■ **technique of analysis**
a method used for displaying or manipulating economic models.

■ **technological change**
a change in a production function that alters the relationship between inputs and outputs. Normally, it is understood to be an improvement in technology or technological progress and it is of interest in in-

ternational economics for its implications for trade and economic welfare.

■ **technological difference**

a difference in production functions, usually for the same industry compared between two countries, such that one country has higher output for any given input than the other.

■ **technological paradigm**

model and a pattern of solution of selected technological problems, based on selected principles derived from natural sciences and on selected material technologies.

■ **technological progress**

a technological change that increases output for any given input.

■ **technological trajectory**

the movement of multi- dimensional trade-offs among technological variables that the paradigm defines as relevant. Progress can be defined as an improvement of these trade-offs. One could imagine the trajectory as a 'cylinder' in a multidimensional space (Dosi) or: a pattern of 'normal' problem-solving activity within a technological paradigm .

■ **technological transition**

a state in which firms may find themselves 'whose technology has begun to be constrained by its practical limits and whose rate of economic performance consequently begins to slow down.'

■ **technology**

1. a concept of varying breadth. In its broadest form, technology refers to knowledge of intermediating procedures of all complexities, including procedures involving everyday life, manufacturing, transportation and communication processes, as well as the organisation and management of such procedures. An important function of technology is the leveraging of manpower and brainpower.

2. knowledge which permits or facilitates the transformation of resources into goods and services.

3. the complete set of knowledge about how to produce in an economy at a point in time, including techniques of production that are available but not economically viable.

■ **technology gap**

the presence in a country of a technology that other countries do not have, so that it can produce and export a good whose cost might otherwise be higher than abroad.

■ **technology multipliers**

certain 'classes of technological innovation can induce a matrix of change and progress in other sectors that are thousand times the Keynesian multipliers of the investment in the original innovation. Relatively tiny investments in innovating the first microprocessors, radios, spreadsheets, hybrid corns, personal computers (PCs), antibiotics, the Internet and scientific selective breeding have created economic multipliers millions of times greater than their original investments'.

■ **technology transfer**
the communication or transmission of a technology from one country to another. This may be accomplished in a variety of ways, ranging from deliberate licensing to reverse engineering.

■ **temporary admission**
permission to import a good duty free for use an input in producing for export. See **drawback, export processing zone.**

■ **temporary producer movement**
a mode of supplying a traded service through the temporary movement of persons employed by the supplier into the buyer's country.

■ **tender**
to offer a product for sale at a specified price, usually in response to a specific request from a potential purchaser. Government procurement, for example, that is not open to international tendering is a form of nontariff barrier.

■ **terminal costs**
Transshipment and loading costs which must be paid regardless of the distance involved. See also **linear transport costs.**

■ **terms of trade**
1. the relative price of a country's exports compared to its imports. See improve the terms of trade.
2. terms of trade do NOT refer to contractual conditions of trade, but to price or exchange relationships between exports and imports. Thus, the terms of trade of a region or country improve when the prices for exports increase or those for imports decrease. Yes, the concepts of terms of trade can be meaningfully applied to many exchange type interactions.

■ **terms of trade argument**
same as the optimal tariff argument, which works by restricting the quantity of trade in order to improve the terms of trade.

■ **terms of trade effect**
the effect of a tariff on the terms of trade. By reducing the demand for imports, a tariff levied by a large country causes the prices of those imported goods to fall on the world market relative to the country's exports, improving its terms of trade.

■ **tertiary sector**
economic activities concerned with the organisation and coordination of production and other economic activities and with the exchange (logistics, distribution, marketing, etc.), maintenance (repair etc.) and consumption (retailing, wholesaling) of goods and services.

■ **textiles**
cloth. The textile sector is important for trade, along with apparel,

because with some exceptions (synthetics) it is a very labour intensive sector and it is therefore a likely source of comparative advantage for developing countries. See **textiles and apparel**.

■ **textiles and apparel**
these largely labour intensive sectors are often the first manufactured exports of developing countries. Because of the threat to employment in developed countries, however, they have long been protected there. This is only now changing under the WTO's ATC.

■ **the commons**
a shared resource. Air and water are frequently used examples.

■ **the loss function**
also known as the 'criterion function.' A function that is minimised to achieve a desired outcome. Often econometricians minimise the sum of squared errors in making an estimate of a function or a slope, in this case the loss function is the sum of squared errors. One might also think of agents in a model as minimising some loss function in their actions that are predicated on estimates of things such as future prices.

■ **theoretical proposition**
a property of an economic model that is derived (deduced) from its assumptions. It usually takes the form of a prediction about something that would be true in the world if the world conformed to the model's assumptions and perhaps also to additional assumptions specified in the proposition.

■ **theory**
a systematic explanatory statement comprising a deductively connected set of (inductively/empirically derived) laws or propositions which relate (dependent and independent) variables to each other.

■ **theory of second best**
see **second best**.

■ **third world**
refers to all less developed countries as a group. Term originated during the Cold War, when the 'first world' was the developed capitalist countries and the 'second world' was the communist countries, although these terms were seldom used.

■ **thread**
a hierarchical arrangement of linked notes in which each successive contribution is written as a response to an earlier note in the discussion (to organise discourse). Usually used by online conferencing forums and called 'threading'.

■ **tied aid**
aid that is given under the condition that part or all of it must be used to purchase goods from the country providing the aid.

■ **time-space convergence**
refers to the diminishing time needed to connect two places by

transportation due to improving transport technologies.

■ **time-use surveys**
surveys that measure how citizens spend their time. Time-use surveys are an important tool for measuring unpaid work and have been used in Canada since the 1996 Census.

■ **tort**
in law, a private or civil wrong.

■ **total factor productivity**
the growth of real output beyond what can be attributed to increases in the quantities of labour and capital employed.

■ **Total Factor Productivity (TFP)**
a measure of the output of an industry or economy relative to the size of all of its primary factor inputs. The term and its acronym TFP, often refers to the growth of this measure, as measured by the Solow residual. See also **Hicks-neutral technical progress**.

■ **Trade Adjustment Assistance (TAA)**
a program of adjustment assistance for workers and firms in industries that have suffered from competition with imports. In the US, TAA began with the Trade Act of 1974 and has been renewed and expanded since then, including as part of the NAFTA.

■ **trade and investment**
the interactions between and the rules and policies governing international trade and foreign direct investment. One of the Singapore Issues.

■ **trade balance**
balance of trade.

■ **trade barrier**
an artificial disincentive to export and/or import, such as a tariff, quota or other NTB.

■ **trade bias**
see **bias of a trade regime**.

■ **trade creation**
trade that occurs between members of a preferential trading arrangement that replaces what would have been production in the importing country were it not for the PTA. Associated with welfare improvement for the importing country since it reduces the cost of the imported good. Concept due to Viner (1950).

■ **trade credit**
1. an amount that is loaned to an exporter to be repaid when the exports are paid for by the foreign importer.

■ **trade deficit**
imports minus exports of goods and services. See **deficit**.

■ **trade deflection**
entry, into a low-tariff member of a free trade area, of imports that would otherwise have gone into its higher-tariff partner.

■ **trade dispute**
any disagreement between nations

involving their international trade or trade policies. Today, most such disputes appear as cases before the WTO dispute settlement mechanism, but prior to the WTO, some were handled by the GATT while others were dealt with bilaterally, sometimes precipitating trade wars.

■ **trade diversion**
trade that occurs between members of a preferential trading arrangement that replaces what would have been imports from a country outside in the PTA. Associated with welfare reduction for the importing country since it increases the cost of the imported good. Concept due to Viner (1950).

■ **trade flow**
the quantity or value of a country's bilateral trade with another country.

■ **trade imbalance**
a trade surplus or trade deficit.

■ **trade in services**
the provision of a service to buyers within or from one country by a firm in or from another country. Because such transactions do not involve a physical product crossing borders, they were not regarded as "trade" and were not covered by GATT. In the mid-1980s they were recognised as a form of trade and were incorporated into the WTO's GATS.

■ **trade indifference curve**
in a diagram measuring quantities of exports and imports, a curve representing amounts of trade among which a freely trading country is indifferent, based on its community indifference curves and its transformation curve. Due to Meade (1952).

■ **trade integration**
the process of increasing a country's participation in world markets through trade, accomplished by trade liberalisation.

■ **trade intensity index**
for a group or bloc of countries, usually in a PTA, the ratio of the bloc's share of intra-bloc trade to the bloc's share in world trade. If greater than one, this is said to suggest that the bloc displays trade diversion. Index seems to be due to Frankel (1997).

■ **trade liberalisation**
reduction of tariffs and removal or relaxation of NTBs.

■ **trade liberalisation**
the direct reduction in trade barriers or the easing or elimination of policies that indirectly restrict or distort international trade, especially policies which protect local production (tariffs, import quotas, export subsidies) and restrictive licensing regulations and practices.

■ **trade minister**
the government official, at the ministerial or cabinet level, primarily responsible for issues of international trade policy; the min-

ister of international trade. In the US that is USTR.

■ **trade negotiation**

a negotiation between pairs of governments or among groups of governments, exchanging commitments to alter their trade policies, usually involving reductions in tariffs and sometimes nontariff barriers.

■ **trade pattern**

what goods a country trades, with whom and in what direction. Explaining the trade pattern is one of the major purposes of trade theory, especially which goods a country will export and which it will import.

■ **Trade Policy Review Mechanism (TPRM)**

the periodic review of the trade policies and practices of the member countries of the WTO, conducted and published by the WTO.

■ **Trade Restrictiveness Index (TRI)**

a theoretically consistent index of the restrictiveness of trade policy — both tariffs and NTBs — developed by Anderson and Neary (1996).

■ **trade round**

a set of multilateral negotiations, held under the auspices of the GATT, in which countries exchanged commitments to reduce tariffs and agreed to extensions of the GATT rules. Most recent were the Kennedy, Tokyo and Uruguay Rounds.

■ **trade sanction**

use of a trade policy as a sanction, most commonly an embargo imposed against a country for violating human rights.

■ **trade surplus**

exports minus imports of goods and services or balance of trade. See **surplus**.

■ **trade theory**

the body of economic thought that seeks to explain why and how countries engage in international trade and the welfare implication of that trade, encompassing especially the Ricardian Model, the Heckscher-Ohlin Model and the New Trade Theory.

■ **trade triangle**

in the trade-and-transformation-curve diagram, the right triangle formed by the world price line and the production and consumption points, the sides of which represent the quantities exported and imported.

■ **trade war**

generally, a period in which each of two countries alternate in further restricting trade from the other. More specifically, the process of tariffs and retaliation.

■ **trade-and-transformation-curve diagram**

one of the most frequently used diagrams of trade theory, using a transformation curve together with one or more price lines and sometimes community indifference curves to illustrate production, consumption and trade and the effects on them of tariffs and other exogenous changes.

■ **traded good**
a good that is exported or imported or sometimes a good that could be exported or imported if it weren't for those pesky tariffs.

■ **trademark**
a symbol and/or name representing a commercial enterprise, whose right to the exclusive use of that symbol is, along with patents and copyrights, one of the fundamental intellectual property rights that is the subject of the WTO TRIPS agreement.

■ **Trade-Related Intellectual Property Rights (TRIPS)**
this was the term used for bringing intellectual property protection into the Uruguay Round of trade negotiations under the pretence that only trade-related aspects of the issue would be included. In practice, that did not constrain the coverage of the resulting agreement.

■ **trade-related investment measure**
any policy applied to foreign direct investment that has an impact on international trade, such as an export requirement.

■ **trade-weighted average tariff**
the average of a country's tariffs, weighted by value of imports. This is easily calculated as the ratio of total tariff revenue to total value of imports.

■ **trade-weighted exchange rate**
the weighted average of a country's bilateral exchange rates using bilateral trade, exports plus imports, as weights.

■ **trading arrangement**
an agreement between two or more countries concerning the rules under which trade among them will be conducted, either in a particular industry or more broadly.

■ **trading bloc**
a group of countries that are somehow closely associated in international trade, usually in some sort of PTA.

■ **transaction**
the exchange of money, goods or services through buying, selling or exchange.

■ **transaction cost**
1. on the foreign exchange markets, this includes broker's fees and/or the bid/ask spread.
2. the lower the transaction costs associated with a particular contractual assembly of inputs, the more likely self-interested individuals will choose that method of organising production.

■ **transaction value**
the actual price of a product, paid

or payable, used for customs valuation purposes.

## transfer payment
1. payment made by the government or private sector of one country to another as a gift or aid, not as payment for any good or service nor as an obligation. Also called a unilateral transfer.
2. social benefits paid to individuals or households by government.

## transfer pricing
the practice of pricing goods and services flowing within a corporation between corporate units located in different tax jurisdictions so as to shift profits into the jurisdiction with the lowest corporate income tax rates.

## transfers
transfer payments.

## transformation curve
same as production possibility frontier. The name comes from the idea that, by devoting resources to producing one good instead of another, it is as though one good is being transformed into another.

## transition
the process of converting from a centrally planned, non-market economy to a market economy.

## transition matrix
a matrix of transition probabilities (p) (probabilities of outcome a on any given experiment/ during a specific period of time, given that outcome a occurred on the pre-

ceding experiment / during the previous period of time).

## ■ translog function
the transcendental logarithmic production function, a flexible functional form due to Christensen et al. (1973). With output Y and inputs Xi, it takes the form $\ln Y = á0 + Si\ ái\ \ln Xi + 1/2\ Si\ Sj\ âij\ \ln Xi\ \ln Xj$.

## ■ Transnational Corporation (TNC)
1. same as multinational corporation, though for some reason this term seems to be preferred by those who don't like them.
2. a corporation whose national identity is a matter of convenience only and that will move its headquarters readily in response to incentives.

## ■ transparency
1. honesty, openness, disclosure propensity and accountability in public and private transactions.
2. the clarity with which a regulation, policy or institution can be understood and anticipated. Depends on openness, predictability and comprehensibility. Lack of transparency can itself be a NTB

## ■ transport cost
the cost of transporting a good, especially in international trade.

## ■ transportation cost
see **transport cost**.

## ■ treasury bills
short-term bonds issued by the

government, used to pay to cover government spending.

■ **Treaty of Rome**
the 1957 agreement among six countries of Western Europe to form the European Economic Community, which went into effect January 1, 1958.

■ **tree**
a fully connected network without circuits.

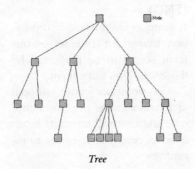

*Tree*

■ **trend**
the long-term movement of an economic variable, such as its average rate of increase or decrease over enough years to encompass several business cycles.

■ **triad**
1. Europe, North America and Japan.
2. The EU, the U.S. and Japan.

■ **trickle-down economics**
an assumption that the benefits of economic growth will eventually trickle-down to the poorest sectors of a society. History has shown that this does not actually happen. Economic growth does not ben-

efit all members of a society equally but rather increases the wealth of the richest while increasing the poverty of the poorest.

■ **trigger price**
see **minimum price system**.

■ **TRIPs Agreement**
the agreement negotiated in the Uruguay Round that incorporated issues of intellectual property into the WTO. It provides a set of minimum standards for intellectual property protection to which all but the poorest member countries of the WTO must conform.

■ **trough**
the point in the business cycle when an economic contraction reaches its lowest point before turning up. Contrasts with peak.

■ **two cone equilibrium**
a free-trade equilibrium in the Heckscher-Ohlin Model in which prices are such that all goods cannot be produced within a single country and instead there are two diversification cones. This or a multi-cone equilibrium, will arise if countries' factor endowments are sufficiently dissimilar compared to factor intensities of industries. Contrasts with one cone equilibrium.

■ **two-ness**
the property of simple versions of many trade models that they have two of everything: goods, factors and countries especially. An important issue, addressed by Jones

(1977), who coined the term and by Jones and Scheinkman (1977) is the extent to which the results of these models depend on this two-ness.

## ubiquitous materials or inputs

materials or production (or consumption) inputs which are available more or less everywhere in a similar quality and at approximately the same price. Still, ubiquitous inputs may have an effect on location: Inasmuch as such ubiquities affect the weight or bulk of the final product, the location of production (ceteris paribus) will tend to be relatively close to the market (in order to save transport costs).

## uncertainty

failure to know anything that may be relevant for an economic decision, such as future variables, details of a technology or sales. In models, uncertainty usually appears as a random variable and corresponding probability density function. But in practice, most international models, especially of trade, assume certainty.

## uncovered interest parity

equality of expected returns on otherwise comparable financial assets denominated in two currencies, without any cover against exchange risk. Uncovered interest parity requires approximately that $i = i^* + a$ where $i$ is the domestic interest rate, $i^*$ the foreign inter-

est rate and a the expected appreciation of foreign currency at an annualised percentage rate.

- **underdeveloped country**
a synonym, not usually used today, for less developed country.

- **under-invoicing**
the provision of an invoice that states price as less than is actually being paid, perhaps to reduce the amount that will be collected by an ad valorem tariff.

- **undertaking**
see **price undertaking**.

- **under-valued currency**
the situation of a currency whose value on the exchange market is lower than is believed to be sustainable. This may be due to a pegged or managed rate that is below the market-clearing rate or, under a floating rate, it may be due to speculative capital outflows. Contrasts with over-valued currency.

- **unemployment**
a measure of the number of workers that want to work but do not have jobs.

- **unemployment rate**
the unemployment rate is the percentage of the population who are willing to work for the current market wage for someone of his or her skill level but cannot find employment.

- **unequal exchange**
trade in which the labour used to

produce a country's exports is more than the labour used to produce its imports, as in the exchange between low-wage developing countries and high-wage developed countries.

■ **uniform delivered pricing**
a common pricing scheme for consumer and other goods in which prices charged at different locations are uniform and independent of transport costs. 'Remote buyers are subsidised by buyers near the production location.'

■ **unilateral transfer**
transfer payment.

■ **unit elastic**
having an elasticity equal to one. For a price elasticity of demand, this means that expenditure remains constant as price changes. For an income

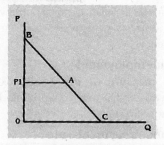

*Unit Elastic*

elasticity it means that expenditure share is constant. Homothetic preferences imply unit income elasticities. Contrasts with elastic and inelastic.

■ **unit isocost line**
an isocost line along which cost is

equal to one unit of the numeraire, such as one dollar.

■ **unit isoquant**
the isoquant for a quantity equal to one unit of a good. The unit isoquant is useful for relating the price of a good to the prices of factors employed in its production.

■ **unit labour requirement**
the amount of labour used per unit of output in an industry, the ratio of labour to output. In a Heckscher-Ohlin Model this varies along an isoquant as different techniques are chosen in response to different factor prices. But in a Ricardian model these are the constant building blocks for defining comparative advantage and determining behaviour.

■ **unit of account**
a basic function of money, providing a unit of measurement for defining, recording and comparing value. i.e., one dollar signifies not only a one dollar bill, but also a dollar's worth of money in other forms (deposits), of wealth in other forms than money and of any good or service with a market value.

■ **United Nations (UN)**
an organisation of countries established in 1945 with 51 members, expanded to 188 countries as of July 2000. Its purpose is 'to preserve peace through international cooperation and collective security.'

*United Nations*

## United Nations Commission on International Trade Law (UNCITRAL)

a legal body created in 1966 to formulate and harmonise national rules on international commercial transactions. It includes 36 member states elected by the UN General Assembly, representing various geographic regions and economic and legal systems. It differs from the WTO in its more technical focus and its broad representation.

## United Nations Conference on Trade and Development (UNCTAD)

an intergovernmental body established in 1964 within the United Nations, responsible for trade and development. Historically, it has often been the international voice of developing countries.

## United Nations Organisations (UNO)

the complex and extensive system of organisations that exist under the umbrella of the United Nations. Several of these, like the WTO and the IMF, play critical roles in the international economy.

## United States Trade Representative (USTR)

the cabinet-level official of the US government 'responsible for developing and coordinating US international trade, commodity and direct investment policy and leading or directing negotiations with other countries on such matters.'

## unit-value isoquant

the isoquant for a quantity of a good worth one unit of value. This is meaningful only if the nominal price of the good is given, for some specified currency or numeraire. Unit-value isoquants are central to the Lerner diagram for analysing the Heckscher-Ohlin Model.

## unskilled labour

labour with a low level of skill or human capital. Identified empirically as labour earning a low wage, with a low level of education or in an occupational category associated with these, sometimes crudely proxied as production workers.

## upstream subsidisation

export of a good, one of whose inputs has been subsidised.

## urban-growth boundary

a politically specified line around cities beyond which development is discouraged or prohibited. Sometimes also called urban-limit lines or rural-limit lines, urban growth boundaries exist in many cities, counties and regions across the US, particularly in California.

- **urbanisation economies**

  benefits accruing to individual households or consumer-oriented activities resulting from the agglomeration of populations and the urbanisation of an area or to other economic activities benefiting from the access to a general labour force. The population is assumed to have similar or complementary needs for residential infrastructures, schools, health-care and other service activities.

- **utility function**

  a function that specifies the utility (well-being) of a consumer for all combinations goods consumed (and sometimes other considerations). Represents both their welfare and their preferences.

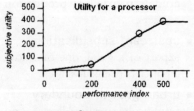

*Utility Function*

- **Utility Possibility Frontier (UPF)**

  in a diagram with levels of individual utility on the axes, a curve showing the maximum attainable levels of utility in a given situation, such as free trade or autarky

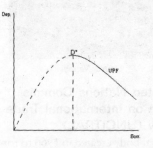

*Utility Possibility Frontier*

- **validity**

  the extent to which a statistical instrument measures what it was designed to measure, for example IQ tests may have a high reliability (people tend to achieve similar scores over time). However, they might have a low validity when it comes to measuring certain competences, such job skills.

- **value**

  what something or someone is worth. In terms of economics value is judged solely by monetary value, what something or someone is worth in money.

- **value added**

  the value of output minus the value of all intermediate inputs representing therefore the contribution of and payments to, primary factors of production.

- **Value Added Tax (VAT)**
  a tax that is levied only on the value added of a firm. A VAT is usually subject to border tax adjustment.

- **value chain**
  refers to a business as a 'collection of interdependent activities, which in turn, form part of a continuous system that stretches back to suppliers and forward to channels and customers.'

- **value marginal product**
  marginal value product.

- **value network**
  the communications network of relations between all individuals and organisations who add value to a product.

*Value Network*

- **value quota**
  a quota specifying value — price times quantity — of a good.

- **variable cost**
  the portion of a firm or industry's cost that changes with output, in contrast to fixed cost.

- **variable levy**
  a tax on imports that varies over time so as to stabilise the domes-

tic price of the imported good. Essentially, the tax is set equal to the difference between the target domestic price and the world price.

- **variance**
  a measure of how much an economic or statistical variable varies across values or observations. Its calculation is the same as that of the covariance, being the covariance of the variable with itself.

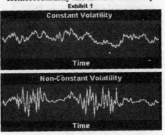

*Variance*

- **variety**
  the multiplicity of differentiated products that are available in some industries, a multiplicity that tends to become larger with trade.

- **vehicle currency**
  the currency used to invoice an international trade transaction, especially when it is not the national currency of either the importer or the exporter.

- **vertical integration**
  production of different stages of processing of a product within the same firm.

- **vertical integration**
  corporate mergers involving firms which are involved in forwardly

or backwardly related production stages, i.e. they buy each other's inputs or outputs. A merger accomplishing an internalisation of such linkages increases control of input or output markets and thereby over prices and other market facets.

■ **vertical intraindustry trade**
intraindustry trade in which the exports and imports are at the different stages of processing. Contrasts with horizontal IIT.

■ **vertical mixing**
ensures a variety of different ages, experience sets and skills on design teams.

■ **vertical specialisation**
another term for fragmentation.

■ **vicious cycle (or circle) of poverty**
a conceptual reference to the complex, self-reinforcing interdependency of poverty-causing and sustaining factors in multi-causal, chain-like processes. Often referred to in the context of 'underdevelopment'.

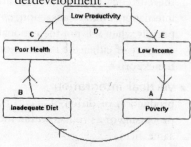

*Vicious Circle of Poverty*

■ **visible**
in referring to international trade, used as a synonym for 'good'. 'Visibles trade' is trade in goods. Contrasts with **invisible**.

■ **volatility**
the extent to which an economic variable, such as a price or an exchange rate, moves up and down over time.

■ **Voluntary Export Restraint (VER)**
a restriction on a country's imports that is achieved by negotiating with the foreign exporting country for it to restrict its exports.

■ **Voluntary Import Expansion (VIE)**
the use of policies to encourage imports, in response to pressure from trading partners. Due to Bhagwati (1987).

■ **Voluntary Restraint Agreement (VRA)**
same as a **VER**.

■ **wage**
the payment for the service of a unit of labour, per unit time. In trade theory, it is the only payment to labour, usually unskilled labour. In empirical work, wage data may exclude other compensation, which must be added to get the total cost of employment.

■ **waiver**
an authorised deviation from the terms of a previously negotiated and legally binding agreement. Many

countries have sought and obtained waivers from particular obligations of the GATT and WTO.

# Walras' Law

the property of a general equilibrium that if all but one of the markets are in equilibrium, then the remaining market is also in equilibrium, automatically. This follows from the budget constraints of the market participants and it implies that any one market-clearing condition is redundant and can be ignored.

# Walrasian adjustment

a market adjustment mechanism in which price rises when there is excess demand and falls when there is excess supply. Strictly speaking, these excess supplies and demands are those that would obtain without any history of disequilibrium, as with a Walrasian auctioneer.

# Walrasian auctioneer

a hypothetical entity that facilitates market adjustment in disequilibrium by announcing prices and collecting information about supply and demand at those prices without any disequilibrium transactions actually taking place.

# Walter Christaller

German Central Place Theorist (Book published in 1933 on Central Places in Southern Germany).

# WARP

Weak Axiom of Revealed Preference.

# water in the tariff

the extent to which a tariff that is higher than necessary to be prohibitive.

# weak axiom of revealed preference

the assumption that a consumer who reveals strict preference for one bundle of goods over another will not, in other circumstances, reveal their preference for the second over the first. That is, if $q_i$, $q_j$ are the vectors of goods purchased at prices $p_i$, $p_j$ respectively, then $p_i q_i > p_i q_j$ Þ $p_j q_i > p_j q_j$. Used in proving correlation results.

# wealth

the total value of the accumulated assets owned by an individual, household, community or country.

# Weber, Alfred

German economist and location theorist. Brother of Max Weber. Made significant contributions to the development of industrial location theory in his book (1909) Ueber den Standort der Industrien (Engl. Title: Theories of the Location of Industries).

*Weber, Alfred*

■ **weight-loss ratio**

an important concept in Alfred Weber's theory of location: The relative loss in weight of production inputs during the production process. A large weight-loss ratio will favour (proximity to) the source location(s) of the materials for the location of the production activity in order to save transport costs.

■ **welfare economics**

the branch of economic thought that deals with economic welfare, including especially various propositions relating competitive general equilibrium to the efficiency and desirability of an allocation.

■ **welfare proposition**

in trade theory, this usually refers to any of several gains from trade theorems.

■ **welfare triangle**

in a partial equilibrium market diagram, a triangle representing the net welfare benefit or loss from a policy or other change. In trade theory it often means the triangle or triangles representing the deadweight loss due to a tariff.

■ **Western Hemisphere Free Trade Area (WHFTA)**

name sometimes proposed for a preferential trading arrangement including most or all of the countries of the western hemisphere. Now called FTAA.

■ **willingness to pay**

the largest amount of money that an individual or group could pay, along with a change in policy, without being made worse off. It is therefore a monetary measure of the benefit to them of the policy change. If negative, it measures its cost.

■ **World Bank**

World Intellectual Property Organisation the United Nations organisation that establishes and coordinates standards for intellectual property protection.

■ **world price**

the price of a good on the 'world market,' meaning the price outside of any country's borders and therefore exclusive of any trade taxes or subsidies that might apply crossing a border into a country but inclusive of any that might apply crossing out of a country.

■ **World Trade Organisation (WTO)**

a global international organisation that specifies and enforces rules for the conduct of international trade policies and serves as a forum for negotiations to reduce barriers to trade. Formed in 1995 as the successor to the GATT, it had 136 member countries as of April 2000.

■ **X-Efficiency / X-Inefficiency**
The ability of a firm to get maximum output from its inputs. Failure to do so, called X-inefficiency or technical inefficiency, may be due to lack of incentives provided by competition. Improvement in X-efficiency is one hypothesised source of gain from trade. Managers are merely x-efficient due, to
(1) selective rationality
(2) individual inadequacies
(3) discretionary effort
(4) pervasive inertia
(5) organisational entropy

■ **zero degree homogeneous**
homogeneous of degree zero.

■ **zero profit**
a situation in which profit in an industry is zero, usually as a result of free entry and exit. It may, if firms are not identical, refer only to the marginal firm. And it always means zero excess profit, not that all returns to capital invested in the industry are zero.

# NOTES

_____
_____
_____
_____
_____
_____
_____
_____
_____
_____
_____
_____
_____
_____
_____
_____
_____
_____
_____
_____

# NOTES

# NOTES

# NOTES

240

# NOTES